TELL IT TO LOUELLA

LOUELLA O. PARSONS

Tell It To Louella

≪ ≪ ≪ ≪ ≪ ≪ ≪

G. P. Putnam's Sons
New York

*To my daughter, Harriet, my cousin, Margaret Ettinger,
and my friend and associate, Dorothy Manners*

⟫ *Foreword*

"THE first to know" are the most beautiful words in the dictionary to me. That I even own a dictionary might come as a shock to the many people who prefer to think of me as a caricature of a Hollywood columnist who has malapropped and misspelled her way through millions of words about the life and times of Hollywood, its births, deaths, romances, marriages and divorces.

Hollywood is news and Hollywood is my town. For nearly four decades, I've been the "first to know" and the first to tell it too if I think it should be told. If anyone wants to challenge that statement or me, I'll choose the weapons. Telephones and typewriters at forty paces.

In reporting my facts, I've never had to resort to fiction. For me, the truth always has been and will be more fascinating than fiction, especially if you know the truth. The things I've seen and heard would fill a book.

That's what I'm doing now.

Once before, during World War II, I wrote a book, *The Gay Illiterate,* which as the title suggests with a dash of self-humor, was about myself and the people whose lives were interwoven with mine; some famous, some infamous.

7

This second effort will be less about me and *more* about the famous and infamous. Gossamer spun though it may be on a silver screen or a silk typewriter ribbon, Hollywood is and has been my life. My house on Maple Drive in Beverly Hills is not only my home, it's my office, and sooner or later anybody who is anybody, or anybody who hoped to be somebody in Hollywood, has walked those fifty paces to my front door. Greta Garbo never trod the walk. If someone like the legendary Garbo wanted to be alone, I respected that desire, providing of course I couldn't reach her by telephone, telegraph, Wells, Fargo, Jet or Space Ship.

If I knew for sure I could get back in time to telephone the scoop to my city editor, I'd willingly be the first lady Astronaut to volunteer to go to the Moon. Although I know all the Hollywood stars, I'm not so good on Celestial Navigation, so meanwhile I'll stick to the stars I really know—and knew—so many of them tragically gone from our midst; Clark Gable, Gary Cooper, Tyrone Power, Humphrey Bogart, Jean Harlow, Rudolph Valentino, John Barrymore, Douglas Fairbanks. The list is endless and sad—for I, who think of myself first as a reporter, also think of myself as a friend; reporter-friend intermingled. Any writer will tell you that frequently the choice is hard; whether to be a reporter or a friend.

The best thing is to be both, for the alertness of a reporter can be blended with the affection and insight of a friend. I think it makes for a better story.

This then has been my credo; to report the facts, with a fondness for my friends and a responsibility to my readers.

Contents

TELL IT TO LOUELLA

⟶ Chapter 1

THE FIRST TO KNOW

I'VE always claimed a story wasn't a story unless I got it first. Ask Bob Hope. He knows.

During World War II, when our beloved Bob—truly our Ambassador of Good Hope and Cheer—was on the first of his many trips to entertain troops and bring laughter to them, he had to fill out an official form that asked the question: "Who should be notified in case of accident?"

"Louella would never forgive me if she wasn't the first to know," Bob quipped as he wrote down my name.

I've never been hauled into court to reveal the source of any of my stories, but if I were I wouldn't tell. I'd have to incriminate too many people—volunteer tipsters from all over the world in all walks of life, government bureaus, travel agencies, a lowly clerk, a high official, a beauty parlor operator, a hotel clerk, a justice of the peace, a laboratory technician. You name 'em; they've all called me.

One day I received a report that Teresa Wright (who was married to writer Niven Busch at the time) was going to have a baby.

I immediately called Teresa to congratulate her; instead of thanking me, she said somewhat angrily, I thought, for an expectant mother, "That's not true, Louella."

"But, Teresa," I protested, "I have it on good authority."

"I think I'm the best authority," she said, emphasizing each syllable.

I was about to retreat as tactfully as possible, when she said, "Excuse me a moment, my other phone is ringing." A minute later, she was back on the line, laughing uproariously.

"I'll never doubt you again, Louella," she said. "You were right. I *am* going to have a baby. I'm glad you told me first. That was my doctor on the phone. He just got the lab report."

Love and marriage, love and marriage. They go together like a horse and carriage. Well, in Hollywood, they do come first—even before the horse and carriage. (Pardon me, Jimmy Van Heusen, for using your song title.) I've been described—and I suppose a lady shouldn't object when so many people go out of their way to write about one whose business it is to write about people—as "Love's undertaker," because I've written so much about broken marriages, smashed romances, shattered engagements and crushed hopes.

A small-town girl at heart (born in Freeport, Illinois, and raised in Dixon), I'm an incurable romantic. Unfortunately, life doesn't work out that way, on or off the screen. Especially off the screen and right in Hollywood; my adopted home town. Those klieg lights which Hollywood is so famous for shine brightest on our own luminous folk.

What do they eat? Why do they eat what they eat? Where do they sleep? How do they sleep? Why do they sleep? How much money do they make? How do they spend their money? Why do they spend their money? Why do they fall in love? Why do they fall in love with the people they fall in love with? Why do they fall out of love?

The why's go on and on. I'm interested in the wherefore's.

Happily, the younger generation of stars has continued to tell me its secrets. Fortunately, the walls of my playroom can't talk. They might tell too much. I have held back news, too; confidences I have heard within those confines. I never resorted to the trick of secreting tape recorders around to catch the unwary. My own built-in tape recorder is my memory which predates by more years than I care to remember, the invention of the electronic gadgets which so many reporters rely on today.

My playroom opens on my sunny garden which in semitropical

California has flowers blooming most of the year. This sunlit room wherein I have been told so much has become sort of a confessional.

It was here years ago that Carole Lombard told me she loved Clark Gable and gave me the story, first, that she planned to marry him. Here, too, Natalie Wood confided that she was going to marry Bob Wagner, a handsome young man who tells me all his news. However, neither she nor Bob gave me the news of their broken marriage face to face. They knew I would be unhappy for both of them, so they talked with me over the telephone where they could better conceal their emotions.

A surprising visitor one evening was young Bobby ("Mack The Knife") Darin, who as a rule shuns the press with any personal news although the singer makes colorful copy. Bobby wanted to tell me that he and Sandra Dee were engaged. This was a complete scoop and big news with Bobby's teen-age fans and Sandra's many admirers. Six months after their marriage, I was in New York when Sandra telephoned me the happy news that the stork was flapping its wings and would bring the Darins a Christmas gift.

In this room Barbara Hutton shyly told me that she was engaged to Cary Grant, and did I have a scoop! The richest girl in the world marrying the debonair and dashing Cary. But they didn't live happily ever after. There were other marriages to come for both Cary and Barbara.

Of all the stories I've had and heard within those walls, perhaps none rocked the world with sensationalism and repercussions as much as the headline news that Ingrid Bergman was going to have a baby—born out of wedlock—by her director Roberto Rossellini. But I'll have more to tell about Ingrid, The Fallen Angel, in a later chapter.

Charles Chaplin came to my home to tell me his secret plans, but they were to be kept so secret he wouldn't trust the muted walls of the playroom. Instead he accompanied me to my boudoir, locked the door and whispered to me the entire story that he was going to marry Oona O'Neill, the young daughter of the famous playwright, Eugene O'Neill. He extracted my promise that I wouldn't print the story until after he eloped to Santa Barbara the next morning with his young bride-to-be.

15

Nearly a generation later, a young man telephoned me with news that excited him so, his baritone became an octave higher than usual. "Louella, I just . . . that is . . . we . . . that is . . . Nancy and I are engaged. We want you to be the first to know."

The Nancy was "Nancy of the Smiling Face," Frank Sinatra's oldest daughter. The jubilant young man was singer Tommy Sands, who modestly says he would like to sing only half as well as his famous father-in-law. I can tell you this. No one ever had a prettier, nicer mother-in-law than Tommy Sands has. Nancy Sinatra, Frank's divorced wife, has conducted herself in Hollywood with a charm and dignity that are beautiful to behold. I relished getting this story from Tommy for two reasons; the first was downright selfish—I plain like exclusive stories—but the second was that these two youngsters, who were born so long after the birth of my first Hollywood column and belonged to a world so different from my own youth, used the words so dear to my heart. "We want you to be the first to know."

So many scoops; so many memories, like the time Norma Shearer, the most exquisitely groomed woman in Hollywood—Joan Crawford notwithstanding—came to see me. I had known her and her late husband Irving Thalberg very well, and shared her grief at his untimely death in his thirties. Norma, one of the richest women in Hollywood and the mother of two children by Thalberg, told me she was going to marry ski instructor Marty Arrouge whom she had met at Sun Valley.

"Louella," she said matter-of-factly and most practically, I thought, "Marty and I have signed a prenuptial financial agreement." But so wise was Norma Shearer that she settled a sizable amount of money on her husband to avoid his having to dive under tables when checks were presented to them. Their marriage is one of the happiest in Hollywood.

For one scant edition, I had the exclusive story that Clark Gable, for long the idol of so many, was going to be a father by his fifth wife, Kay Williams Gable.

When I talked to Clark, who was then making *The Misfits* in Reno, he and Kay, in the midst of their excitement, took the time to ask me to be the baby's godmother. Although I have other godchildren, this baby—John Clark Gable, born posthumously to one of the most

16

famous fathers in the world—is something special; not only to me, but to the Gable fans. When I held little John Clark Gable in my arms for the first time and looked into that tiny yet strong face, so like his father's, I said a silent prayer in thanks that he had weathered the travail of his father's death which had put an aching strain on his beautiful mother's already weak heart. Oh, how I wished that Clark could have held his son in his arms, as I was doing.

I was one of the five people who knew that dear, dear Gary Cooper had such a short time to live; a matter of weeks before cancer would prove the only villain he could not overcome. Every day I telephoned Gary's devoted wife Rocky, the former Veronica Balfe who had given up an acting career because she felt she had no talent (yet for those last hopeless weeks of Gary's illness she gave a magnificent performance of courage and cheerfulness for her husband). Physically his body had deteriorated, but his spirit was strong and relentless to the end, so typical of the virile, he-man roles which kept him a star for thirty years. Elsewhere in the book I will tell more about the Gary I knew so well.

When Lana Turner decided to marry good-looking Fred May, she came to see me. I had known her well since she was the brown-haired, naïve teen-ager; the first sweater girl, whom Mervyn LeRoy catapulted to stardom in *They Won't Forget*. Lana's meteoric career and the stormy personal life of her multimarriages, romances and divorces—the tragedy of her daughter Cheryl's stabbing Johnny Stompanato and the heartbreak that followed, wherein a mother and daughter tried to find each other—was to my mind the greatest tragedy in Hollywood. Yet that day not long ago when Lana visited me she looked young and beautiful again, dressed in a champagne-colored suit with a matching mink collar almost the exact shade of her golden hair.

Lana is like Hollywood itself, I thought: glamorous, unpredictable, resilient, always able to bounce back after defeat—stronger, more vibrant than ever. Such is the heart of Lana and Hollywood.

It is my proud boast that I have never broken a trust when it was given to me in confidence. But when I protect my sources, I ask for truth in return.

17

I have my own code of ethics.

I don't want to be lied to.

I don't want to be double-crossed.

I don't want to be "used."

I won't stand still for "double-planting," which means giving the same story to two or more reporters while telling each of them "this is an exclusive."

When any of these occur I burn up and hell hath no fury like Louella O. scorched. In return, she's perfectly willing to start a conflagration that Mrs. O'Leary's cow would envy.

Only recently an incident of this "double-planting" centered around Jean Simmons. She had split up with Stewart Granger and was working in *Elmer Gantry* which was being directed by Richard Brooks. There were whispered stories that the actress was taking direction offscreen as well as on, but I hadn't printed those whispers. Now Jean was on the phone and told me in a sugary voice, "I'm going to dinner with Dick tonight. It's our first public appearance. . . ." Then came those words so dear to my heart, "I wanted you to be the first to know."

It was hardly an earth-shaking story, but it was news of a sort on a day when news was short. So I printed it.

That evening when the first editions of the newspapers came out, I discovered that Hedda Hopper had also used it. I called up and had the item yanked after the first edition.

The next morning the same item, almost word for word, was in Harrison Carroll's column and in a trade paper.

Miss Simmons had not only "double-planted." She had quadruple-planted and played me for a sucker. In the future, Miss Simmons, now Mrs. Richard Brooks, will mean it I'm sure when she says, "Louella, I wanted you to be the first to know."

A number of times the first word on the breakup of a Hollywood ménage has come from a moving man, called in to estimate the cost of moving "his" and "hers" out of "his" or "hers." Bad-debt collectors have told me of the celebrities they were dunning. Salespeople in stores have let me know when a prominent personality has bought a gift for someone.

In most instances the callers identify themselves, because as I learned long ago, few people give you something for nothing. Occasionally I get anonymous phone calls that have provided news stories. One Saturday morning not long ago, a strange male voice said over the phone, "I thought you ought to know that Lindsay Crosby's baby has just been born." He hung up before I could find out who he was.

My staff and I took the classified directory and started calling all the hospitals and maternity homes. No luck with any of them. They knew nothing about Lindsay Crosby and his baby. Then I thought of one of the best reporters I know; Kate Crosby, Bing's amazing, wonderful mother, Lindsay's grandmother and the new baby's great-grandmother—providing there was a new baby. My hunch was right. Kate Crosby had all the vital statistics; weight, name, time of birth, mother and child and great-grandmother doing well.

Another exclusive. Not big, but exclusive.

Apropos of babies—years ago, upon what I considered good authority, I ran an item that Margaret Sullavan, then married to Leland Hayward, was expecting her first baby. Some days later I ran into Margaret, and she took me aside.

"Please, Louella, do be careful what you print about me in the future," she said, smiling wryly. "When you wrote I was going to have a baby, I wasn't going to—as far as I knew. Right afterward I found I was pregnant, after all."

A good reporter is a better reporter if she's a lucky one. I've been lucky, and frequently managed to be in the right place at the right time. Of course, it wasn't always coincidence. My nose for news has led me to some pretty queer and distant places. For this next story, I didn't have to go very far—only to Pickfair, the most famous residence in Hollywood, the love nest of the world's most adored married couple, Mary Pickford and Douglas Fairbanks.

I had known Mary and Doug for years. During World War I, when I was a movie columnist for the Chicago *Record-Herald* (this was another first for me, I was the first movie columnist in the world —and don't think I'm as old as Adam. Eve maybe, but not Adam), I went on a bond-selling tour with Mary and Douglas and Charles Chaplin. Later when I went to New York and became the Motion Picture Editor of the *Morning-Telegraph,* I remember an incident at the Astor Hotel where Mary and Doug were staying. She was so petite and so besieged by fans that the swashbuckling Doug used to carry her in and out of the hotel on his shoulders, to keep her literally head and shoulders above the surging crowds.

One afternoon Mary was the only woman invited to a luncheon given by Thomas Alva Edison. She told me she wouldn't go unless I went with her. So I went and sat right up at the head table with Mr. Edison, who was so deaf he couldn't carry on much of a conversation. Later I received a note from the great inventor saying, "Isn't Mary Pickford sweet?"

Later when I moved to Hollywood, the Fairbanks and I were part of a small group who saw each other often. One day four of us were lunching at Pickfair. I had arrived last and one of the other guests said, "Mary, aren't you going to tell Louella what you told us?"

Mary took a long breath. "I'm divorcing Douglas, Louella."

I almost choked. This was world-shaking news, for Mary and Doug were the darlings of the world—the Tristan and Isolde, the Arthur and Guinevere of their day. They not only ruled Hollywood socially and professionally but economically, as well.

"But why?" I finally managed to ask, still aghast at the news.

Mary gave me a long look. "Do I really have to tell you?"

I supposed that she didn't. I had heard rumors that Douglas was smitten with Lady Sylvia Ashley, whom he had met abroad when he went to make a picture; but I never did think he would divorce Mary.

"Don't divorce him, Mary," I counseled. "Give him another chance. He loves you."

Little Mary was adamant. "I'm getting a divorce."

I went back home but I didn't write the story. I hated to write the story. As I said before, I'm an incurable romantic and if I had my way all romances would lead to the altar and would be happy forever after. The twenty-three years that my beloved Dr. Martin and I were married were the happiest of my life.

I kept thinking that if I didn't print Mary Pickford's decision to divorce Doug it might never happen, but it was Mary herself who changed my mind. She called me later that night and said, "If you don't use the story, Louella, I'll give it to someone else."

20

Well, friendship was friendship and big exclusive stories were something else again. "You darned well won't," I said. "As soon as you hang up, I'll call the paper."

It was the front-page headline. Every wire service in the world picked it up and poor Mary was swamped by a flood of newspapermen who dogged her footsteps constantly, even following her into church; the first time, I'll bet, that many of them had been in church in a dozen years.

The other reporters berated Mary for having given me the story first, and at least one suggested that I had forced Mary into her decision by telling her of Lady Ashley. Mary defended me, saying we were old friends, and dismissed the other implication as ridiculous.

Another example of Parsons' luck involved Gene Tierney, that beautiful, tragedy-beset girl who is making such a gallant effort to pick up the pieces of her life and put them together again in her marriage to Howard Lee, Hedy Lamarr's ex-husband.

When Gene was married to Oleg Cassini, they separated at one time, then reconciled. They were among the guests at a big party at Gary Cooper's where Hedda Hopper and I were also guests.

I told Gene, "You've never looked happier."

"I've never been happier," she glowed. "I'm going to have a baby."

That was my cue to rush to the nearest phone. Another first. When I returned, I chatted a bit more with Gene. Then she spotted Hedda and said to me, "I really should tell Hedda, too, shouldn't I?"

"By all means," I reassured her, "but there's no hurry. You'll have a chance to tell her sometime this evening."

I saw them talking together about an hour later. Now, this was at a time when Hedda wasn't as hep in her newspaper ways as she is now, and I smiled as I saw her make notes and stash them in her purse. I knew that by the time Hedda got around to writing that story it would be—pardon the expression—"old hat."

My so-called feud with Hedda Hopper is more apocryphal than actual. (Arthur Brisbane taught me that word a long time ago and I'm quite proud of it.)

Hedda and I had been very good friends for many years when she was an actress. I have been entertained at her house in Hollywood and when I was sick in Palm Springs she came to see me. I didn't take her role as a columnist very seriously until, to my utter amazement, she started making cracks about me on the radio. According to many widespread rumors, she was to be used primarily to offset me and my influence. Hedda, so the story went, "was going to put Louella in her place." As far as I was concerned, my place was right at the top and I intended to stay there, Hedda and her hats notwithstanding.

Despite the competition, I still continued to get the exclusives. It increased my prestige both with the public and my bosses. It proved I was a good reporter, and the phones kept right on ringing and the first words I continued to hear were "I want you to be the first to know."

Mr. William Randolph Hearst, my boss, once told me I was his best reporter but I wasn't his best writer.

If all the words I've written in my lifetime were laid end to end, well—who could count that far? I think they'd be as many as the light miles to the sun. And when you write as much and as fast as I have had to write, you can't make each phrase a pearl of perfection. But I'd rather make a deadline than an epigram any day.

Through no fault of our own, the Parsons-Hopper feud has been sustained by the press agents and a few double-crossing acquaintances who would like to play both sides of the street. Every so often we get together and say we're not going to pay any attention to them.

Time has been a mellowing force. I am a lot less competitive than I used to be—and I've learned to admire more about Hedda than her hats (I started liking her hats more than forty years ago when she was an established actress). I admire her nerve, and she has earned a place for herself in Hollywood. There are times when I'd cheerfully doff one of my own fancy hats to her.

One instance was when both she and I were served notice by a firm of lawyers that Benita Hume Colman Sanders, the remarried widow of Ronald Colman, was planning to sue each of us for remarks we had printed in our separate columns. We had both reported that Ronald Colman's ashes had been left at the San Ysidro home where he and Benita once lived. We both added the comment that many persons felt this was not very considerate of his memory and were saying so.

Benita's lawyers sent photographs of a tombstone which she had designed to mark Ronnie's grave. That tablet was erected after our items appeared. I immediately called the newspaper's lawyer, asking him to reply to Mrs. Sanders' lawyers.

He ridiculed the idea of a lawsuit, but said he would attend to it.

Hedda, on the contrary, didn't even call her lawyer. Instead, she took her own case to court, writing a brilliant answer, sarcastic and logical. She called to read the letter to me, and I must say she showed more courage than I did. But then, I have always dreaded lawsuits.

Of the many "I want you to be the first to know's" that I have heard so happily in my career, none amused me more than the scoop Tallulah Bankhead gave me. At the time, stories were being circulated that the famed Tallulah was desperately ill and might not survive.

Early one morning, her husky voice greeted me over the phone, "Louella, dahling," she confided, "I've been very, very sick. Never been sicker in my life. My enemies have been saying vile things about me—that I'm going to die—of all things. Don't believe them. I have no intention of making any exit without a curtain call. I'm positively not going to die. I want you to be the first to know."

➤➤➤ *Chapter 2*

LONG LIVE THE KING

JOHN CLARK GABLE was born in March, 1961, and it seems to me that this was the supreme irony in the story of his father, Clark Gable. Clark had been dead four months when his son was born. Everyone who loved Clark—and that came close to being everyone who had ever known him—was torn between two deep, conflicting emotions. Happiness that Kay Gable had borne the son whom both she and Clark wanted so much. And sorrow that Clark would never see his boy.

To Hollywood, Clark Gable was "The King." But he was, to me, the type of king I had read about in my high-school days when my assignment was Shakespeare's *King Henry V* and I remember the sentence: ". . . The king is but a man, as I am; The violet smells to him as it doth to me."

In writing about Gable, I must begin at the end. With a news broadcast that I tuned in as I was preparing to go to bed on the night of November 17, 1960. I flipped the radio switch and there was that long moment of dead stillness before the machine came to life. Then the single, short sentence. "Clark Gable is dead."

First there was a shock, as if I had been struck a numbing blow. Then my reaction was to shout back at this mechanical, disembodied voice, "You're lying. Clark can't be dead." And next, of course, the realization that it was so. A friend was dead. A legend was dead. An era was dead.

Part of me wanted only to mourn, but there was another part that forbade mourning. I had a job to do and Clark would never forgive me if I welshed on it. I believe this was one of the reasons that, even as I thought this, I was dialing the number of the *Examiner*. Another phone started ringing as I waited for my connection and I let it ring.

I got the city editor. The story was true. Gable was dead. And someone was even then calling me to tell me that I had to write a story. That was the reason my other phone was ringing.

"Write it fast," the city editor said. "Write it as long as you want. But write it in a hurry."

"I'll get to work," I said.

When I hung up, I began to weep. It took me long minutes to pull myself together, yet even as I wept I had gone to the typewriter, slipped paper into it. But now, facing the typewriter, I found there were no words at all.

Just memories.

I had to take thirty years of friendship, of events, of a rippling pool of relationships and put them on paper. There wasn't a single human emotion, in one form or another, that we had not experienced.

Usually symbolism has little meaning for me. It's not my way of expressing myself or of understanding people or happenings. This time, however, one symbol kept recurring. The symbol of a tree. No, not one, but three.

Clark and Carole Lombard brought the first tree to Doctor Martin and me soon after we bought our ranch in the San Fernando Valley. I saw the pair of them, handsome, vital, so much in love, as they came through the gate. Clark was carrying a stripling olive tree.

"From us to you," Clark said.

"When you pick the olives," Carole said, "think of us."

We took the slender tree and searched for just the right spot, where it would have space to grow strong and free and bear its fruit. When we found the place, we dug a hole and planted it.

25

Some years ago I visited the ranch, which Jimmy Cagney had bought. There was the olive tree, its trunk thick, its spreading branches blue-green with life, the olives growing.

And the second tree was a memory of Christmas, 1959.

Now I was alone. Doctor Martin was long gone. Carole, too, was long gone. But Clark came to visit me, accompanied by Kay, his new wife, who was—in so many ways—like Carole. They brought a gift, an evergreen tree, sparkling with many lights.

"Plant it in the garden after Christmas," Clark said. "The wonderful thing about a tree is that it keeps living—and living—and living."

All during that holiday season the bright lights strung on its branches beamed a greeting to the world through the front windows. And after New Year's it was stripped of its bright baubles and planted, as Clark had suggested, in the garden.

And the third tree?

Clark himself. An oak; strong, dependable, rooted deep in the earth. But nothing outlives its time, not even an oak.

I found that my fingers were working almost of their own volition. They were typing the story of Clark Gable. I have that story before me now as I write this chapter. It is a good story by newspaper standards. It tells a great deal about Clark Gable. But it doesn't really explain him. I know that now, because in the months since his death, in the shorter time since the birth of his handsome, laughing son, I have been trying to find an explanation for Clark.

What was there about him that separated him from others who were handsomer, as successful, just as good actors? What was the quality he possessed that made people his friends?

What was it that permitted him to be son, lover, husband and father to those who watched him on the screen?

Was it because he was the perfect shadow image of them all?

Nothing so completely exemplifies this as the posthumous fatherhood that came to him.

For many years I had known that Clark wanted, more than anything, to have children. He had been married four times and was childless.

Then he married a fifth time and it was happy news for all of us that after all the years of wanting and hoping, he would finally experience fatherhood.

Kay had two children by her marriage to Adolph Spreckels and they lived with Clark and Kay. He loved those two children and they reciprocated. I remember seeing his face light up when one of them called him "Pa." He may even have settled for this adopted parenthood and been satisfied with it, but then a special happiness came to him.

Kay became pregnant. And Clark, sixty years old, man of the world, sophisticate, was a juvenile again. It was as if his coming parenthood was the first in the history of mankind. One of our mutual friends told me soon after the news broke, "He's a blooming idiot about becoming a father. Ever since the doctor gave him the news, he's been up on a cloud and he won't come down."

He was in Reno, Nevada, making his last movie, *The Misfits,* with Marilyn Monroe, when he got the news. I talked with him almost immediately afterward and he was almost incoherent. He kept repeating, "What do you know about it? What do you know?"

It was he who called the two children—Bunky and Joan—to tell them that they would have a little brother or sister in the spring. He wanted them to share his happiness and they did.

His happiness was touching. In anyone else it might have caused jests, laughter, mockery. But Clark was different. A whole industry, a whole town and a whole world seemed to join with him in his joy.

This stemmed, I think, from the fact that Clark was always himself; a man without pretense. That doesn't mean he wore his emotions and feelings for all to see. It meant that he never lied, either in words or emotions. It meant that he always did his best in his life and in his work. It meant that he believed he was the equal of any man and that all men were his equals.

The box-office measuring rod, for what it is worth, rates Clark Gable as the greatest money-making star of all time. He made sixty-one movies and these have grossed, to date, more than $750,000,-000. More than 2,000,000,000 people, it is estimated, have seen him on the screen.

It was fitting, if not inevitable, that he should have appeared in

27

the biggest money-making film of all time, *Gone With The Wind*. Margaret Mitchell, who wrote that book, said that she created the character of Rhett Butler with Clark in mind. Certainly the public believed so for, from the day the book hit the best-seller lists and became a sensation, it was obvious that the public would accept no one but Clark in the part.

The film has grossed more than $4,000,000. It is in re-release now and will add many millions more to its gross. For those who think in terms of money, I suppose that will be their epitaph for Clark Gable. "He filled the movie houses."

But I still would like to probe more deeply. "Why?"

Certainly he epitomized virility on the screen. He was all man and the fans, male and female, loved him for it. For the past thirty years his name has been a symbol. How many times has a gal squelched her guy with an acid, "Who do you think you are? Clark Gable?" And it is evidence of Clark's standing with his own sex that no man resented *that* squelch.

The first time I ever saw Clark was on the stage in Los Angeles the night *The Last Mile* opened. He had a dynamism, a force, an aura of the male animal that leaped across the footlights and affected all of us.

And there was a quality he lacked which endeared him to me from the first. There was no ham in him. He was not then, nor ever, a peacock. He didn't think of himself as a lady-killer. Not then. Not ever. But, take my word for it, he was.

He was signed for pictures almost immediately afterward. Only Clark was surprised. He didn't think he was the type. I'm not sure that MGM believed he was either. Certainly in his first couple of parts, he was cast as a heavy. This was in *The Painted Desert* and in *A Free Soul*.

In this second picture he rudely pushed Norma Shearer into a chair and the audience cheered him. When, near the picture's conclusion, Leslie Howard—the hero—shot Clark, audiences stood up and booed.

Irving Thalberg, then head of production, got the message. It didn't matter that Clark's ears were outsized or that he didn't fit the

28

formula for heroes in facial appearance. Thalberg realized that Clark didn't have to fit a formula, he had created a new one.

Clark was the publicity man's dream. Stories began to come from MGM about Clark's boyhood on a farm in Cadiz, Ohio. Of how he had worked as a mule skinner, as an oil driller, in a rubbermill.

Clark wasn't too happy about those stories. "Sure they're true," he told me, "but they don't tell the important thing. That I always wanted to be an actor. In my teens, I got a job as a callboy in a theatre and I never got the theatre out of my ambition after that. I did lots of other kinds of work and I made pretty good money, but I wasn't happy. I wanted to be an actor."

And an actor he became.

"Hell," he said, "before I came to Hollywood I'd had almost ten years of stock-company experience. I worked backstage, I stage-managed and I played all kinds of parts. I'd even been in a couple of flops on Broadway. A man can do lots of things, but I guess there's only *one* thing he wants to be. I've always wanted to be an actor."

He worked hard at being—or learning to be—an actor. When, through the years, he was asked how one became an actor, his answer was always the simple, "By acting. It's a job. It's a trade. It's a profession. It's an art. And you have to learn it, like all other trades and professions and skills."

He didn't speak a great deal about himself. Just bits and pieces. And through the years I'd forgotten most of them until the time came when I had to write of him through tears and memories. Those things that had been details—small, seemingly unimportant details—suddenly became important.

Writing my daily columns, my weekend features, my magazine stories, I reported on the career of Clark Gable. He was news, big news; and what was important was the new picture in which he had been cast, the latest woman with whom he had been seen, his determination to enlist in the army even though he was overage. But it wasn't important that his mother had died when he was seven months old. It wasn't important that he had been brought up by a stepmother whom he adored.

What did it matter, when I talked of Clark on my radio show,

29

that he had grown up in farm country, a surprisingly lonely boy, who had felt in himself a lack of those social graces that city boys had? Or that, as he told me—his face wrinkled into a smile—of how he had been the one boy back home who never seemed able to adjust to girls, but was always shy and diffident and a little frightened by them?

No, what mattered when I talked of Clark over the microphone was that studios were willing to pay $500,000 to MGM just to borrow him for one picture.

But now, I wonder about that. I wonder if the things I didn't mention—the facts that seemed so unimportant—weren't the factors which shaped his life, made him into the man he was?

How else, for instance, explain his first two marriages?

It was while he was still learning to be an actor that he met Josephine Dillon. She was a drama coach, an elocutionist, a teacher of acting. She was some fifteen years older than he; a charming, quiet woman. And they married before Clark came to Hollywood.

I met them soon after they arrived here and I liked Josephine. But I couldn't help wondering what chance their marriage had of survival. I could see they liked and admired each other, that they respected each other. But their relationship had little of man and woman in it. Instead, you couldn't help but feel that here were teacher and pupil. And pupils have a tendency to graduate.

These thoughts weren't unkind; they were realistic. I knew the romantic jungle of Hollywood and the effect it could have. I knew, too, that fame and success are harder to take than obscurity and that they impose emotional penalties. I'd seen it too often. My heart has ached for a great many first wives and first husbands.

So I wasn't surprised when, soon after Clark's career went into orbit, it became apparent that their marriage was ending. When it did end, it appeared to be without bitterness. (Proof of this would seem to be the fact Clark left her the house she lives in, in his will.)

I took it for granted that when Clark married again it would be someone in the film world. It was just a case of playing percentages. But I was wrong. Clark's second wife was Ria Langham, a widow with children who were almost grown up, who was—again—an older woman.

30

She was poised, charming, handsome. She loved to entertain and she enjoyed bright, sophisticated people. It was a new world for Clark but he became part of it effortlessly by just being, as always, himself. However, once more I had the feeling whenever I was with them that theirs was not essentially a man-woman relationship to which everything else was subordinate.

Again, it seemed, Clark was a pupil, a son, a junior. He was learning the social graces, was being indoctrinated by an older woman into her world. I'm not trying to write as a psychologist, but as an observer.

And so it came as no great surprise to me when, after a relatively short time, they separated. I got the exclusive story of their contemplated divorce and told it in *The Gay Illiterate*. I hope I'll be pardoned if I retell it briefly.

One of the lawyers involved happened to let it slip that the divorce settlement had been arranged, and the person who heard this called me. Clark was in New York and I telephoned him to verify the story.

"It's true," he said, "but I wish you'd get the story from Ria. I don't want to say anything that will embarrass her."

I immediately called her, told her what Clark had said and was delighted when she said, "I'll be right over."

This was all I could ask for. I immediately began to make plans not only to get the story, but to make sure that no one else got it until mine was in print.

When Ria came to the house, I insisted that she tell me her side of the story. Then, as I sat down at the typewriter, I looked up at intervals to check a point with her or to ask her advice. When the story was done, I called for a messenger to pick it up.

Ria said it was time for her to go but I insisted that she stay and have dinner with me. She agreed. After dinner we talked some more. I showed her some new hats I had bought. We listened to a radio program together. We played cards. And I watched the clock. I knew how long it would take for the story to get on the wires; how much time I needed to assure me of my "exclusive." To that time I added an extra hour just for safety's sake. It was a tired Ria Gable who finally left my house to go home.

When a reporter from a rival syndicate did finally reach her, after

31

my story was long in print, he complained that he had not been able to find her although he had tried everywhere. "Where did you hide out?" he asked.

"At Louella Parsons' house," she told him.

"My God."

Oh, those were the days.

But, back to Clark. Within two years after he appeared in his first picture, he was one of the "Top Ten" box-office draws in pictures. He was to remain at, or near, the top all the rest of his active career. People liked him.

Wherever he went, he was mobbed. He had to give up deep-sea fishing off Santa Monica because he turned out to be bait for eager crowds, and the bait he was using was tangled and cut. He caught fans, not fish. When he made an appearance at a public function, the police had to be on hand to prevent his being mobbed.

This was, of course, in the period when movies had no rival such as TV, and the glamour had not rubbed off the stars as it has in the years since. But the reaction to Clark was so much bigger, so much more spontaneous, that it set him in a class by himself.

One oft-reported aspect of his influence had to do with a scene in *It Happened One Night*, the wonderful comedy in which he appeared with Claudette Colbert in 1934 and for which he won an Academy Award. In this scene Clark removed his shirt and revealed only a hairy chest, but no undershirt. Almost overnight the men's undershirt business ran into a depression from which it has not recovered to this day.

There is an interesting high light to this picture. It reveals the element of luck in the picture business.

MGM had borrowed Frank Capra, one of the outstanding directors in Hollywood, from Harry Cohn at Columbia, and in return was to lend Robert Montgomery, then a far bigger star than Gable, to Columbia. The terms of the deal called for Capra to work at MGM for three months. However, at the end of three months Capra still had not made the MGM picture. Nevertheless, Cohn insisted that Capra return to Columbia.

This angered MGM and Columbia was told that Montgomery would not be available to Columbia for any time in the near, or even distant, future. However, MGM was willing to let Columbia have Gable, who at the time was having some trouble with his MGM bosses. Cohn was all set to insist upon Montgomery when Frances Manson, then story editor at Columbia, said she had a perfect picture for Gable and that she felt he would be better in it than Montgomery.

The picture was *It Happened One Night,* and there was a further irony here. MGM, by reason of its relations with Mr. Hearst through Cosmopolitan Pictures, had first call on all stories which appeared in *Cosmopolitan* Magazine. It was in that magazine that the story appeared on which *It Happened One Night* was based. The MGM story department had recommended it but L. B. Mayer had turned it down because the millionaire father of the heroine was depicted in an unfavorable light.

Columbia had then purchased the story for $5,000.

Frank Capra, of course, directed it and Gable, who had been temporarily marked down by MGM, suddenly became its biggest star and was not to lose that position for many years.

Not long afterward Clark was called "The King" for the first time. This was no press-agent stunt, no carefully evolved publicity stratagem. I believe it was Spencer Tracy who first called him that but soon everyone was referring to him by the title. It was one he appreciated but one that also embarrassed him.

But if he was a king professionally, he didn't rate very high in the *Almanach de Cupid.* This was the period between his separation from Ria and his next marriage. It was a time when he had few public dates and his spare time was taken up with that most masculine of pursuits, hunting.

This was an enthusiasm he shared with his father who was now living near Clark. The two spent a lot of time together and it was remarkable how much alike they looked, except that Clark was so much bigger than his father; a kind of giant-economy size. They would have Sunday dinner together—strictly red meat and potatoes—and discuss hunting and fishing.

But the routine of picturemaking and the sporting life was suddenly exploded by a woman—Carole Lombard.

I knew Carole well—my husband was her doctor and so the relationship transcended the film business—and she was one of the most enchanting of women. She looked like an angel and behaved like a gamin. She was lusty, but it was a healthy, 100 per cent womanly type of lustiness. And beneath an appearance of bravado, of bounce, she was a "giving" woman. In a place where so many are takers, this was enough to set her apart from the majority.

She was an important star, a big box-office name, when she and Clark began their romance. They had known each other for some time and had played opposite, some two years earlier, in *No Man of Her Own*. That was during Carole's brief, and hardly happy, marriage to William Powell.

And here I would like to make a point about Clark. He had romances, a great many of them, but it was always with women who were free. He was no poacher, in the hunting field or in the arena of romance. He respected another man's wife.

But now Carole was free and that meant he could enter the lists.

I recall the night that their paths crossed again—and their stars. It was at the fabulous White Ball, given at the old Mayfair Club. Carole, who had been in charge of arrangements, was an angel in white. The doctor and I were sitting with her at her table when Clark came over and asked her to dance.

We watched them, Clark dark and handsome, Carole blond and truly beautiful, as they moved in time to the music. It seemed to us that they weren't so much dancing together as blending together, as if they were two parts of a perfect whole.

My husband and I exchanged a quick look and later, when we talked about it, it seemed we had had the same thought. How wonderful it would be if these two, who had known little happiness in their personal relationships, could find some of that happiness together.

Carole, in addition to her unhappy marriage to William Powell, had been through the tragedy of her love for singer Russ Colombo. All Hollywood knew how much these two had cared for each other and how an accidental, pointless shooting had killed Colombo, leaving Carole grief-stricken and so broken that she required medical care for a long time.

The next morning Carole was on the telephone. "Louella," she said, "I think I'm in love."

I had no answer for that. But I wondered how Clark felt. The answer came, not in words, but in action. He began courting Carole with the fervor of a young man involved in his first love affair. This was it. This was for real. This was forever.

And yet there was, in my mind, the thought that these two people were basically so different.

Carole was a comedienne. She was irreverent. She knew a lot of impolite terms and used them. She had no show, no pretense; did what came naturally.

Clark, for all his apparent worldliness, was still quite naïve. He had a sense of humor, but it was a passive one. He could appreciate humor a great deal more easily than he could join in it. And he shocked easily.

One of them would have to give, if not both. It turned out that both of them wanted to give.

Carole enjoyed practical jokes. She bought an old truck and had it painted white with big red hearts splashed all over it, and sent it to Clark as a Valentine's Day gift. His reaction was to stop driving his own car and start driving the truck all over town.

Carole appeared in a picture directed by Norman Taurog, and a live bear was one of the characters in the film. Taurog had his troubles with the bear and when he finished the picture announced, "I never want to see that—bear again."

Carole, hearing this, arranged with the trainer for him and the bear to be waiting on Taurog's lawn the next morning; her gift to the director. (The bear, not the trainer.) When Taurog saw the bear he was first flabbergasted and then decided to turn the tables on Carole. He pointed out he had no place to keep the bear and that it should be returned to the animal farm from which it had come. "Miss Lombard loves animals and she would want the bear to have nothing but the best. So provide it with steaks. And send the bill to her."

When Gable heard this story, and learned that the bear had already eaten about $800 worth of steaks, he suggested that it be turned loose on one of his hunting parties. That almost broke up the romance.

For, from the beginning, Carole was aware that if she had any rival, it was Clark's love of the outdoors. She was a city girl herself at that time.

Not long after they started romancing, Gable told her he was going hunting for wildcats in Arizona.

Carole gave him a rough time. She told him she didn't want him to go hunting. She told him that there weren't any wildcats in Arizona, so the whole hunting business was a fraud. And she told him that hunting was for Boy Scouts.

Clark went anyway but he did leave a telephone number through which he could be reached in case of an emergency.

Carole decided that she would prove her point. She immediately began to check with wildlife authorities on the subject of wildcats in Arizona. And, as he told me, "They say the country is full of them. I've got to apologize to Clark."

"You really should," I said.

She called the emergency number and asked that Clark be found and asked to return her call. Two days later he did call. "What's the matter? Are you sick? Is anything wrong?"

"No. I just wanted to apologize. I've found out there really are wildcats in Arizona."

The receiver at the other end banged down. "I'll never speak to that—again," she told me and Fieldsie and Walter Lang, her two closest friends. Fieldsie (Madeline Fields) was her secretary and lived with her before she married Walter Lang, a famous director.

But she did speak to Clark when someone who had been hunting with Gable told her that it had taken more than a day for the message to reach him and that, as soon as he received it, he began an eight-hour horseback ride in a rainstorm through rugged terrain, to return the call. She apologized for a second time.

Not long after that she followed the old axiom, "If you can't beat them, join them." She decided that if she had to hunt to be part of Clark's life, she would.

She was always a perfectionist. She had learned to be an expert swimmer, tennis player and horsewoman, and now she set out to become an expert hunter and fisher. She was never one to do things halfheartedly and this was no exception. She found the best teachers and with their help mastered marksmanship and fly casting.

Later she bought a trailer in which she could live when she went on trips into the wilds with Clark and his cronies. This was her home and she stayed in it while the males enjoyed their stag fun in camps and lodges.

Carole was always a woman of contradiction to me. So feminine on the surface, she had a strong will and determination. And when it came to her work she was as single-minded as Clark. Like him, she had a great respect for their profession and would never sell it— or herself—short.

When she and Clark first became serious, he was separated, but not divorced, from Ria. There was a long period during which attorneys sought to work out a settlement between the Gables. When, as it seemed at times, there were insuperable roadblocks and even Clark grew dispirited, Carole was always certain that things would be worked out. When I asked her how she could be so certain, she said, "It's in the numbers."

She had great belief in numerology, and as long as the numbers were on her side she never had any doubts. As she pointed out to me, it was numerology which had caused her to change her name from Jane Peters (not good) to Carole (with an "e") Lombard (very good). "And you see what happened," she said.

When things were finally straightened out, she said, "I told you they would be."

She and Clark bought a ranch in Encino, not far from where we were living. During the three years they were there, the friendship between Carole Lombard, Clark Gable, Fieldsie, Walter Lang and Dr. Martin and me continued to be a warm one. We saw a great deal of each other.

In 1937, Dockie and I went to Europe. We spent my birthday in Venice with Sally Eilers and her then husband, director Harry Joe Brown. I was in some inexplicable way, homesick. When we returned to our hotel, the Lido, there was a cable from Carole, Clark, Fieldsie and Walter, saying: WE ARE THINKING OF YOU TODAY. YOUR GIFT IS A SURPRISE. YOU WILL GET IT WHEN YOU RETURN HOME. Dr. Martin was in on the secret, but beg, borrow or steal, he wouldn't tell.

You can imagine my surprise when I returned home and walked into my bathroom, to find a card reading: HAPPY BIRTHDAY FROM

37

CAROLE, CLARK, FIELDSIE AND WALTER. Carole had personally done over my bathroom—the walls were mirrored—the doors painted pink—the walls hung with pictures—and all new plumbing installed. It was an unusual present but I had admired Carole's bathroom, and she wanted to give me something I wouldn't give myself.

It was interesting and exciting to see their relationship develop. They had been in love when they married, but that love grew deeper each year. It seemed to me that she added an extra dimension to Clark, as if by being his wife, she was proof to the world that he was the strong, dominant, conquering male.

And then came Pearl Harbor.

Carole took it on herself as a personal responsibility to aid the war effort. When a request was made for stars to go on tour to sell war bonds, she immediately volunteered. She was asked to start on such a tour early in January, and immediately agreed. Just before she left she and Clark had, as he told me, "a silly disagreement." It was something minor that they blew up into more importance than it possessed.

After she left, Clark moped. Finally he was able to reach her on the telephone and they made up with their "Hello's." He was exuberant and started to make preparations for her return. She, in turn, was altering her plans so that she could get back at once.

The plane in which she was flying home struck a mountainside near Las Vegas, Nevada. Everyone on board was killed in one of the most shocking tragedies that has ever struck Hollywood.

Clark rushed to Las Vegas with his closest friend, Howard Strickling, head of publicity at MGM, and Eddie Mannix, MGM executive. Together they went to the barren waste where wreckage of the plane was strewn. Somehow they got separated in the early evening and Strickling went looking for Clark. He found him finally, sitting beside some of the wreckage, weeping like a child.

In every such tragedy there are always "it might have been's," always feelings of guilt that are baseless, but nonetheless existent. I remember how often Clark talked about that last phone call and how, if it had not been made, Carole might not have been on the plane. This undoubtedly added to his grief. Certainly few men have ever been as inconsolable about the loss of a wife as he was.

He didn't make a public show of it, of course. That wasn't in character. But those of us who knew him well were aware of what an effect the loss had on him. It occupied all his thoughts, dominated all his memories. And he sought consolation in the only way he could —through work.

Then he told us that he was determined to get into the service. He was then forty-one, overage for enlistment, but was able, despite this, to enlist in the Air Corps. He made it plain that he was going in as "Clark Gable, citizen," not "Clark Gable, movie star." He wanted to fight.

Of course he couldn't change what he was. But, at the same time, he never took advantage of it. He took the same training as other enlistees. When he went to Officers' Training School, he took the same courses, was held to the same discipline as all the others attending. When he received his bars as a second lieutenant, it was because he had earned them. No one was more vociferous about reporting this than the men who were in OCS with him.

He was a major—a rank he had earned—when he was discharged in March, 1944. It was a blow to him not to be able to remain in the service until the end of the war, but he was getting the same treatment as other men of his age. War, it seemed, was for young men.

When he came back to Hollywood, he was almost a recluse until the war finally ended. He didn't want to cash in on his fame, his war record or the fact that other men were fighting his war. Instead, he went off hunting and fishing and kept to himself otherwise.

After the war he was cast in a picture titled *Adventure,* with Greer Garson. He was very unhappy about the script. "It's just no good," he told me. "I wish I didn't have to do it." He was a big enough star to have fought against doing the role, but he was under contract to MGM which wanted him to do it. Unlike some other stars, he respected his contract.

I have always believed that what really embittered him was not so much the picture as the advertising campaign that MGM used. He writhed every time he heard or saw the words, "Gable's Back and Garson's Got Him."

It was a bad picture but it made money. I'm certain that was because movie fans all over were so happy that he *was* back.

He was still adored by women. That went for the biggest names in Hollywood as well as for the millions of anonymous fans; but he kept himself uninvolved.

"I had something so perfect with Carole," he told me, "that I can't expect ever to have it again. I don't ever expect to marry again."

He did, however, start to go out again, and one of the women with whom he was often seen was lovely Kay Williams—as blond as Carole had been—who looked a little like her and who possessed the same high spirits, the same love of fun, the same pixie sense of humor.

And she seemed able, as Carole had, to house-tame Clark. He loathed cards but Kay could even get him to play gin rummy or old maid, and it seemed to Dr. Martin and me, greater love hath no man than to play old maid.

Then, just when it looked as if these two might be getting serious, Clark went East. He went without saying good-by to Kay and she didn't hear from him all the time he was gone. That hurt her terribly but she never spoke a word against Clark.

I felt that Clark was caught up in some kind of internal struggle. That he felt that getting involved with any other woman would make him faithless to Carole. And I felt too that somehow he wasn't quite ready to face marriage again; as if marriage was too much of a challenge for him at the time.

But that, of course, was only a guess.

At any rate, after his return he did not see Kay. Instead, he dated a series of women. There was Virginia Grey, a quiet, serious young actress with great ability. She was a girl with a gentle and apparently forgiving character, because it was no secret that Clark was dating other women, yet when he started dating her again she always seemed happy to see him.

However, it was Virginia who finally broke this off. She said that Clark would have to make up his mind. If he wanted to play the field she was dropping out of the race.

Next came Dolly O'Brien Dorelis, a society personality who was part of the international set. She was more a contemporary of Clark's and she did represent a new element in his life, a step beyond the world he had known when he was married to Ria. When Clark went to Florida to be her house guest over Christmas everyone said, "This is it."

But it wasn't. I hadn't believed it had much of a chance because I had never been able to imagine Dolly packing in and sloughing through the wilds on a deer hunt.

Other women figured briefly in his life. Paulette Goddard, with her flair for publicity, announced that Clark was The Man in her life when he saw her off on a plane trip to Mexico. He wasn't at the airport when she returned.

He escorted such beauties as Anita Colby, Joan Crawford and Marilyn Maxwell. Romance, yes; marriage, no—if I may paraphrase a slogan of today.

And then Sylvia Ashley Fairbanks Stanley returned to town. She had married into the British peerage twice and the Hollywood peerage once, when she became Mrs. Douglas Fairbanks, but was now free.

For those who may not recall Sylvia, here is a brief rundown.

She was born Sylvia Hawkes, daughter of a London stableman. She was, from childhood, a very beautiful pale blonde and again, from childhood, knew the power of her beauty.

Her first job was as a manicurist in a London barbershop. One of her regular customers was Lord Ashley, a handsome blade-about-town whose democratic heart had often caused anguish to his aristocratic relatives. When Sylvia changed from manicurist to show girl in a London revue, the knowing ascribed this to Lord Ashley's—influence. But the real shocker came when Lord Ashley married the show girl.

And now Sylvia proved her mettle. She made no effort to hide her beginnings. People would have to take her for what she was and if they didn't, that was too bad. This didn't help her with the bluenoses, but it did with that section of British society which is analogous to our own "café society," and in Britain that included—at the time—most of the famous names, including some of royal background.

There was a freedom in that group that shocked many who were hardly bluenoses. They laughed and loved and lived carefree lives. They made their own rules and broke them when the occasion arose and it suited their purpose.

41

Perhaps Lady Sylvia fitted into this group too well. Whatever the reason, it soon became known that the Ashleys were estranged. And Lady Sylvia began to be seen in the company of Douglas Fairbanks, Sr. It was not long afterward that Mary Pickford announced that she was divorcing Fairbanks and that Lady Sylvia was the reason.

After Mary divorced Doug he returned to England. Soon Lord Ashley sued for divorce, naming Doug as correspondent. After that divorce, Sylvia and Doug were married and they returned to take up life in Hollywood.

I had a grudge against Sylvia. Mary had long been one of my closest friends and I knew what the breakup of her marriage had meant to her. (Had I been she, I would have gone to England, grabbed Doug by the ear and dragged him back to Hollywood, thus putting an end to such nonsense. But I wasn't Mary and, as I now know, only those involved can ever know the reasons why a marriage ends.)

I wasn't surprised, however, when I received a call from Douglas asking me to come to his home and meet Sylvia. He wasn't inviting Louella Parsons, his ex-wife's friend. He was inviting Louella O. Parsons, columnist and syndicated writer. And as a newspaperwoman I had to accept the invitation. It was my job to meet this siren who had first married a titled Britisher and then married Hollywood's top male star. Off I went to their home on the beach front at Santa Monica.

I was unprepared for the charming, vivacious woman I met. She had humor and wit and, if I didn't leave the house won over, I certainly left it neutral. I felt that here were two people who loved one another and that was almost enough for me.

(I'm like Alexander Throttlebottom and Mr. Wintergreen. I believe that love is the answer to almost all the problems the world faces. If everyone in the world were happily married, as I see it, there would be less hate and viciousness and misunderstanding. Happy, loving people don't make wars.)

After that visit, I again saw the Fairbanks and, coincidentally, Clark and Ria Gable, who moved in much the same circles.

Then Douglas died. For a time Sylvia stayed in their home but finally left for England. There some five years later, Sylvia married Lord Stanley of Alderley. I met Sylvia and her new husband briefly in New York. That marriage lasted two years. For a time afterward, Lady Sylvia traveled about and there were many stories of romantic involvements that filtered back to Hollywood. And then Lady Sylvia returned.

If this were fiction, I might try to show that a long time before, when Clark and Sylvia first met, some spark had been ignited that had smoldered all these years and now burst into flame when they met again. But it isn't fiction that I'm writing and so I'll have to say that there was no sign that they were anything more than friends when, after Sylvia's return, she was seen occasionally with Gable. Clark was seemingly engrossed with handsome Joan Harrison, the blond producer who later became noted for the Alfred Hitchcok TV shows.

By this time I wasn't regarding any of Clark's romances as serious; there were just too many of them and they all followed the same pattern of a quick beginning and a sudden end. And Sylvia had told me, at a party at the Charles Vidors, "I shall never marry again. Douglas is the only man I ever loved or will love." It was quite a renunciation scene and I would not have been surprised if, shortly afterward, she had taken vows.

I was surprised—and flabbergasted—when, on December 20th, 1949, a "flash" reached my office: "Clark Gable and Sylvia Ashley are being married this very minute at a ranch near Santa Barbara."

Here is where I wished that I had been given the old "I want you to be the first to know!" treatment. Instead, I had to make do with what information trickled in to me. (Within an hour after the story hit the wires, I had received two magazine assignments for stories on the marriage, and my paper had instructed me to write a one-shot paperback book. I learned that this had been an impetuous elopement, with only enough notice for Howard Strickling to go with them to San Luis Obispo, California, to get the license.

The marriage had taken place at Alisal, a dude ranch owned by one of Clark's friends, and the couple spent the wedding night there. Next day they drove down to the Encino ranch and, according to report, Clark carried his bride over the threshold. It was probably true; Clark, at least, was full of sentiment.

That evening they called me. "Sylvia and I want to thank you for your wire and good wishes," Clark said. "We'll see you when we get back from Honolulu."

This marriage just didn't have a chance. Looking back, I can see all the handicaps that the pair faced. I know, for instance, that Clark had not only married a bride, but also what he hoped was a substitute for Carole. And he was wrong, for never were two women as different as Carole and Sylvia.

Where Carole had changed and altered her life to fit the pattern that suited Clark, Sylvia expected Clark to change his way of life to suit hers. Where Carole had been a "giving" woman, Sylvia—spoiled and petted by at least two husbands—was a "taking" woman. (I'm not implying that she was "taking" in a material sense, though she ultimately did get a fine divorce settlement.)

And Sylvia had expensive tastes. Clark balked at these, especially when bills came rolling in for changes that she insisted upon making in the ranch, so long his home. Clark, by the way, was always conservative about money, what the Scotch call "canny."

They broke up rather quickly and, after the divorce, Clark said, "It's good to be free again. And this time I'm going to stay free."

He never talked about their differences. They were personal and not to be discussed with anyone, for which I respected him. However, I always felt that the basic reason that their marriage was so short lived and unhappy was that Sylvia did harm to Clark's male ego. Instead of building this up, she tore it down. And since he was always sensitive about this, it was a booby trap from which there was no happy escape.

That same day, as Clark and I talked in the playroom of my home, he did delve more deeply into himself than I had ever heard him do. He had just left MGM, after twenty-three years at that studio, and was now free-lancing. "I'm fifty-four years old," he said and I've worked hard—very hard—for a quarter of a century. It's time to slow down, take inventory and see where I'm going."

"You're going," I said, "to keep on breaking hearts." There was a touch of silver at his temples, but he still looked as handsome and youthful and virile as ever. "Don't tell me you're going to give up women."

He broke into laughter. "I'll always enjoy the company of any lovely ladies who will have me. But no more wedding bells. As far as they're concerned, I'm tone deaf."

There were plenty of lovely ladies, I knew, who would be delighted to enjoy his company. The most beautiful was probably Grace Kelly, who had played in *Mogambo* with him. That film had been made in Africa and there were rumors that more than the weather had been heated during the filming. "What about Grace Kelly?" I asked.

"She's a lovely kid," he said, "but still a kid." He smiled. "There's nothing there, Louella, except friendship."

And apparently there was nothing but friendship for Clark with other women. Suzanne Dadolle, a French model, took a leaf from Paulette Goddard's outdated notebook and announced she might have a statement for the press. Clark and the lady from Paris were never seen together again. And when the newspapers started to couple Clark's name almost constantly with that of a charming Arizona widow, Betty Chisholme, the pair quickly uncoupled.

Yes, I must say that at the time it looked as if the King didn't intend to marry again.

Almost at the same moment Kay Williams came back into his life. It had been a long time between dates for them. A long time since Gable, tormented, uncertain, had left her without even a good-by.

In the years between, Kay had been married to millionaire Adolph Spreckels and borne him two children. Theirs had been one of the stormiest marriages on record, replete with quarrels and separations. Once, after a violent disagreement with Kay, Spreckels told newspapermen, "Kay never got Clark Gable out of her system." Kay heatedly denied this and, at the time, must have felt that it was true.

They were finally divorced, after Kay walked into court with proof of physical injury at the hands of Spreckels.

And some time after the divorce, Kay and Clark got together again. It was, I suppose, a form of unfinished business in their lives.

I think the years of their separation really made it possible for them to marry. Each had matured in that time. Each had known

45

more unhappiness than happiness. Each was, I feel, prepared to do a little more to make the other happy. And certainly after they married they succeeded.

Kay gave him the best home life he had ever known. Her two children were a boon to him. He was able, for the first time, to live the life of a family man. And at the same time, because Kay wanted only to make him happy, he was married to a woman who thought only in terms of him. Not even Carole had been able to do that because, in addition to being a wife, she had been a great star and, as such, an individual with her own separate existence.

Yes, this was a period of contentment for Clark. Unlike so many of his contemporaries, he accepted the fact that he was no longer young. The parts he played in pictures suited him because of this. And for that reason his career was continuing to roll in high gear.

When he was asked to play in *The Misfits,* written by Arthur Miller for his then-wife, Marilyn Monroe, Clark was offered the highest pay ever; $750,000 advance against 10 per cent of the gross of the picture, for a straight sixteen weeks' work. In the event the picture took longer, he would receive a salary of $48,000 a week!

It was while he was making this picture that Kay told him that she was pregnant. I have told how this affected him. This was the high light of his life and he wanted, more than anything, to get to his ranch to be with her. He counted the days and, unfortunately, these lengthened. It soon became apparent that the picture would go over schedule.

This was nothing new with a Monroe picture but, because this one was costing both her and Miller money, there had been the hope that the normal Monroe delays, breakdowns and diseases would not happen. But they did.

This galled a professional like Clark. All his acting life he had appeared on the set on time, his lines carefully rehearsed, ready to give all his talent and effort to the job at hand. He had worked with the greatest and he certainly was one of the greatest himself, and this was the way a picture should be made. But now he found himself the victim of Marilyn's temperament and psychosomatic stresses.

Of all the company, he was the one who seemed least affected. He was a great actor to the end.

46

For, three days after he returned from the Reno location which had weeks overtime, he suffered a heart attack. He was rushed to a hospital and all of us who knew him personally, as well as the hundreds of millions who knew him only on the screen, started hoping and praying that he would recover.

It seemed as if our hopes and prayers would be answered for, shortly, word came that he was recovering. And some of us prayed again, this time prayers of thanks.

And then I turned on the radio and heard, "Clark Gable is dead."

I am looking, once more, at the first paragraphs of the story I wrote that night.

"The heart of the world aches today in sorrow over the death of virile, popular, sports-loving Clark Gable, called 'The King' by his adoring public.

"To us, who loved him well, he was more than 'The King'—he was our pal; someone to laugh with and listen to as he told his tales of hunting and fishing.

"Something has gone out of our lives with Clark's death that will never return. It's hard to imagine a world without Clark Gable, who has been my friend from the time he arrived in Hollywood. . . ."

And now, once more, I am saying good-by to a friend. I have sought to explain what he was, as much to myself as to anyone else. I have tried to tell those things he was, those qualities he possessed, the things that happened to him; so that I could better understand him.

He was a remarkable man and if I have done nothing else, I hope I have shown some of the qualities that made him that.

Some day a child who never knew his father may want to learn something about the kind of man that father was. Perhaps what I have written will help. I hope so.

➤➤ *Chapter 3*

THE FOUNDING FATHERS

IT is an eerie feeling to call the roll and have so few answer "Here." Among them: Harry Cohn, Harry Warner, Winfield Sheehan, William Fox, Jesse Lasky, C. B. De Mille, Louis B. Mayer, Lewis Selznick, David Wark Griffith, Mack Sennett—all founding fathers of our fabulous industry.

It is stranger still to hear these names mentioned and be answered by a blank stare from some youngster whose fame and fortune rest on the foundation that these men built.

In compiling material for this book I had intended from the start to devote a chapter to the astonishing pioneers, the men of dreams and steel who founded the motion-picture industry.

"Don't do it" said some of my solicited and unsolicited advisers. "The readers of today aren't interested in the founding fathers. Most of them are gone from the scene anyway. Stories about them would be *dull.*"

Ha!

Is the story of Edison dull to the electric light; Ford or Dupont to the automobile; Marconi and Lee De Forest to radio?

Believe me, some of the most exciting stories of our industry have to do with these early-day giants of the movies whose daring gambles equaled the most extravagant exploits of our historical forefathers.

I do, however, agree that my purpose in this book is not to recount biography but to give a respectful review of these veterans as I found them. And I found them plenty exciting!

Yes, giant ghosts parade through my memory.

I think back to the days of open warfare when the late Myron Selznick, brother of David, son of the powerful Lewis Selznick, and first of the mighty agents, nearly brought on the wreckage of my radio show.

I think back on the bitter vendettas I have carried on with Sam (the one and only) Goldwyn. Of my clash of swords with Louis B. Mayer and the flamboyant Cecil B. De Mille; in the case of the latter, not his fault nor mine.

The personal fight I waged for D. W. Griffith's immortal *Birth of A Nation* comes back to me now as a chapter of courage and integrity —although it almost cost me my newspaper job at the time, high-mindedness or not!

Of all those who founded the motion-picture industry as it is today, only Sam Goldwyn and Jack Warner are still active.

But every now and then, as I walk through the lobby of the Beverly Hills Hotel, I run across a wonderful friend, Adolph Zukor, the spryest octogenarian I know and still Chairman of the Board of Paramount Pictures, his eyes twinkling and his zest for "his movies" as great as when he "dared" to make a picture with Sarah Bernhardt!

We always stop and talk and *remember*. He once told me, "I like being with you, Louella. You remember all the people I remember."

Not too long ago, Mr. Zukor invited me to lunch with him, just the two of us. Of course we talked movies—past and present.

"The French have a saying," this charming gentleman said over our luncheon table, " 'The more things change, the more they remain the same.' Now everyone talks of the movies moving to Europe. Almost everyone has forgotten, or never knew, that my first company made some pictures in Europe; the first made because I was in love."

"With moving pictures?"

49

"No." And, as always, his eyes crinkled when he smiled. "With an actress. With Sarah Bernhardt. For years I had been in love with her —my wife knew about it and thought it was very nice as long as Madame Bernhardt and I remained strangers.

"I felt all the world should love the Divine Sarah as I did. So I suggested that we star the French tragedienne in a full-length picture."

Mr. Zukor chuckled. "As it was my company and *my* suggestion— I was the boss you see—the plan was carried out. Privately, I think my associates and many of our exhibitors thought I was dotty. This I fully sensed—and went ahead anyway. We made *Queen Elizabeth*, starring Bernhardt, and it was a great success. So you see, foreign pictures with foreign stars are nothing new. I could well say, 'That's where I came in.' "

I joined Mr. Zukor in his laughter, then asked, "And did you stay 'in love' with Bernhardt?"

He shook his head gently. "Louella, I think the only way to stay in love with a great actress is not to meet her."

But Mr. Zukor has never fallen out of love—with motion pictures.

"The industry is still young," he says. "Its future is brighter than its past. Just wait and see." Only then does he grow somber. "My one regret is that I won't be around when it really reaches its greatest heights."

Among those who competed with Mr. Zukor in those early days were Carl Laemmle and Lewis J. Selznick. Selznick was a rugged individualist, a trait he passed on to his sons, the late Myron Selznick and David O. Selznick.

The story of Lewis Selznick's battles against the rest of Hollywood, his determination to be himself and his own boss, are a vivid part of the Hollywood legend. In the end he was beaten, but his two sons carried on the fight for him.

I first met Lewis Selznick in Chicago when I was writing my first movie column. At that time he was producing one-reelers and marketing them himself. It was a small business at the time but he told everyone who would listen, "The moving-picture business is going to be great. It will make a millionaire of anyone with faith in it."

It did make him a millionaire and, as has happened so often, it also took him from the top of the financial heap to the bottom. But he never changed as an individual. He was a friend of mine from those early days and remained my friend until his death.

He gave me some of my first exclusive stories and, when my paper was sold and I lost my job, he was one of the producers who continued to think of me. When he heard that I was going to New York to try to start over again, he came to see me. "Whom do you know in New York?" he asked.

"Very few people."

"I know a lot of people. I have written letters to some of them and I want you to use these letters." He pressed a thick stack into my hands. "Louella, don't be too proud. When you need help, call on your friends. That's why we have friends."

Years later, when Lewis Selznick was engaged in his great battle, I reminded him of what he had told me and said, "Don't be too proud to ask the help of friends."

"I'm not," he said. "It's just that I don't seem able to find those friends."

I was equally fond of his wife, Florence Selznick. She was one of the most beautiful women I have ever met, with enormous brown eyes that were always filled with kindness and gentleness.

There came a time when my felicitous relationship with the Selznick family was really put to the test.

I was on radio with my "Hollywood Hotel" program. The biggest stars in Hollywood had long been appearing on the program, taking their payment in the publicity value of their appearances and to their pictures. I know many persons have implied that I used the pressure of my circulation to get them to appear, but that was not true.

Of course, the stars wanted to be on my good side. Some of them, I believe, because they liked me. Some because they wanted me to like them. And many because they decided, after weighing the pros and cons, that any publicity was good publicity. Furthermore, it advertised their current movies and the motion-picture companies were in favor of it.

I realize now, looking back, that they should all have received payment. However, the budget for my show was very high for those days and the only way the show could stay on the air was for the stars to appear gratis.

I was unprepared at the time, though, for an ultimatum that I either pay the stars or none of them would be available for the show. This was the result of a decision made by the then outstanding agent in Hollywood, Myron Selznick, who had the majority of them as clients.

I appealed to my sponsors for a larger budget but they refused. It appeared that this meant the end of my radio show. I was most unhappy, of course, but it seemed that there was no choice. Dr. Martin had a suggestion. "Why don't you go directly to Myron and see if you can get him to change his mind?"

We drove to Santa Monica where Myron was living with his widowed mother. Myron was charming, friendly but adamant. "No money, no stars."

He was repeating this when Florence Selznick came into the room. She listened to him for a moment and then interrupted her son. He was at that time about as powerful as any man in Hollywood. The largest studios were in awe and terror of him. But not Florence Selznick.

"Myron," she said, "I'm ashamed of you. Louella is an old friend of your father's and mine. You know you're supposed to help your friends; not hurt them. Besides, why should you keep her from making money when you're making so much yourself?"

When he tried to answer, Florence stopped him. Instead, she said to me, "Don't worry, dear. You'll get every star you need."

Myron started to protest, then stopped. "You win, Louella. I'm licked. Just don't ask me for too many."

And that explains how I was able to continue with my show when a great many people were convinced—some of them gloatingly so— that I was going to be forced off the air. These same people started the rumor that it was Mr. Hearst and his influence that had saved the show. But the truth was something entirely different, as you know now.

The radio show had been saved because of a very gracious lady and

52

a very generous one, who placed friendship above profit and had a son who respected her feelings. When I tried to express my thanks to her, she said, "Why, Louella, I only did what Lewis would have done."

Myron Selznick is gone now also. I lost a good friend when he died. In a sense, he left a deeper mark on Hollywood than almost anyone in its history. It was Myron Selznick who made the stars aware of their power. It was he who laid the foundation for today's Hollywood which is run by the stars and their agents.

Until Myron came along, agents were usually more responsive to the studios than to their clients. And contracts between stars and studios were loaded in favor of the studios. But he changed all that. Myron Selznick was aware of the tremendous drawing power of the stars and that the studios needed them and their box-office appeal.

The agency of which he was a part set out to tie up as clients as many big names as possible. Before Myron was finished he had almost a monopoly. And he was able to impose his will on the studios.

In this way, as was so often remarked, Myron was the final winner in the battle his father had lost.

David Selznick, the other son, also left a mark on Hollywood. No producer, I believe, has ever outshone David. As a boy in his late twenties, he was head of production at the old RKO studio. A short time later he was producing such pictures as *Dinner at Eight, Tale of Two Cities, Anna Karenina* and *David Copperfield*, as boss at MGM.

It was David who produced *Gone With The Wind*, still one of the best pictures ever made. It has been re-released and is again playing to crowded movie audiences. This and *Rebecca*, in successive years, won the Academy Awards. A record no other producer has equaled.

David is regarded as the one producer in Hollywood to whom money is a tool, not an end. He has said that he is interested in making great pictures; not in making big money. As a result, the Hollywood story is that David is carrying on his father's feud with the great production companies. As it is put, "Lewis Selznick couldn't beat them, but give David enough time and he'll break them."

Hardly true, but still worth repeating.

Personally, I'm waiting for David to return to active production again. Hollywood needs him.

Another Hollywood victim was David Wark Griffith, the first great picturemaker and still regarded by many as the greatest.

D. W. Griffith was truly the master. This was what I called him in the days when I was writing my first columns. His technical innovations really turned pictures into "moving pictures." It was he who took the camera, until then stationed solidly before the stage like a Cyclops, and made it mobile.

D. W. Griffith invented the close-up, the fade-in, the wipe. He made the camera an actor and a spectator at the same time. He was the inventor of intercutting—that device by which various threads of a story are told simultaneously.

It was with Griffith's *Birth of a Nation* that the motion picture attained maturity.

I have never been known as the Carrie Nation of Hollywood, but there was one time when I was the leader of a crusade when *Birth of a Nation* was first shown, in Chicago.

There were riots and fights outside the theatre where it was advertised to open. Passions were at white heat and everyone was partisan.

My paper, the *Record-Herald,* took a violent anti-Griffith position. James Keeley, the publisher, wrote editorials condemning the picture and demanding that it be withdrawn from the screen.

I felt that this was wrong. I believed that *Birth of a Nation* was a great picture—the best made up to that time—and that if it were not freely shown it would be calamitous. I said so to Mr. Keeley and, talking to him, realized that he had taken his position without ever having seen the picture.

"Please see it," I asked him.

"It won't change my mind. This picture should be banned."

"I think you're wrong, Mr. Keeley. And have you thought that if *you* can censor what appears on the screen, what's to stop other people censoring what appears in the newspaper? You've always fought this kind of censorship and now you're approving it."

I was really on my white horse, charging into the fray. I found myself passionately defending the freedom of the screen and saying things I didn't even know I had ever thought. Somehow my intensity paid off. Mr. Keeley agreed to look at the picture.

After seeing it, he said, "You were right, Louella. This is not an evil picture, but a great one. From now on I'm on Mr. Griffith's side."

Griffith needed every friend he could find. The picture was the biggest issue in Chicago, with the matter finally going to the courts. It was the first great test of screen censorship and Mr. Griffith's attorney called on a group of "experts" to testify. I was among them.

He won his battle. And I earned his friendship. A friendship that endured until his death.

It was never an intimate friendship for he was not a man who had intimate friends. He lived for and in his work. He was, if there ever was one in motion pictures, a true artist.

His finest films—*Broken Blossoms, Heart of the World* and *Intolerance*, among them—were trail blazers in content and technique. Every picture he made was an advance on the one before. He was never content to merely repeat past successes. He had to surpass them.

And he was the first of the great star-makers. It was Griffith who brought the Gish sisters, Mae Marsh and Richard Barthelmess to the screen; who gave her first important film role to Mary Pickford.

Yet this man spent his last years a lonely wanderer in the world which he had helped to create. I was as guilty as so many others for allowing this. But the knowledge did not strike me until it was too late; until that day in July when, like that of countless others, his death reminded us all of our omissions.

D. W. Griffith belonged to us here in the movie world and it seems to me that he should be something more than a name imprinted on the sidewalk of Hollywood Boulevard.

Another great—but one who never allowed himself to be forgotten—was Cecil B. De Mille. He produced many spectacular and successful pictures through the years and it is an odd commentary that his last picture, *The Ten Commandments,* should be another version of the Biblical story which brought him his first fame—and me my first contact with him.

I had just gone to work for Mr. Hearst when the first *Ten Commandments* was released. It seemed to me that this was truly a masterpiece.

I was overwhelmed by its magnificence, its unusual production values, the stunning costumes and sets, the grandeur of the presentation. I rushed to the typewriter to peck out the most glowing review I had ever given a movie.

The next day I saw my review in print. The shock unnerved me; almost knocked me out.

Gone were the superlatives, the lavish adjectives. Instead, the picture was torn apart, ripped, mangled. This was just the opposite of the review I had sent to the composing room. The only thing that remained of that review was the by-line.

When I got my wind back, I rushed to write my letter of resignation. I wrote to Joe Willicombe to tell Mr. Hearst that I did not write reviews only to have them rewritten, the opinions reversed and my name implanted above words with which I disagreed.

I then went home to sulk—and try to think of ways to get another job. I had saved my integrity but lost my place on the payroll. I was determined, however, that my daughter Harriet and I would not live on money basely earned. I had my editorial honor to preserve.

The next day the phone rang. It was Mr. Hearst. He apologized for the way my review had been altered. He promised he would personally punish the culprit who had been guilty of this worst of journalistic crimes. He assured me that it would never, never happen again. Even my most outrageous commas would be safe from copy editors forever and ever.

This soothed my ego and my ruffled feathers. I was happy to withdraw my resignation. I went back to work and waited for the heads of the guilty to fall.

Like all tragedies, this one was forgotten after a time. It was not until many years later that I learned who had changed rave to ravings, applause to boos, altered my language so that it said just the opposite of what I had written.

It had been Mr. Hearst himself!

When the first *Ten Commandments* was released, Mr. Hearst was angry with C.B. He felt that De Mille had double-crossed him on a story purchase, and Mr. Hearst was not one who would let anyone double-cross him without taking action. His action had been the altered review.

(My reaction, however, did have one lasting effect. Never again was a review, or my column, altered without my first having been consulted. Sometimes this has resulted in some rather glaring errors because every copy editor was aware that my copy was untouchable!)

But, back to C.B.

He was magnetic, delightful, intelligent and an actor at heart. There was a big streak of ham in him and it came out in the way he dressed. The old prototype of director in puttees, with megaphone in hand, is really an accurate picture of C.B. Once he went on the set he wanted everyone to know he was the boss. And he had no hesitancy in saying so.

There have been those who felt that his attraction to Biblical subjects was not based on any religious drive, but on the ground that if pictures made from best-sellers have the biggest chance of success, then why not make pictures from the greatest best-seller of all time and thus increase the chances of success?

I know that C.B. was religious. I went to Mass with him one Sunday when both of us were guests at the Hearst Ranch, and although he was not a Catholic he knew the ritual enough to follow the priest. Not in any sectarian sense, but in a larger, grander way. It was as if he envisioned a Creator who was a Master Director and who was able to impose His will, His imagination, His sense of the spectacular on the universe. And, if there was such a Master Director, why not C.B. as His own Prophet?

He made many other types of pictures, and among them were outstanding successes. But his reputation will probably rest on those that derived from his version of the Bible—the Bible according to King C.B.—and he would probably be content with that. He would, I am sure, point out other reputations that have derived from that source and be willing to join that company. Complete with megaphone.

C.B. was a man of strong opinions and always had a crew of press agents at hand to spread those opinions. He was in favor of God, of country, of profits.

There was a deep sincerity in his beliefs. He had these convictions —these first principles—and was willing to fight for them. His attitude toward unions was not based on an antipathy to labor, but

57

rather on his belief that labor unions tended to weaken the basic democratic and capitalistic principles in which he believed and to which he was devoted.

He was willing to deprive himself of the opportunity to earn hundreds of thousands of dollars rather than pay even one dollar under duress, so that he could honestly say that the payment had been made out of necessity, not choice.

He was an autocrat on the set, but could and did justify that autocracy on the ground that it meant better pictures, and better pictures were not only important artistically, but at the box office.

He spent thousands of dollars to research his films to give them authenticity. Then he would disregard all the research for the sake of a scene or a shot that appealed to him as better movie-making.

Hollywood misses C.B.

And Hollywood also misses another great movie-maker. Louis B. Mayer.

"L.B.," as he was known the length and breadth of Hollywood, and to most of the world and the public, was in my opinion the most powerful man ever to reign in the realm of make-believe.

He had his weaknesses, many of them. He was part charlatan, part mountebank. Given the right occasion, he could out-emote any star on the MGM lot. He was given to outbursts of temper, to histrionics and crocodile tears.

But he had qualities of leadership, creativeness and daring that I believe far overbalanced these personality traits.

As boss supreme of the famed Metro-Goldwyn-Mayer studio in its greatest days, L.B. exhibited the Lion-like courage of the MGM trademark—and an inspiring imagination. He had a sixth sense where talent was concerned and when he waved his wand, great stars sprang into being: Greta Garbo, Jean Harlow, Greer Garson, Clark Gable, Robert Taylor, Spencer Tracy, Joan Crawford, Katharine Hepburn, Wallace Beery, Marie Dressler, Mickey Rooney, Judy Garland, Lana Turner, Walter Pidgeon can all thank their lucky stars for the careers L.B. built for them!

He was a vain man and autocratic, but his was not a vanity that precluded his seeking the "best" of talent and technicians for MGM productions. It was he who gave the "boy genius" Irving Thalberg the opportunity to run MGM. L.B. was willing to share credit with Thalberg and David Selznick and anyone else who could make finer pictures for his company.

Anything derogatory that was ever said about any MGM product or possession was regarded by L.B. as a personal insult.

I found this out shortly after I started working in Hollywood.

In New York, after that first experience with my De Mille review, I was never again questioned about any opinions I expressed. I took it for granted that I had the same freedom in Hollywood. So I expressed my frank opinion of a minor MGM picture. Frankly, I didn't think much of it. (The critic of the rival Los Angeles *Times* praised it; I couldn't understand why.)

At this time Cosmopolitan Pictures, those produced by Mr. Hearst, were being released by MGM. There was a most friendly relationship between Mr. Hearst and Mr. Mayer.

I was to discover this a few days later when I heard from Mr. Hearst about my "panning" review. At Mr. Mayer's request, my boss had seen the movie in question and disagreed with my evaluation. He thought it a good picture and was surprised that I should think otherwise. I remember he concluded our little talk by saying, "You must remember, Louella, that Cosmopolitan and MGM are partners."

My answer was, "Does this mean that I'm supposed to praise MGM pictures whether or not I think they are good?"

"I didn't say that," Mr. Hearst replied. "Let's say that I suggest you temper your judgment with—judgment."

A few minutes later there was another telephone call. From Pete Smith, then in charge of MGM publicity. (Later Pete would become a producer and make a series of Oscar-winning shorts.) "Louella, Mr. Mayer would like to see you."

I snapped, "I've had about all I can take from Mr. Mayer."

Pete begged, "Do it for me, Louella. Please."

I agreed to go to MGM. I've always been a sucker for people I like and I had always liked Pete. But I was determined to stand up for my right to criticize, my freedom as a critic, and the "freedom of the press."

In view of my fighting stance, I walked into Mr. Mayer's office with a plank—not a chip—on my shoulder.

In place of the ogre I expected, I ran smack into an animated bundle of *simpatico* hospitality. L.B. leaped from his desk, came toward me with outstretched hands and said with deepest solicitude, "I'm sorry that I caused you trouble."

Later, when I repeated this to people who knew L.B., they found it hard to believe. They had never known him to apologize for anything. But it did happen—and it happened to me.

Immediately mollified, the "plank" slipping from my shoulder (what a smoothie he was!) I smiled. "That's all right, Mr. Mayer. Let's forget it."

But I didn't yet know my man. He wasn't about to let me forget it. He led me to a chair and stood over me. "I'm sure you didn't know what you were doing," he began in the tones of a schoolteacher talking with a bright, but difficult child. "You couldn't have despised the picture as much as you said you did. You must remember—we have a lot of money in that picture. That's what made me lose my temper."

I said, "Well, Mr. Mayer, every picture can't be a good one."

He gave me a quick, piercing look. "Miss Parsons, let me tell you one thing. *Every* MGM picture is a *good* one."

I realized that he sincerely believed this. This was his creed and he lived by it.

But I wasn't about to give any ground. I said, "I'm a critic, Mr. Mayer, and I have to write my reviews the way I feel about the pictures I see."

He nodded polite agreement. "Of course. Of course. But MGM pictures are always good—and I'm sure you will understand this from now on. You're new here, Miss Parsons, so let me explain something about reviewing pictures."

I could have bitten nails in my righteous indignation. I think this might have been the end of our friendship before it began. But before I exploded, Mr. Mayer continued soothingly.

"We're all in the picture business together," he sermonized. "You and I and everyone else who has anything to do with it. It is our combined job to defend and protect the picture business. Any time anyone says anything bad about a picture, he is only hurting himself"—he paused for another long look before adding significantly—"or *herself*. Just remember, some pictures are better than others, but there are no really bad pictures!"

L.B. was not a man of great humor. But now a smile whisked across his bespectacled face for the first time. "At any rate, there are no bad MGM pictures!"

With what I thought was a marked tinge of sarcasm, I said, "Thank you, Mr. Mayer." If he noticed my mental curled lip, he ignored it.

"I'm glad we understand each other," he said, sitting down for the first time since my arrival and giving indications of relaxing. "Louella, I want you to know one thing: if you ever have any problems, any troubles, come straight to me. I'll help you. You must think of me as a father!" What I was thinking of "father" at that moment couldn't be printed.

(Years later, Robert Taylor told me about a similar experience with L.B. Bob had bearded L.B. in his Lion's den to ask for a raise he thought his fast-growing popularity warranted. After just a few minutes, the eager-beaver Mr. Taylor had come out of the boss' office shaking his head. He was asked, "Did you get the raise?"

"No," replied the star. "But I gained a father!")

This "father" bit was one of the most effective of L.B.'s gambits. He firmly believed in the sacredness of motherhood and the omnipotence of fatherhood—not always to commercial advantage. L.B. had a strong patriarchal sense about those who worked for him and if he figured his "children" deserved a raise, or a certain story, he was an indulgent father. If not—like the father in the TV series many years later—L. B. always "knew best."

Despite our rocky start, L.B. and I became very good friends. Through the years he was the source of many exclusive scoops I broke. When he and his first wife, Margaret, were divorced after many years of marriage, I was given the story long before any other reporter.

Some years later, when he and Lorena Danker, the beautiful widow of my old friend Danny Danker, were married, I was told of their plans to elope even before the details were revealed to Howard Strickling, then head of MGM publicity.

Many were the delightful evenings I spent as a guest in the Mayers' beautiful Bel Air home during the ten years of their marriage which ended sadly in L.B.'s death of leukemia.

And I find I now think of this powerful man in his most becoming role, that of a gracious host, welcoming the greats of all walks of life from his and my close friend Francis Cardinal Spellman and later, James Francis Cardinal McIntyre, President Herbert Hoover, such captains of industry as the automotive Ford clan and K. T. Keller of Chrysler, to his beloved "flock," the MGM stars he created.

I remember him vividly standing in the door of his home graciously giving greeting or godspeed to his guests, great or small. More and more, I forget the piercing roar of the *real* MGM Lion!

In any rating of so-called Hollywood so-and-so's, over the years, I suppose the late Harry Cohn, head of Columbia Pictures, would top most lists. The worst he could come in is second on most polls—but not on mine.

Personally, I never had a better friend than Harry, the Horror, as he was frequently and unsentimentally referred to. For my money and in my book, Harry was a Honey—an opinion which may have originated in his habit of telling me every bit of Columbia news first. But I learned to feel deep affection for the man himself.

"Guts" isn't a pretty word for a lady writer to use. But if ever a man in Hollywood had intestinal fortitude, it was my friend Mr. Cohn.

He not only battled the competition where Columbia pictures were concerned; he was frequently embroiled with his own bankers and New York advisers getting such high-quality movies as the Oscar-winning *It Happened One Night* and *Bridge on the River Kwai* to the screen.

Harry loved a good fight. But most of all he loved a great picture—if turned out by Columbia.

His enthusiasm for something big knew no office hours. I recall the day that Cohn saw the first completed print of *Bridge*. Actually, it was the night—and early morning. He telephoned me from a Columbia studio projection room just as I was getting ready for bed at 2 A.M. "Come on over here, Louella. I want to show you the picture that's going to win the Academy Award."

"At this hour?"

"Why not? I've just seen it and I'm going to run it again."

I bowed out of this post-midnight "treat" but agreed to see the picture the next afternoon. Which I did—with the excited Harry by my side. I had to admit it was a great picture though I wasn't as sure as my host that it would win the Oscar scramble.

"Take my word for it—it will," he pronounced. And then this man who had the far-flung reputation for hogging the whole show, said a (to me) typical thing:

"When you write about *Bridge* make sure to give Sam Spiegel [the producer] the credit he deserves. He's taken plenty of raps—from me as well as elsewhere—and he's entitled to the praise."

That was Harry Cohn. He was tough and hard. But like L.B. Mayer he loved the motion-picture business with an ogre's fierce pride and he was the first to place the crown on the head of a winner!

And now we come to Samuel Goldwyn. Let me retype that to read *Sam* Goldwyn!

Still with us, although less active, the name of Sam Goldwyn is branded in my memory—and sometimes, I have thought, in my *hide* —with both bitterness and blessedness. Over the years we have fought outrageously via telephone and nose-to-nose.

There's nobody like Sam, in or out of pictures. A producer and maker of great "class" picture product, commercially a dreamer who makes dreams turn into millions, he is also the purported creator of more slips of the tongue than any human being since Mrs. Malaprop. "Goldwynisms" they call Sam's slips.

And far-flung are such "typical" Goldwynisms as:

Introducing world-famed Field Marshall Montgomery, the Goldwyns' honored guest at a party, he is quoted as calling the mighty military man "Marshall Field Montgomery."

Leaving with his wife on a trip to Europe, Sam is said to have rushed to the rail of the ship and waved to his cohorts on the dock, "Bon voyage—bon voyage!"

Truth compels me to add that I repeat these yarns purely as rumor. I personally have never heard Mr. G. give out with a Goldwynism and he swears the stories are tacked on him—that he has never uttered a word of this nonsense.

Not that any of it is too serious compared to his exalted reputation as a leader of Hollywood and a magnificent producer.

My recollections of Sam are far more concrete veering from encounters in which he seemed to me to be the Devil with horns—or an Angel complete with halo.

I can tell you this. As a friend in need, Sam is without peer. As I recounted in detail in my previous book, *The Gay Illiterate,* when I was taken ill with tuberculosis in New York, it was Sam who came to the hospital and whispered in my ear, "Louella, if you need anything, call on me. If you have too much pride to take financial help from me, let me lend you money until you can recuperate in California."

Luckily, thanks to the wondrous generosity of Mr. Hearst, my newspaper boss who kept me on salary the full year I was on leave of absence in California recovering my health, I didn't have to avail myself of Sam's offer. But I shall never forget it!

Neither shall I easily forget the long series of TNT encounters we have weathered over 40 years.

Like L. B. Mayer and most of the other captains of the good ship Movies, Sam could never abide the slightest criticism. Once, he became so enraged over something I had written that he ran screaming about me to headquarters, to Mr. Hearst himself. Knowing Sam, and being slightly irritated with his antics, Mr. Hearst chided severely, "Sam, if you didn't like what Louella wrote—there's a simple way to solve it. I'll tell her not to mention your name—favorably or unfavorably!"

Quothe Sam, "That's what I want, Mr. Hearst." Like a hole in the head he wanted it. After a long period of being treated to the *persona non grata* style throughout the entire Hearst syndicate on the boss' order, Sam had had enough.

As always in times of trouble, Same called on his lovely, tactful, charming former-actress wife Frances (Howard) to make a trip to San Simeon to see Mr. Hearst in his behalf.

Mr. Hearst was gracious to Frances, as he was to every guest, but he did not immediately rescind his order. "Tell Sam to call Louella—and henceforth let's make a deal. Tell him I said, 'If I let you produce pictures your way—you'll have to let my star reporter call them *her*

64

way.' " That was my wonderful boss at his most wonderful best, in my eyes.

Of course we made up and lived to battle through many more frays. I adore Frances Goldwyn, the only person in the world who really understands Sam, and I repeat, I have enormous respect for the explosive Mr. G.

If the enormous number of fine movies he has turned out were not sufficient criterion of Sam's superlative taste, his selection of Frances would be the ultimate proof. Not only is Frances his wife and constant companion, she is his business partner and in recent years he has turned over all rights, movies or TV, to use as her judgment sees fit. No mean responsibility, such great movies as Sam's *Dark Angel, Stella Dallas* and many others.

At their 36th wedding anniversary I asked Frances the secret of her success with Sam. She laughed. "Oh, I put him in his place. I let him go just so far." And Sam beamed as she said it. It was a warm and gracious evening in the home of my good friend and noble enemy —Sam.

Some of the latter-day movie giants come quickly to mind, particularly Darryl F. Zanuck and Jack L. Warner.

Fewer men have made a deeper mark than Darryl, the pint-sized bundle of nerves and activity who has written screen history with the smoke of his titled cigar. A salute is in order for this man who started out as a film cutter and editor and who rose to the top rung of the ladder of success, controlling the motion picture fate of Warner Bros. and then 20th Century-Fox studios.

Lately, his independent pictures, mostly made abroad, have not been so successful. But never count Zanuck out. He has forgotten more about movie-making than many men ever learn.

As for Jack Warner—the genial production boss of Warners is at once a brilliant movie-maker, and perhaps the most persistent cracker of good and bad jokes in Hollywood. Part genius, part "ham," Jack can and frequently *has* outshone Jack Benny, Bob Hope and other wits of Hollywood across the dais tables!

I once said to Jack, "I think you'd rather be complimented on being a comedian than on one of your pictures."

He looked at me quizzically. "Louella," he said, "don't fool yourself!"

I promised. I hardly ever do, really, where these Captains of moviemaking are concerned.

⇢ *Chapter 4*

FALLEN ANGEL

"Movie idol" is almost a literal description of the status to which some of Hollywood's greatest have risen.

Fans idolized them, placed them in lofty niches and adored them out of all proportion.

It is a peculiar thing that, in the creation of goddesses, the public has drawn a distinct line between those whom they held to be symbols of purity and those who represent the heathen goddesses entitled to have quite mortal appetites and adventures.

These latter have been forgiven much. When their weaknesses have become public knowledge, the general sentiment has been that it was only what might have been expected. Certainly no better example of this is possible than the public's attitude toward Marilyn Monroe, Ava Gardner and Lana Turner.

But let one of the stars endowed with purity reveal the endowment false, then the iconoclasts go to work with everything from mud pies to atom bombs.

A conspiracy of a type has long been in operation to protect the peccadillos of these lily maids of the movie lots. As a result, only a few have long known that one of the sweet, pure and demure mothered

67

a child out of wedlock and later went through the motions of publicly adopting the infant. Or that a second has been having a love affair for a score of years with another top star. (It was of this affair that someone remarked, "How dare people say that there is no fidelity in Hollywood?")

But there are times when this curtain of secrecy is pierced. There are times when the truth will out to the accompaniment of glaring headlines.

It happened to that gamin, Mabel Normand.

It happened to Mary Miles Minter, the Shirley Temple of the early 20's.

Both of these women were caught up in the eddies that developed from the murder of William Desmond Taylor.

It happened to Mary Astor, she of the pure profile and manner of a gentlewoman born, when her private diary became public knowledge during her bitter divorce suit.

These were fallen angels, but none of them was ever regarded as so angelic—nor was any other to fall so far—as Ingrid Bergman.

It is a curious commentary on both motion pictures and the public that when Ingrid sinned she should have to be the scapegoat for the sins of all; either committed or contemplated. Millions of persons reacted as if they had been the victims of a personal betrayal.

Every husband felt wronged.

Every wife felt guilty.

I wish I were psychologist enough to explain this, but I know I'm not and I am not going to make any attempt to do so.

Instead, I am going to tell Ingrid's story from my point of view. The point of view of the reporter who broke the exclusive story of Ingrid's approaching motherhood and had to suffer, along with her, for quite a while, "the slings and arrows of outrageous fortune."

For a long period of time it appeared that many people felt that, if Ingrid had sinned, the fault was mine for revealing it. Frustration, anger and bitterness all resulted in attacks on me for having done my job as a reporter.

It was all these, I think, that resulted in so many foolish attempts to prove that my story that Ingrid was to bear Roberto Rossellini's child was untrue.

68

It was not so much that other reporters and newspapers resented my exclusive story as it was that they did not want to believe it.

To understand this it is necessary to give the story of Ingrid's impact on Hollywood.

I would say that only three foreign actresses have become really great American stars. They are Garbo, Marlene Dietrich and Ingrid Bergman. The first was the eternal woman of mystery. The second was femininity incarnate. And the third, through some peculiar chemistry, the perennial virgin.

She came to the United States in late 1939, brought here by David O. Selznick after she had attained her first success in the picture *Intermezzo,* starring with Leslie Howard.

David told me, "You must meet her, Louella. She is going to be the greatest star in films."

I took this for the natural enthusiasm of any producer about to make a large investment in a star. However, I had then, as I have always had, a great respect for David's judgment, and said I would like very much to meet Ingrid.

She came out for lunch to the ranch in the San Fernando Valley where Dr. Martin and I spent our weekends. The moment we saw her we knew that here was somebody different, somebody out of the ordinary mold. She had a natural beauty, an inner glow. Later, Dr. Martin said, "You know, I was sure there was a halo around her."

She was vibrant and exciting and ingenuous. This was her first visit to a ranch and her eyes opened wide when she saw the orange trees with their loads of fruit. "I've never seen an orange tree before," she said. "Might I have one to send to Sweden?"

"Take as many as you like."

"Just one," she said.

She chose a large orange, left a few leaves on the stem. "I will send it," she said, "to Peter, my husband. It will be a sign of my remembrance."

It was hard to believe that this child was married, that she was already a mother.

Some time later, when I next saw Ingrid she told me what had happened to her gift. "It got there black and shrunken. It didn't even smell like an orange. It was—was—dead."

69

She imparted tragedy to this orange and what had happened to it and I felt, as she told me of it, that a great calamity had taken place. This was part of her gift of intensity, of being able to transport you from the real world to the world she created for you.

David Selznick's forecast of her success proved true. From the first her career rocketed. She was able to rise above some bad pictures and to make good pictures seem superlative. She added something to whatever she appeared in.

I used to see her at parties. By this time Dr. Peter Lindstrom had joined her and I met him.

He seemed to me dour. He was formal, unsmiling, cold. His intensity and drive were directed at getting his medical degree. And I sometimes felt, when he looked at us in the course of a party, that he was envisioning us as objects for dissection in some laboratory.

The world of Hollywood is a small one, of course. And a world which, like all worlds, is given to gossip and rumor. But there was no gossip, although there was much talk about Ingrid and her husband. People regarded them as mismated, ill-matched. They could not understand this union of beauty and the boor.

Ingrid attained greater heights with each picture. There was only one disappointment in those years. In 1944 many in Hollywood felt that she would receive the Academy Award for her performance in *For Whom The Bell Tolls*. Instead, it was voted to Jennifer Jones who had starred in *The Song of Bernadette*.

Ingrid was disappointed, but generous. When she was asked her reaction she said, "When I saw *The Song of Bernadette* I cried all the way through because Jennifer was so moving and because I knew that I had lost the Award."

But the next year, Ingrid won her first Oscar for *Gaslight*. It was, as has so often been the case, a retroactive award. I feel that she received almost as many votes for *Bell* as for *Gaslight*. However, I think she rightfully deserved the Award.

She followed this up with *The Bells of St. Mary's*, with Bing Crosby. This, I feel, was the picture which resulted in her first being thought of by the world at large as the symbol of feminine purity.

She played the nun with such grace, with such inner fire, that it seemed she was playing herself rather than playing a part. She was not a Catholic. She was a married woman with a child. Yet, to so many millions, she became the idealization of a nun.

And this was followed, and added to, by her appearance on Broadway in the Maxwell Anderson play, *Joan of Lorraine.*

There are few purer idealizations than the Maid of Orleans and when Ingrid appeared in the part, she once again seemed to have incarnated it in herself. She wasn't an actress playing Joan. She was Joan. And the popular concept of Ingrid was enhanced.

She was separated from her husband all the time she was on Broadway which caused some talk. The talk died down, however, on her return to Hollywood. Dr. Lindstrom was still deeply immersed in his medical studies. He had become a neurologist and, I was told, a fine one. But he hadn't warmed up any.

Then it was announced that Walter Wanger, one of Hollywood's better producers—a man of taste and discrimination—was going to make a film of Joan of Arc and that Ingrid would, of course, play the title role. I do not think that, even if he had wanted another star, the public would have permitted him any other choice.

Ingrid was Joan, and Joan was Ingrid.

When the picture was completed Ingrid was at her zenith. She was, without question, the star of stars in Hollywood.

But, unknown to most, she was also a trifle unhappy, a trifle restless. At this moment Roberto Rossellini came into her life.

Rossellini had attained world-wide fame and renown soon after the end of World War II with a pair of fine, naturalistic pictures, *Open City* and *Paisan.* These had been great critical successes and Rossellini had been hailed as the greatest director since Griffith and the greatest innovator since the days of the nickelodeon.

(This happens sporadically. Foreigners have attained this type of praise and cashed in on it. I can think of René Clair, Fellini, De Sica, Renoir and others and, today, of Ingemar Bergman. There will be someone else tomorrow, I suppose.)

When Ingrid had seen the Rossellini pictures, she had written him to compliment him on his work and to say that if ever he had a

71

part for her she would be available. Now Rossellini came to Hollywood and he was a house guest of the Lindstroms.

He was quite a social lion and we all met him. I first saw him at a dinner party that the Lindstroms gave in his honor. I went to meet a genius and met a superegotist. I have encountered quite a number of these in my time, but Rossellini stands near the top of the list.

Personally, he was fairly attractive, with penetrating black eyes that seemed to burn with some kind of bitter fire. Otherwise, he was just a man of about medium height, balding and thickening through the middle from too much *pasta* and success.

He had verve and gaiety, though little humor. However, since I knew little Italian, it could be that the humor was there, but out of my reach. One thing I must say for him and that is that he possessed great warmth. Even I felt it.

But when word began to spread that Ingrid was romantically interested in him, I found it hard to believe. I knew of all the famous, handsome, talented men who had fallen in love—or believed they had—with Ingrid through the years. I knew of the way she had managed to evade any sort of entanglement without losing the friendship of these men. It didn't seem to me that Rossellini could prevail where so many others had failed.

I was surprised, frankly, when I was told that Ingrid was going to Italy to make a picture with Rossellini.

Then came a series of shocks, one after the other. Like a good reporter, I printed the stories that came to me. Stories that Ingrid's marriage was finished and that she wanted her freedom. There was evidence of why—pictures showing her with Rossellini in Stromboli where they were making their fiasco of a picture.

Repercussions came quickly.

St. Joan had turned sinner.

The entire world reacted. There was no limit to the anger because it was based on a form of self-delusion and no one likes to appear the fool. Especially the self-created fool.

The newspapers echoed the general anger. Editorials castigating Ingrid appeared in newspapers, not only in the United States, but throughout the world. Radio commentators joined in the general stoning, forgetting an admonition of some 2,000 years earlier.

Motion-picture producers and exhibitors were damned for showing any pictures in which she appeared and threats of boycott and worse were common.

Thousands of individuals throughout the world wrote to Ingrid directly, filling their letters with scorn, invective, threats and scurrility. It was as if a later Eve had tasted of the apple and had brought sin to a pure, chaste, innocent earth.

Ingrid's reaction was a public statement which read:

"I have instructed my lawyer to institute divorce proceedings immediately. Also, at the conclusion of my present picture it is my intention to retire into private life."

This did not stop the demand that her pictures be banned. I received thousands of letters demanding that I join this holy crusade. I asked, in my column, "How can you ban the pictures of someone who is retiring? The time to talk about a ban is when—and if—she makes other pictures."

I did not believe that she would retire. I felt that her drive to act was stronger, more vital than this grand passion. In addition, I somehow felt that this idyl had some overtones of comic opera. I just couldn't see Rossellini as the symbol of enduring passion. Time has proved that I underrated him, but that I was right about other aspects of this affair.

At the height of the scandal, I was queried by *Quick* magazine about Ingrid's future. I ventured a guess that ran against the general tide. I said, "If Ingrid ever decides to continue with her career, she will be the success she has always been."

At the time, my forecast was derided. Later it was, of course, proved correct.

Meanwhile, Dr. Lindstrom was hiding from the press in Hollywood. At the start he was the object of sympathy, because on the surface he was the wronged party. But there is a tradition of gallantry in the United States. A man must also be a gentleman. And Dr. Lindstrom, it appeared, was uninterested in being Galahad. Hell had no fury like a neurologist scorned—and held up to ridicule.

73

Dr. Lindstrom, I suppose, had right on his side. But right was hardly enough. He had to forego righteousness and this he would not do.

So, slowly, some of the anger and bitterness were diverted from Ingrid toward her husband.

Then came the shocker—and I was the one who revealed it!

One Sunday night as I went on the air with my radio show, I was given a message from a man of great importance not only in Hollywood, but throughout the United States. He was close to Ingrid and had been close to her for a long time. He had connections in many parts of the world—including Italy—whose sources of information could not be questioned.

I had no idea what he wanted to talk to me about and it came as a shock when, after my radio show, this man picked me up at the radio station and said, "Louella, Ingrid is going to have a baby."

I just stared open-mouthed at him for a moment and then said, "Why didn't you tell it to me earlier, so I could put it on the air?"

"What! Waste a story as big as this one? The only place to break it is in the newspapers."

Then I had a second thought. "Are you sure?" I demanded. "How do you know?"

"I'm sure," he said. "And I know. You have to take my word for it."

There were few people whose word I would have taken on a story such as this. I realized that if I wrote the story and it turned out to be untrue, the repercussions could well destroy me. But I knew that my informant would never put me in such a position. I had every reason in the world to trust him.

I have been asked many times who this person was. I gave my word that I would never tell. I even refused to tell Mr. Hearst. I must say that my trust in him—and keeping my word to him—have both been repaid many times.

Now that I had the story, I also had an unexpected problem. As a reporter, I knew that this was really a page 1 story. But as a woman and a friend of Ingrid's, I knew this story could only do her harm.

Common sense, however, told me that if I didn't break the story, someone else would. It was not the kind of story that could be kept secret forever. And while I felt deep compassion for Ingrid, I realized that it was she, not I, who had placed her in this unconscionable position.

I started to write the story. It was a hard one for me to put down on paper. Finally, I finished. In it, I wrote:

"Few women, or men either, have made the sacrifice the Swedish star has made for love. Mary, Queen of Scots, gave up her throne because of her love for the Earl of Bothwell. Lady Hamilton gave up her position in London to bear a child out of wedlock to Lord Nelson. King Edward VIII renounced his throne to marry the woman he loved, Wallis Simpson. . . ."

And if anyone thinks that my analogies were farfetched, let him remember that Ingrid, too, was a queen with subjects throughout the world. That she was an ideal. That she was an idol.

The Los Angeles *Examiner* put two great lines of type across its front page:

INGRID BERGMAN BABY DUE
IN THREE MONTHS AT ROME

The story created a sensation. The greatest ever, I believe, in relation to a story about a movie personality. And resulted in the greatest effort I have ever known by other newspapers and newspaper people to deny a story.

Newspapers, syndicates, foreign correspondents, friends and intimates of Ingrid all hastened to report that Ingrid was not pregnant.

There were so many denials from so many apparently authentic sources, that for the only time in the years that I worked for him, Mr. Hearst felt that he had to check a story with me. He called me and asked, "Are you sure about the facts?"

"As sure as I have ever been about anything in the whole, wide world."

"You know what can happen if the story isn't true? You will be liable privately and so will all the newspapers which carried the story."

"I know that," I said. "I'm sure of my facts."

"Then I'm sure of them too."

So sure that when he heard that the Los Angeles *Herald-Express,* the Hearst evening paper, had printed one of the many denials, he called the editor and demanded, "How dare you deny a Louella Parsons story?" The denial was yanked in the next edition.

The phone kept ringing all day. Everyone sought to throw doubt on the story. Some of my "best friends" called me to say that I should try to extricate myself as best as I could from a serious predicament.

That evening, when I went into my husband's bedroom, I found him bent over his rosary. "I'm saying my beads," he said, "and praying your story is right."

I, too, prayed that the story was right. And I also prayed for Ingrid, who had followed her heart down such a long, agonizing road.

The next day it looked as if I had gotten myself into trouble. Art Cohen, a newspaperman then working in Stromboli, reported that he had seen Ingrid and that she definitely was not pregnant!

Cohen was regarded as reliable. He was right there in Stromboli. It was a bombshell and it resulted in much gloating.

All I could do was stand by my story.

(Some time later Art told me that at the time he wrote his denial, he knew my story was true. He was trying to protect Ingrid! I felt then that he had performed a shameless act and one that I could not condone. However, my bitterness has long been dissipated and poor Art is dead. He was in Mike Todd's plane when it crashed and he was killed with Mike.)

At this time Joseph Steel paid me a visit. He had been Ingrid's personal press agent for years and one of her most devoted friends. He told me that my story was true and that he had been trying for some time to get Ingrid to confirm it. He suggested we put in a call to Ingrid in Rome. We did, but though we waited for hours we were never able to get Ingrid on the phone.

Joe had been playing hide-and-seek with reporters, editors and press services from the moment my story had appeared. He was worn out and his nerves were about gone. I asked him if he would like to stay in our house and rest and he gratefully accepted.

Dr. Martin gave him a sedative and loaned him a pair of pajamas. Then Joe was put into the guest room. He slept until late in the evening, and when he woke up I scrambled some eggs for him because it was the cook's day off.

Later, I was accused of having kidnapped Joe and hidden him from other reporters. But I didn't have to do that. Some people have implied that he was the source of my story. He wasn't. And I believe it has long rankled with him that I broke the story without his aid or knowledge. If that were not so, I think that some of the things he wrote in his biography of Ingrid might have been both kinder and more factual.

A story, even a big story, tends to diminish in importance when nothing new happens. For some days Ingrid and her coming motherhood were big news. Really big news. The denials, at first so loud and positive, softened and became dubious. Finally, the confirmation came.

Once again Ingrid became the target for abuse. The guns that had been trained on me, were reloaded and turned on her.

But it has always been a matter of gratification to me that many persons stood stalwartly by Ingrid. They did not condone what she had done, but they would not condemn her. It took courage for men like Gary Cooper and Cary Grant to make it plain that they were on Ingrid's side and would not turn their backs on her.

For a little time the venom was diluted and was spread out. Then the story went into the inside pages. After a time, it disappeared entirely.

And I had a daily column to turn out, special stories to write and newsbreaks to cover. So that I was unable to grasp the meaning of the words that Seymour Berkson, then head of INS, shouted at me some weeks later when he met me as I arrived in New York from Florida where I had been spending some time with my husband.

Seymour shouted to me, "It's a boy, Louella. We just got the news."

"What's a boy?" I asked, trying to collect my thoughts.

"What's a boy?" Berkson's face broke into a big smile. "Ingrid's baby," he said. "That's what's a boy. I've ordered all our papers to print your original story and the denials of all the other papers side by side."

I'm human enough to feel that it was no more than I deserved. I had had to take attacks from many sources. My professional and personal reputations had been attacked by other papers and other reporters. Some columnists, whose records for veracity were nonexistent, had written vicious and distorted stories about me.

Now they had to look at their words in print. They had to suffer the same type of professional scorn they had attempted to inflict upon me.

I don't believe anything gave me greater satisfaction than the sour-gripes (stet!) editorial which was printed in the Los Angeles *Times*. The *Times* declared:

"Well, Louella knows more about such clinical things than we do. We're interested in other news."

I had to laugh out loud.

But the satisfaction I got from having been proven right, was not equal to the later satisfaction I got when Ingrid made her glorious comeback.

Her own personal troubles and humiliations did not end with the birth of her son. Dr. Lindstrom continued to balk her attempts to get a divorce so that she and Rossellini could marry. It appeared to many of us that poor Pia, their daughter, was being used as an instrument of vengeance against Ingrid.

She finally obtained a Mexican divorce and married Rossellini. Dr. Lindstrom got his own divorce in California.

At that time, it appeared that Ingrid's career really had come to an end. *Stromboli* had proved a flop. The public condemnation that she had suffered was supposed to be partly at fault, but I thought that it was just a bad picture; that the fault lay with Rossellini.

I got some confirmation of this from George Sanders, who had made a picture with Rossellini in Italy.

"Never again," Sanders told me. "We worked from day to day, never knowing what our lines would be because Rossellini was writing them each night. Sometimes he made them up in the course of shooting. Ingrid suffered as much as any of us. She didn't seem like Ingrid at all."

It was shortly after that that I went to England. I found when I checked into the Savoy, in London, that Ingrid was also staying there. She had just played in *Tea And Sympathy* on the stage in Paris; a role she had taken, it was reported, against the wishes of Rossellini.

I had not seen her, or spoken to her, since she had left the United States. In the intervening period I had written the story of her pregnancy. I did not know how she felt toward me, though we had been friends. There was only one way to find out.

I called her and asked if I might see her. Her response was warm and immediate. "Of course. Come right up."

When I saw her I was struck by the lack of change in her appearance. She was just as lovely; still had that same aura of purity and innocence. It was I, not she, who was stiff and embarrassed. It took time for me to adjust. I asked her, finally, how it had happened that the pictures she had made for Rossellini had turned out so badly.

"I think," she said, "it was because we are too close to each other. It prevented either one of us being objective. I do not believe a husband and wife can work well together."

That broke some of the ice. She showed me pictures of her son and of the twins, who had been born to her and Rossellini later. Finally I said, "Ingrid, I've always been sorry that I had to write that story. I didn't want to harm you and yet I knew if I didn't write the story, someone else would."

"I understand," Ingrid said. "I don't hold it against you. It was news and you wrote it. You had to."

There were other questions I suppose I should have asked her. This was at the time Rossellini was in India and there were reports that he was making a picture and trying to make the Indian beauty Sonali Das Gupti. But I decided that Ingrid had suffered enough pain and that I would not be the one to cause her more.

Only a short time later, my prediction that she would survive all the bad publicity—all the scandal—was also proven correct. The late Buddy Adler insisted upon her playing the lead in *Anastasia* and when I saw the picture I felt that it would win her an Academy Award.

In all the years I have been in Hollywood, I don't think I ever saw a more emotion-filled moment than that one when the Price-Waterhouse envelope was opened, a stillness filled the Pantages theatre, and then the words, "Winner—Ingrid Bergman."

There was bedlam. It was as if all those people in that theatre felt that they had somehow undone harm, cleansed themselves of viciousness and prudery and prejudice by voting the award to Ingrid. It was fitting that one of those who had never condemned, who had always stood up for Ingrid—Cary Grant—should be the one to accept the award for her.

Then, a few months later, I read some purported remarks by Ingrid in a magazine. According to the magazine article, Ingrid held me responsible for much that had happened to her. There was an implication that I had, somehow, done her harm and done this voluntarily.

A short time later Ingrid returned to Hollywood to be present at the 1957 Academy Award ceremonies. A dinner was to be given for her and I was asked to attend. I sent my regrets in a curt note.

Buddy Adler called me. "You must come, Louella."

"I hardly think that Ingrid would agree. Not if the things she said in that magazine article represent her feelings."

"They can't, because she specifically asked that you be placed at her table. She said you were one of the few people she really wanted to sit with. Besides, as a reporter you have to attend an affair like this. It's your job."

Buddy had hit a tender spot. This was a news event and one that had to be covered. If I didn't go, someone else would. So of course I went. But when I entered the dining room and took my seat, the people in my immediate vicinity probably got frostbitten. I was going to be aloof, cold and highly professional. I was present as a reporter and that was all.

It took exactly two minutes for all my haughtiness to depart. Ingrid, seeing me, came over, threw her arms around me and said, "Louella, you don't know how happy I am to see you." There was a touch of moisture on her eyelids and, I know, more than a touch on mine.

A few minutes later she introduced me to Lars Schmidt, the gifted producer to whom she is now married. I liked him the minute I met

80

him and hoped that he and Ingrid could, sometime, find the real happiness that they now appear to enjoy. Now too her relationship with Pia is back on its old, loving basis.

Time seems to have proven Ingrid right when she said she felt that she and Rossellini were too close together to make good pictures. His latest, *General Della Rovere* is being called the equal of his first hits, *Open City* and *Paisan*. However, Ingrid has certainly had her problems with him over their children—Roberto and the two little girls. But she showed how big she was when she sent hearty congratulations to him on the success of the new picture.

It seems so long since I first met Ingrid. Yet, I am sure one thing has not changed about her and never will. I can only put it as Dr. Martin put it at the time. Somehow she will, I am sure, still have a halo about her.

It is that quality which permitted her to become the only fallen Hollywood angel to rise again.

➤➤➤ *Chapter 5*

MOVIE MYTHOLOGY

I WOULD be willing to bet that Hollywood ranks just behind Abraham Lincoln and Franklin Delano Roosevelt as the subject matter of modern-day writing. It seems to me that not a day passes without announcement of some new books dealing, in one way or another, with the town in which I live and work.

I've read much of what has been written (Oh, yes, I do read) and I've concluded that most of the fiction is filled with barely disguised fact and most of the fact books are undisguised fiction.

It was when I was a schoolgirl, back in Dixon, that I first heard the term *"roman à clef."* My English teacher explained that it meant a novel about actual people without the disclaimer that Sgt. Friday made famous, to wit: "Only the names have been changed to protect the innocent."

Perhaps that is because these books tell of persons who are lewd, lecherous and libidinous. Because the characters are ignorant, illiterate and untaught. Because they are tasteless, vulgar and uncouth.

But none of them are about the innocent.

The works of fiction have been appearing for about a generation. It has been a standard Hollywood game, as each of the new novels was published, to start a guessing game as to the actual characters

82

upon whom the fictional characters were based. In almost every one of them there has been a gushing, semiliterate movie columnist, and my schizophrenic ego has forced me to lay claim to being the model for the various "Lollipops Marsons" who have malapropped their way through thousands of pages.

I called my ego schizophrenic because none of these characters was admirable, but they were all columnists and as the founder of the club I have to take the bitter with the sour.

I think the first of these Hollywood novels was *Queer People*, written by Carroll and Garrett Graham. I believe the best of them all was *What Makes Sammy Run?* written by Budd Schulberg.

Budd was able to give the feel, the smell, the touch of Hollywood to what he wrote. And why not? Of all the writers who have chosen Hollywood as a locale, he had the best background for it. He was born into Hollywood and was part of it. So were his parents and other members of his family.

Budd's father was the famed and talented B. P. Schulberg, who once headed Paramount. His mother is Ad Schulberg, a fine and successful agent. His uncle is Sam Jaffe, another fine agent.

Budd was an onlooker during that dizzy era when his father was one of the deities of this town. He saw the adulation that was heaped upon him then. And saw, as he so brilliantly wrote in one of his short stories, how fleeting that could be. In Hollywood, as everywhere, the battle cry of those on the make is, "The King is dead! Long Live the King!"

When the first copies of Budd's book reached Hollywood, it set the town on its ears. Everyone started to substitute the names of real people for the fictional characters. And, of course, everyone had his or her own choice for the prototype of Sammy Glick, hero (?) of the novel.

Hollywood accepted the fact that no one individual had served as the sole basis for Sammy. But the town felt that one person, more than any other, did come close. And, after the most secret ballot in town, the choice for prototype was Jerry Wald.

Now, I like Jerry. He's one of my favorite people for the simple reason that Jerry performs the one basic function on which Hollywood depends. He makes pictures.

83

Jerry has made good ones, including a number which have received Academy Awards. He has made some real stinkers. But, one way or another, Jerry has made pictures.

Jerry had a background similar in many respects to that of Sammy Glick, in that he had worked as a sort of columnist in New York, come to Hollywood and risen rapidly.

In one way Jerry certainly resembled Sammy Glick. That was in his drive, his determination to get ahead. He was—and still is—willing to work long hours at top speed, without sparing himself, to attain success. He has used the old Hollywood trick of blowing his own horn and, when this was not enough, hiring a brass band to do the blowing for him. Jerry knows that sweet are the uses of publicity and he is not afraid of saccharinity.

When the novel appeared I happened to encounter Jerry in the Green Room at Warner's, where he was then employed. "Have you read Budd Schulberg's book?" I asked.

"Great book. Great." He just bubbled with enthusiasm. "I can't imagine whom he used to draw Sammy from, though. Can you?"

"I have an idea," I said.

"I haven't. Tell you one thing. I'd like to make a picture of the book. I'm going to talk to the front office about it."

Was Jerry the prototype of Sammy Glick? Your guess is as good as mine.

What Makes Sammy Run? has become a modern classic. It has run through many editions, both in hard cover and paperback. It has been adapted and shown on TV. But no one has made it into a picture—not even Jerry. Perhaps, after he succeeds in licking James Joyce's *Ulysses*, he may recall his old enthusiasm for the book and make it.

A favorite subject for so-called Hollywood fiction has been the family saga. And many of the books that have dealt with Hollywood families have been called adaptations of the story of the Laemmles; the elder Carl, his son and his numerous relatives.

In 1946 *The Golden Egg*, written by James S. Pollak, was published. Jimmy Pollak had been part of the Hollywood scene most of his life and had the knowledge and background to write a good book. Personally, the old grandmother, one of the characters in *The*

Golden Egg, has long been one of my favorites in Hollywood fiction.

About three years later, the novel *The Dream Merchants*, by Harold Robbins, was published. Robbins, who at that time worked for Universal pictures—the company which Carl Laemmle founded —also chose the Laemmle story as the background for his novel. His new book, *The Carpetbaggers,* is a thinly disguised story of a well-known Hollywood millionaire. It's a vulgar, shocking Hollywood tale.

Another Hollywood notable who has reportedly been turned into a fictional character is John Huston, writer, director and individualist. Talented Niven Busch's novel *The Actor*, about an actor and his director son, was believed to have been based on John and his late, wonderful father, Walter Huston.

And Peter Viertel, now married to Deborah Kerr, wrote a novel titled *White Hunter, Black Heart* which was believed to be based on his experiences while working on a picture with Huston.

Richard Brooks, writer, director and producer, wrote *The Producer* shortly after having worked for the late Mark Hellinger, and the protagonist in that book bore far more than a superficial resemblance to Mark.

When Stephen Longstreet's book, *The Beach House*, hit the stands a great many people maintained that it had to be about David O. Selznick. (I disagreed with them.)

Budd Schulberg has written another book with Hollywood as its locale, *The Disenchanted*, which is part of a peculiar daisy chain of Hollywood literature.

The Disenchanted, it is generally agreed, concerned itself with the last days of a great writer, F. Scott Fitzgerald and Fitzgerald's and Schulberg's partnership as a writing team working for Walter Wanger.

But at the time that Fitzgerald was working with Schulberg, he was writing (but never finished) his own story of a Hollywood producer, *The Last Tycoon*. This was supposed to be based on the late Irving Thalberg.

Meanwhile, Jerry Wald was subsidizing the writing of *Beloved Infidel*, the story of Sheilah Graham, a Hollywood columnist who had been Fitzgerald's last love.

It was a race to cash in on the sudden interest in Fitzgerald, and

85

Wald won it. His motion picture of the Graham book hit the screen —before any of the others could be made. But it was not a hit at the box office.

And as a sidelight, while all this was going on, Robert Carson's book, *The Magic Lantern*, was published and everyone in Hollywood decided that it was about a father like B. P. Schulberg and a son like Budd Schulberg.

It has always seemed to me that these books—the good and the bad alike—have with few exceptions failed to catch the real story of Hollywood. Truth has been stranger, more interesting and more human than fiction.

The true story of Uncle Carl Laemmle, whom I knew so well and loved, had far more drama than the fictional attempts to recreate it. No one has been able to tell how Uncle Carl survived and triumphed over all his faults, his relatives and his weaknesses by being forced into making *All Quiet On The Western Front*, only to go down into defeat a few years later at the hands of the bankers who took over his studio.

And try as they might, those writers who sought to depict John Huston's "one-man-against-the-world" way of life never could bring it off as well as John has been able to do it by simply being himself.

The novels about—or supposedly about—David O. Selznick and Mark Hellinger never really got beneath the surface; never reached the core of those two many-sided men. David Selznick has survived many Waterloos and will, I think, come back to conquer once again. The true story of his battle with both himself and Hollywood has not been written, either as fact or fiction.

And Mark Hellinger, who was really a Don Quixote who never ran out of windmills, was very different from the character in the books that I have read.

The simple fact, to my mind, is that all these writers of fiction weren't really interested in writing about Hollywood. They wanted to write about themselves, about their places in Hollywood, their adventures in Hollywood, their reactions to Hollywood. Many of them have been writers only too anxious to bite the hands that fed them caviar.

In many ways these books have been surrenders. The writers

were unable, for one reason or another, to cope with Hollywood and were taking their revenge.

Neither an intentional satire, like *Dirty Eddie*, written by Ludwig Bemelmans, nor an unintentional one which showed up its author more than the movie world, like *Deer Park*, ever had the ring of honesty.

The simple truth is that not the books written about Hollywood, nor all the plays, beginning with *Once In A Lifetime*, but the movies themselves have provided the true story of Hollywood. Only the movies have had the guts and intellectual honesty to present Hollywood as it really is.

Think of the candor, the understanding, the depth of such motion pictures as *A Star Is Born, Sunset Boulevard* and *The Bad and The Beautiful*. Here, in these pictures, were studies of our town and its people. Not the surface. Not the obvious. But the motivations that make Hollywood tick and that make the people of Hollywood tick.

Certainly these pictures come a lot closer to telling the real story than the so-called "fact" books; the sociological studies and psychological studies that live off Hollywood while, at the same time, seeking to destroy it.

There is quite a roster of these books, among them Leo Rosten's *Hollywood, The Movie Colony, The Movie Makers* and Hortense Powdermaker's, *Hollywood, The Dream Factory*.

In their own fashion they explain everything about Hollywood. But, while they are filled with impressive statistics, charts and tables, they ignore the basic facts about Hollywood which can't be put into charts.

That is the effect that this place has had in so many different spheres. Its influence has been economic and aesthetic. It has been both national and international.

Hollywood has influenced the public taste in books, in fashions, in interior decoration.

Neither Mr. Rosten nor Miss Powdermaker could find a chart to show the impact that a dress worn by Joan Crawford in the picture, *Letty Lynton*, had on the women's fashion field. Yet it became a national favorite overnight and laid the groundwork for mass-produced style in women's clothes.

It was Marlene Dietrich who created the demand for women's slacks. (She had the legs and figure for them. Alas, too many women who copied her didn't.)

On another front, it was Bing Crosby and the casual Hollywood actors who made a big business of sports clothes for men. Not until these well-publicized figures appeared in trousers and jackets that didn't match did the men's clothing industry have any market for these articles of apparel.

A very great part of the clothing industry bears the mark of Hollywood and I maintain that it is for the better.

Men like Cedric Gibbons, who were among the first outstanding designers and set decorators, have revolutionized the décor of American homes. American women owe them a great debt for the lessons they taught on the screen.

Once again, there are no charts to show how much Hollywood had to do with the growth of mechanical aids in the home for the housewife. The sales records of the big companies, however, can offer evidence as to the effectiveness of Hollywood as a molder of the American scene.

In another sphere Hollywood also deserves credit. Of course the cry is always heard, "the book was better," when a classic is transcribed to the screen, but the record shows that not until such great books as *War and Peace, The Red and The Black* and *Sons and Lovers* became moving pictures was there any demand for them in the libraries.

Actually, the sales of these books, and other fine books classified as literature, have gone into the hundreds of thousands in cheap editions after they were made into pictures.

There is a third class of books which is being written these days. It takes the form of the crassest sensationalism and Hollywood is always the villain.

The books by ex-alcoholics, ex-drug addicts, ex-libertines and, mainly, ex-stars, are always filled with attacks on what Hollywood did to these people. It seems to me that these same people would have been the victims of their own weaknesses whether or not they ever came to Hollywood. The fault was not in my town, but in themselves.

I find such books a form of pandering and I have little respect for those who have to turn to them.

Nor, for that matter, do I have any great respect for those who look down the ends of their noses at Hollywood and proceed to write "biographies" of Hollywood personages. They seem to have adopted the motto, "If you can't knock, don't write."

Recently there appeared another book "debunking" Hollywood. This latest collection of sour gripes ran 452 pages and was titled, *The Fifty-Year Decline and Fall of Hollywood,* and was written by a former film critic, a former *Time* correspondent and, may I add, a former reporter, Ezra Goodman.

To be charitable, let me characterize this effusion as fiction parading as fact. Even the title is a misrepresentation. Hollywood has had its sinking spells over a half century, but right now it is enjoying one of its most prosperous periods. Motion-picture stocks are at their highest and financial statements reveal that the producing companies are heavy with profits.

Mr. Goodman made a considerable number of references to me in his book and one of my more courageous friends asked me if I was angered by them.

My reactions, for those who care, are mixed, but anger isn't one of them. I reserve anger for those who are worthy of it. However:

I resent Mr. Goodman's misstatement of facts.

I was bored by his rehashing of so many baloney "legends" about me.

I am indignant at his attacks on members of my family and those close to me.

And I'd like to set the record partially straight. If I tried to do it completely, I'd need more pages than Mr. Goodman used.

During my long, and without false modesty, not inconspicuous career I have been sniped at by experts. And why not? Almost everyone who has ever attained any kind of public stature in his or her profession can expect sometimes to see a reflection in a cracked mirror. It would be strange indeed if Louella Parsons were to be the exception.

I've never held myself up as a paragon of even *half* the virtues. (I have a temper, as many press agents, stars and directors can attest with a vehement "Amen.") I have made mistakes in my daily column, which is not always couched in pure Webster. (Ask any reporter faced with a deadline if every sentence parsed and every pronoun had an antecedent.) And on the purely personal side, at various times I have not sported sylphlike lines on my figure. (Some critics feel that *Marilyn Monroe* is too fat.)

However, I can read about myself as "plump and prattling" (*Time*'s favorite description for me) with a fair degree of patience. I have learned to accept being called a "Mrs. Malaprop" and being described as "terrible tempered." (I've already entered a guilty plea to that one.)

But, as a sop to my female vanity, I'd like the world to know that I am no longer plump. I've worn a size twelve dress for the past ten years and, quite often, a size ten.

It was not repetitions such as these which annoyed me with Mr. Goodman's book. It was the lies, the BIG lies. And I'll mention a few of these in justice to other people as well as to myself. Some of them are dead and can't ask for that justice.

The late writer Richard English did not give me an "assist" in writing my autobiography, *The Gay Illiterate*. Dick did not even insert a comma in that book. He acted as the representative of the publishers; keeping me pepped up, keeping me on the job, making sure that I got it done in time to meet the publishing deadline.

Of course it was edited. All books are. Or should I make an exception of Mr. Goodman's book? I can hardly believe that any responsible editor would have permitted all the errors, distortions and misquotations. No, I'll give him credit for a "do-it-yourself" job.

Mr. Goodman repeated an old and false story that one year all my Christmas gifts were stolen from my car and that I demanded they all be replaced. Now Mr. Goodman knows better. He knows, as a former critic and *Time* correspondent, that the studios send their gifts to the homes of the recipients. I wouldn't for the world suggest that he send his car on a Santa Claus tour.

I said earlier that I didn't get angry at anything in his book. However, I came mighty close to anger when I read his remarks concerning my late, beloved husband Dr. Harry Martin, my daughter Harriet and my cousin Margaret Ettinger.

Here, again, Mr. Goodman used the word "assist." Only, this time I am supposed to have done the assisting. The implication was that I used my column and what influence I had in their behalf and made their successes possible. Mr. Goodman is a liar.

Let me "assist" him in stating these facts:

Dr. Harry Martin was a distinguished and successful urologist before I ever met him.

Harriet obtained her first writing job while she was in college. I did not know about it until after she had signed a contract. She made her own way in Hollywood and took the setbacks as well as the successes without any interference from me. And I would have resented it had she disowned me or changed her name.

Margaret Ettinger was already established as one of Hollywood's leading press agents before I ever came to the Coast. For years her largest and most profitable accounts have had little or no relationship to the movie business.

So much for Mr. Goodman. Too much in fact.

But it is books like his which point up one of the great failures of the motion-picture industry. Hollywood has developed the art of press agentry and public relations to its zenith in dealing with its product. Why should it have done such a bad job in relation to itself?

⋙ *Chapter 6*

A TOUCH OF ROYALTY

I HAVE attended only one royal wedding—the literal not the Hollywood type—in my life.

When I saw the lovely bride, it seemed to me that no movie script would ever have dared tell her story because it would have lacked believability. To me, watching and listening, the marriage had an aura of unreality because I kept thinking of the first time I had ever seen the bride and all the things she had been, and done and which had happened to her in the years between.

Yet I knew it was happening. Happening to the girl I had first seen in 1935 in Agua Caliente, Mexico, whose name was Marguerita Cansino. On this spring day in 1949, we were on the French Riviera and in a few moments she would be changing her name from Rita Hayworth to Princess Marguerita Aly Khan.

In the 30's, Agua Caliente was Hollywood's playground (as Las Vegas and Palm Springs are today). We would go to the Mexican town for the races, the night clubs and general relaxation. This included wide-open gambling.

I had been invited to spend a weekend with Joseph Schenck, still one of my dearest friends, who owned the casino which was the heart of Agua Caliente. Among my fellow guests was Winfield

Sheehan, now dead and almost forgotten in Hollywood, but then the production head of Fox Films.

The casino had a floor show and one of the acts appearing that weekend was a team of dancers—father and daughter—Eduardo and Marguerita Cansino. As dancers, they were superb. I felt that they had a great potential—as dancers.

But Winnie Sheehan, watching the act, had another idea. He whispered to me, "That girl is a beauty. She could be a great movie star."

I took another look. The girl had grace, of course, but she was also quite overweight. And the promise of beauty was there, but only the promise. She was dark—almost black-haired. And her hairline was quite low. Her skin was good but not luminous, as Dolores Del Rio's is, for instance.

And when she came to our table, she turned out to be painfully shy. She could not look at strangers when she spoke to them and her voice was so low it could hardly be heard. Hardly, it seemed to me, the material of which a great star could be made.

Yet, when we were returning to Hollywood the next day, Sheehan told me, "I've signed her to a contract."

This didn't mean too much, for at this time all the studios were signing actors and actresses to short-term contracts with options and most of these contracts terminated at the first option date. The odds were great against any of these contract players ever being anything else.

I was piqued, however, that Sheehan had paid so little attention to my comments. "What are you going to do about her figure?" I asked.

"We'll put her on a diet."

"And her voice?"

"We'll train it."

"And how are you ever going to get her to look into a camera?"

"By teaching her."

He had an answer for everything, but it wasn't enough of an answer for me to feel that I ought to write a headline about it. I felt that in six months Marguerita Cansino would be forgotten.

In two weeks she was no longer Marguerita Cansino. Sheehan had changed her name to "Rita Hayworth." He explained, "It will look good on theatre marquees."

"You really believe in her?" I asked.

"You bet I do."

I kept getting reports on her progress and I saw her a couple of times in the ensuing months. Sheehan had been right about what diet would do for her. The plump girl had become a willowy one and stares followed her wherever she went. Though it appeared I was right about her potential as a movie actress. The first three pictures in which Rita appeared proved that she didn't come across to the general audience.

She seemed to lack that unique quality which has nothing to do with talent, beauty or intelligence but which, for lack of a better word, is called "personality." That she obviously lacked.

But Sheehan remained confident he had a star in Rita and announced that she would play the lead in Helen Hunt Jackson's *Ramona* which Fox was preparing to make. Right after that was announced (though I do not believe there was any connection) another announcement came out of the studio. Fox had let Sheehan go as production head. And, a little while later, a third announcement. Loretta Young had been given the role of "Ramona."

By all the logic of Hollywood, that should have been the end of Rita Hayworth's career. She had lost her sponsor and her record showed no hits in three times at bat. The chances were that she would be kept at the studio until her next optiontime arrived and then dropped.

The chances are that just this would have happened if Edward C. Judson, a balding automobile salesman and promoter from Texas, had not appeared on the movie scene. He changed the script.

Rita, by this time, had learned the rudiments of acting. She was sincere, hard working, earnest. She applied herself to the job of becoming an actress. But she appeared to lack drive, to lack the egotism that is almost a necessity for a successful Hollywood career. She did not push herself, sell herself, talk about herself. She remained, as she had been, shy and too placid and introverted.

Judson was neither shy, nor placid nor introverted. He was a sales-

94

man who was using the "hard sell" before that term came into common usage. And, as soon as he saw Rita, he decided that she was the commodity he was going to sell.

In this respect—and because it has always played so large a part in Rita's life—I think I should repeat what her father told me about her at the time. "Rita," he said, "likes to be told what to do. If she likes and trusts you, she will accept whatever you tell her. I suppose the fault is mine because from the time she was a baby, I taught her and told her what to do.

"She is a marvelous pupil but she has carried into her personal life this same habit of doing what she is told, rather than making her own decisions. She has remained a child."

In Judson—as she had earlier in Sheehan—she found a new father figure. (Here's Parsons proving that she has read a book again!) He was more than twice her seventeen years, a man of the world, a convincing talker. And he did something that Sheehan had not been able to do. He made Rita believe in herself. He convinced her that she could be a star.

In addition, he altered the product which he had taken under his wing. His first step was to get her to dye her hair the deep, lovely red that it still is. Then he began to act as her agent.

Rita fell in love with Judson and married him. There were few who thought that this could be good for Rita. They were both right and wrong. In so far as her personal life was concerned, the marriage would bring both heartache and unhappiness. But, as far as her career was concerned, Judson proved that he could make good all his boasts.

His start appeared inauspicious. When Rita's optiontime arrived, Judson demanded that she receive a larger raise than the option called for. He was told that the studio had an investment in her and would be willing to keep her under contract, but without any raise. Judson refused and the option was dropped.

Now Judson pulled a master stroke. He sold Rita to Harry Cohn, head of Columbia studios. Somehow he convinced Cohn that she was the material of which stars were made. Of course Cohn must have had some such feeling himself, for few men were so adept at sensing hidden values in an actress. (One doesn't have to go beyond the career of Kim Novak for proof.) He must have felt that Rita would turn out to be worth a fortune for Columbia.

Cohn gave her a contract that started at a high salary, with options that reached astronomical figures. And, in her professional life, he became the dominant father figure.

Judson, however, ruled Rita's life outside the studio. She never bought a dress without his first approving it. She could not make a social or business engagement without his permission. He read every script submitted to her and whatever his decision, she abided by it. He seemed to do all her thinking for her.

It was at this period in Rita's life that I first got to know her well. These were the years when she blasted into orbit as a major Hollywood star. These were also the years when, for the first time, she began to have doubts about herself as a human being.

One time she said to me, "I feel hollow inside. As if I were a puppet."

Such a remark really surprised me. Not that Rita should feel this way, but that she could express it so aptly. To most of us in Hollywood she *was* a beautiful puppet.

She was really torn between two very deep parts of herself. She was grateful to Judson for what he had done for her. She had a deep affection for him; the affection, I think, of a child for a parent. She felt that if she ever left Judson she would be showing the worst kind of disloyalty.

But another part of her had developed during those years. Maturity had come late, but it had come. Judson was her husband and here he had failed her. Or, to be more accurate, here he was out of place, miscast. She was barely twenty-one, her mind filled with romance and a desire for the excitement that youth always craves. But Judson was staid, settled; more interested in financial statements than in valentines.

Rita tried to tell this to Judson but was unable to come to the point. "I keep thinking," she said to me, "how hurt he will be and I hate to hurt anyone. I'd rather be hurt myself."

This unhappiness was having a marked effect upon her. She lost weight continually. She could not eat and many nights found her

96

unable to sleep. Her nerves grew tense and Rita, who had always been able to get along so well with everyone, suddenly found she could not get along with anyone.

She sat in my playroom and wept out her unhappiness. She carried on an argument with herself and I was the interested bystander—a sounding board. She kept saying how grateful she was to Judson, how much she owed him. He was responsible for her success, for her financial security, for her career. "I never had to do any fighting for myself," she said. "He fought for me."

Finally I said, "There's only one question. Are you happy?"

"No." It was a whisper.

"Then all the rest isn't worth while."

"I know," she said, "but I was fighting against admitting it."

Soon afterward she told Judson that she wanted a divorce. At first he refused, but when he discovered that she was adamant he imposed a set of conditions, all of them financial. Rita told me what he demanded and I was shocked. It was as if he were demanding alimony, and I said so.

"You're wrong," Rita said. "Running my career was his only business. He's entitled to a fair return."

Well, I could agree to that. What was "fair"? Certainly not what Judson was asking. Finally I suggested, "Go to Harry Cohn, tell him the whole story and let him advise you."

Rita grasped at this quickly. It seemed so fitting that she should be able to turn to an older—and she was sure, wiser—man for help. She had been doing just that all her life. She went to see Cohn almost at once.

Harry Cohn was apparently able to take quick control of the situation. Within a few weeks Rita and Judson separated and were later divorced. It was done with the minimum of fuss and no scandal—a real rarity.

With the divorce, Judson seemed to be cast out of her life. Where once all her talk and her thoughts had concerned themselves with him, now she did not speak of him at all. And I think that in the years since, I have heard her mention him only once and then it came almost casually.

"Ed regarded me only as an investment," was what she said.

97

The divorce appeared to liberate Rita. For the first time she was on her own. Her first gesture of freedom was a trip to New York where she bought a completely new wardrobe. "I wanted everything I owned to be mine," she said. "As if I were mine—as if I belonged to me—for the first time." On her return, it was as a gay, young divorcee.

Remember that at this time she was one of the biggest stars in pictures. She racked up box-office successes with *Blood and Sand,* in which she played opposite Tyrone Power, and the musicals *My Gal Sal* and *Strawberry Blonde.*

In addition, the plump, dark-haired girl of a few years ago had become a redheaded sex symbol to the men in the armed services. She and Betty Grable were the two top pin-ups of the age. Many an American boy was fighting for Mom, for apple pie and for a girl like Rita. And a lot of them preferred Rita to apple pie.

She was one of the regulars at the Hollywood Canteen. She went on USO trips, visited hospitals and camps. She was a success and the reason, I think, was told me by a homesick marine at Camp Pendleton. "She isn't an actress or Rita Hayworth, Miss Parsons. She's just Her."

At the same time, Rita got around Hollywood and its parties like a debutante in her coming-out year. She played the field, dating every eligible young man in town. When she was criticized for this, she said, "Why shouldn't I? I'm free. I'm young. I love to dance. What do they want me to do? Dance solos?"

For a time it seemed that Vic Mature was first in line in her heart. Certainly he was in love with her and few women ever had a more devoted admirer. And certainly Rita gave up the field and started dating only Vic. I was in New York just before Vic went into the Coast Guard. Rita, Vic and I had dinner at the Stork Club and I might as well have been back in Hollywood as far as he was concerned. Rita was the only person in the world to him.

Later I asked Rita if she were in love with him. She said, "I like him a great deal. But love? I just don't know, Louella. Besides—" she threw a brittle laugh at me—"I don't want to get married in a hurry. I have a lot of years to make up."

98

And then Orson Welles—awesome Orson—entered her life.

He came a-wooing with his press books and his reputation and his air of knowing everything because he had invented everything. He had been the Boy Wonder of Broadway, the *enfant terrible* of radio. The only world left for him to conquer was Hollywood and he came to town certain that this wouldn't take too much time.

As I have remarked, Orson is hardly one of my favorite people. That's one reason I'm bending over backward to be fair to him in retelling the story of his relationship with Rita. I wouldn't want anyone to think I'm sticking a pin in Orson's overinflated tummy.

When Rita met Orson, she reverted to type. She ceased being the new, independent, on-her-own Rita. Instead, she once again became dependent. Here was—by his own admission—The Great Intellect, and Rita made obeisance to this latest inhabitant of Olympus.

Rita entered a new world which was furnished, if not littered, with books, music and art. She was being indoctrinated with "the finer things in life." Orson talked and Rita listened. He was teacher and she pupil. It was, in many respects, a repetition of her relationship with Judson except that Orson proved of little help to her career.

Rita tried hard. She read books and went to art galleries. She played symphonies by the score. But, somehow, she didn't get the same lift from these that she did from just being herself.

She became pregnant and bore a daughter, Rebecca. And, after bearing, she became bored. She and Orson broke up. Her attitude about her marriage was typical of her character. She told me, "I'll never be sorry that I married Orson. He's intelligent and he gave me a new viewpoint on life. Besides, I have my daughter."

Once more liberated, Rita started seeing other men. For a time she was seen everywhere with Jimmy Stewart. She had quite an effect on Jimmy, making him gayer than he had ever seemed before. I recall one night at Irene Selznick's when Jimmy played the piano and Rita sang for hour after hour.

But that romance did not last long and soon Rita was being escorted about town by Tony Martin. He fell head over heels in love (the cliché fits, so I'm using it) and I can recall the hurt and shock in his voice when he called me and said, "Rita is reconciling with

Orson. I can't understand it. I'm in love with her and I was sure she loved me."

I called Rita and asked if this was true. She said it was and explained, "I have our daughter to consider. And besides, I'm going to make a picture with Orson."

Rita had been starred in a series of sensational hits, among them *Cover Girl* and *Tonight and Every Night*. Her position was assured and with Harry Cohn to guide her it appeared that nothing could hurt her career. However, Orson would prove that to be untrue. He came quite close.

Orson made *Lady From Shanghai* with Rita as the star, but he had his own idea of what to do with Rita. He decided to alter her personality and the way he chose was to have her bleach her hair a pale blond and cut it short. She was a different Rita, all right, and the fans didn't like the new Rita or the picture. Soon after she again left Orson, this time for good.

I think Orson's big mistake was getting involved in Rita's career. An actress, especially a star, can forgive anything but a flop. Rita once told me that her reason for leaving Orson for good and all was because "I always came last with Orson. His writing, his magic show, his radio work and his other personal interests always came first. Sometimes he would forget that I existed. He would leave me alone night after night."

Those are all good reasons for leaving a man, but just the same, I feel that the basic reason was the flop movie. It proved to Rita that Orson wasn't all-knowing. It proved that he could make mistakes—and bad ones. (What was worse than injuring her career?) And so she left him.

As if to underline Orson's failure with her, Rita's next picture was one of her greatest successes. This was *Gilda*.

And if Rita's ego had been hurt by Orson's neglect, it certainly should have been soothed by the unbelievable publicity which came with that picture.

Far away from Hollywood, at the atomic-testing grounds in Bikini, *Gilda* made news. A news magazine reported what happened in this manner:

"In christening the deadly missile 'Gilda,' in honor of the russet-haired Columbia star's latest film, a smitten ground crew and technicians had lovingly pasted her pin-up on its side. This spontaneous tribute earned Miss Hayworth nearly as much international publicity as the fearsome Gilda got for itself by exploding on schedule. To Miss Hayworth's studio, it amounted to the most literally earth-shaking free plug in the history of the world."

The picture re-established Rita, made millions and proved that Orson didn't really know everything.

Rita was again seeing Tony Martin but he had no monopoly on her time. David Niven was a rather ubiquitous rival. This was a most interesting contest and a lot of people waited to see which of these two would win out. Neither did.

Instead, Rita decided to go to Europe. "If I stay here," she told me, "I might marry again and I don't want to do that. See you when I get back."

I think, however, her reason was far deeper. She was again involved in an emotional crisis, but this one was internal. Orson's efforts had left a deep mark. Rita couldn't return to being the simple, pleasure-loving girl she had been. Her old values had been destroyed and no new ones had taken their place. The need for new values, however, was with her.

For the first time in her career, she became temperamental. In Paris she kept members of the press waiting for almost an hour before she would see them. London reporters wrote that she had a flunky in a powdered wig and knee breeches announce her arrival to them. The result, of course, was a bad press. The trip to Europe was hardly a triumphal tour.

Then, when Rita returned to Hollywood, she continued to avoid newspaper people. Once she had been voted the most co-operative star in Hollywood by all its working press. In 1947 she received their vote as the most unco-operative.

We had remained good friends and I called her and asked her what had happened to bring about this reversal. Her answer was almost fierce. "My private life is my own, Louella. I'm going to protect it."

101

At this time she left Columbia and formed her own film company. "It's a way to protect Rebecca's future," she said. "I can't do it just working on a salary." She made a picture for her own company, *The Loves of Carmen,* which was a success, and then she left for Europe again.

The next time I saw her was in the summer of 1948. My husband, Dr. Martin, and I were visiting in Cannes and Rita was at Cap d'Antibes, close by. I heard stories about Rita; that she was not well, that she was secluding herself, that she appeared depressed and emotionally weary.

I gave credence to these reports when I learned that Orson had asked her for a reconciliation and she had agreed to see him. He came from Rome to visit her. She saw him and decided that she would continue to live alone even if she didn't like it. This also proved to me that while she might have been depressed, she was certainly rational.

Some friends gave a party for me and invited Rita. I hadn't seen her for some months and her appearance upset me. She was lethargic and drooped. There was none of the vitality, the exuberance that she had always had. Aware of it, she said to me, "I'm just not well."

A short time later I had lunch with Elsa Maxwell at her lovely home, Le Sault, at Auerbreau. Elsa told me she was giving a big party the next Saturday and had asked Aly Khan to come. Then she gave me a quick look. "I've also asked Rita. I believe he's just the man to snap Rita out of whatever ails her. He has money, charm and position."

Aly Khan was one of the best-known members of the international set which was far more Elsa's territory than mine. However, he was hardly a stranger to me or anyone else who ever read the newspapers.

He was playboy and diplomat, lover and soldier, gentleman jockey and racing daredevil. During the war, he had served with the French army, the French Foreign Legion, with the British in North Africa and India and with the American forces during the landings in France. He had won, among other decorations, the *croix de guerre* with palms and the United States Army's Bronze Star.

Aly was best known, however, as the son of the fabulously wealthy

Aga Khan and because in a world of romantics, he was held the champion of ladies' men.

From his youth the slim, dark, vital Aly had been most attractive to women. They fell in love with him and he fell in love with them. He had an Oriental concept of the relationship between men and women and practiced it in the Occidental world. At the age of twenty-four he was named corespondent in the divorce suit of Thomas Loel E. B. Guinness, heir to the British brewing fortune.

A week after the Guinnesses were divorced, Aly and the ex-Mrs. Guinness were married and they had two sons. But when Rita met Aly, he had long been separated from his wife.

I returned to Hollywood shortly after that meeting and reports reached me that Rita had awakened from her lethargy as soon as she had met him. And Aly, never lethargic, was positively volatile. When Rita went to Paris, he followed her there. When she came back to the United States, he followed her to New York. And when she returned to Hollywood, word was that he would soon be out here.

Rita appeared on my radio show but she refused to talk about Aly on the air. However, when the show was over and we were alone she said, "This is it, Louella. I've never known anything like this before."

I started to probe, but Rita stopped me. "When there's something to tell you, Louella, you'll know it. And before anyone else does." However, she did admit that, as of the moment, Aly wasn't exactly a free agent.

Shortly afterward he arrived in town. He had nothing to say to the press. Then Rita flew to Mexico. Aly followed. Rita went on to Cuba. Aly was a plane behind. The romantic chase continued to Ireland, Switzerland and, finally, Cannes. From that last spot came word that Aly was getting a divorce.

This was a big Hollywood story and it was a big story out of Hollywood.

Nobility was not new to the movies. There was a time when it seemed that half the female stars of Hollywood were marrying one of the assorted M'divanis and the other half had married, or were going to marry, the charming Count Henri de la Falaise. And hadn't Doug Fairbanks married Lady Sylvia Ashley?

Aly Khan was a newsworthy figure in his own right.

But, I have to admit, I kept thinking that this would all be much ado about nothing. I just didn't believe that Aly, after all these years, would get a divorce.

I was wrong.

One spring morning in 1949 my phone rang and the international operator told me that I was being called from Cannes. A moment later Rita was on the phone. "I'm getting married, Louella, and I want you at the wedding. We're such old friends. Will you come?"

"You bet I will," was my answer.

I immediately informed my bosses of the invitation and they were delighted. They were even more delighted when it was announced from Cannes that the wedding would be closed to the press. The Los Angeles *Examiner* took the opportunity to report that I had been invited and was, of course, going.

Hedda wrote in her column the next day: "Louella Parsons will not get within a mile of the wedding. Helen Morgan has been assigned to cover it and she will be the only newspaperwoman there."

(Helen Morgan, who had resigned from the editorial staff of *Life* magazine to handle Rita's publicity, was at the wedding only in her capacity as press agent. Hedda continued to report that I wouldn't be there, until pictures of the wedding guests appeared. One picture stifled thousands of words.)

Accompanied by Dottie May, I rushed toward France by way of New York. The column was left in the capable hands of Dorothy Manners. In New York I talked with editors and syndicate managers, and then Dottie May and I flew on to Paris.

My first stop was at the fabulous shop of *couturier* Jacques Fath, who was making Rita's beautiful blue wedding dress. I bought a polka-dot hat to wear at the ceremony.

Next, accompanied by Bob Considine, one of the best newspapermen I know, I went off to buy a wedding present. It turned out to be a full day's work. Rita was, literally, the "girl who had everything" and she was marrying a man whose family wealth was great enough to buy her spares. We searched Paris and finally, in an antique shop, I discovered an embroidered wisp of a handkerchief which, I was assured, had belonged to Marie Antoinette. And that was my wedding gift to Rita.

Rita had made reservations for Dottie May and me at the Carleton in Cannes. When we arrived the doorman greeted me by name. The desk clerk told me, "You are invited to lunch at L'Horizon tomorrow." The rest of the help seemed to know all about who I was and what I was doing.

I quickly learned that there were no secrets in Cannes.

The bellboys, clerks, waiters, chambermaids and other members of the hotel staff were all in the pay of newspaper and magazine correspondents from all over the world. They steamed open letters, eavesdropped on conversations, listened in on phone calls, scavenged in wastebaskets. They sold each other information and there were times when they bought back their own fictions as truth.

Was I grateful that I didn't have to engage in this type of espionage! I was on the inside of the story.

I found the luncheon invitation in my room, the edges of the envelope flap slightly curled.

L'Horizon was a jewel of a home, set against the stunning backdrop of the blue Mediterranean. It had been built by Maxine Elliott, the famous actress from whom Aly Khan had bought it, and was more like a movie set than any movie set ever could be.

Rita and I embraced and I took a good look at her. Happiness and excitement had brought her a new beauty. I must say, though, that she looked more American than I had ever seen her look before. She was wearing blue jeans, a checked shirt and a pair of *huaraches*.

Aly assured me, as he stood with an arm about Rita's waist, that he was deliriously happy and delighted that there no longer were any obstacles to their marriage.

We ate lunch on the terrace and Aly, always the gentleman, did everything he could to put me—*me!*—at my ease. He asked about my work, about my plans for covering the story and about newspapering in general. He seemed completely interested in that and that alone.

Rita ate little, smiled fondly at Aly and looked beautiful. She spoke very little.

Afterward, I was taken on a tour of the château by Aly. It had recently been redecorated, on his instructions, in tones of blue and green, with touches of rose and gold. "Those," he said, "are the sunset colors which make the Mediterranean so beautiful."

I was then shown the presents which had already arrived; among them a painting of Utrillo's which the artist felt belonged in the château because it was done in Mediterranean blues and greens. I liked this piece of art a great deal more than I did a set of dishes especially designed for them by Picasso. I thought the dishes came close to being the ugliest pieces of pottery I had ever seen, but that was only one woman's opinion and that woman knew enough to keep her mouth shut.

During the afternoon, a delegation of Ismaili Indians, subjects of Aly's father, the Aga, came to pay their respects. They wore their native costumes and these were among the handsomest I had ever seen.

When I returned to the hotel, I dictated a series of what I thought were exclusive stories to Dottie May. The next day I received a wire from New York telling me that my stories had been pirated and parts of them were appearing in other stories out of Cannes. Thereafter, Dottie May worked in a locked room, we telephoned our stories to New York and all carbons were carried by me. None of my other stories was lifted until it appeared in print.

The wedding had originally been scheduled for L'Horizon but the French Ministry of Justice decided that it must take place in the office of the Mayor of Vallauris, a Communist.

When informed of this, Aly Khan was enraged. To cool off he jumped into his Alfa-Romeo, rushed off to Cannes Casino and gambled furiously for an hour. His luck was bad.

There were a large number of social events before the wedding and I was included in all of them. I met many of the elite of European high society but by far the most fascinating was Aly's father, the Aga.

A square, stocky man, he had as much charm as his son and a less volatile temper. As spiritual leader of the Ismaili Moslems he had great importance, but he added to it with his political acumen and diplomatic brilliance. He did much to keep relations good between the seat of empire, Great Britain, and the outskirts of the empire.

Most of the publicity about the Aga concerned itself with his wealth and the fact that he had been twice presented with his weight in gold and twice in diamonds. In all four cases, the Aga kept only a token souvenir and turned the rest of the mountains of wealth back to his people to be used for schools, hospitals and other civic purposes. The millions thus diverted, however, did not make too large a dent in his personal fortune.

The Aga, of course, had the same Oriental attitude toward women and marriage as did his son. He had been married three times. His first wife, Aly's mother, died. The Aga then married Princess Irene, divorced her but remained on the friendliest of terms with her, and married the woman who survived him, the Begum, probably the handsomest woman I have ever seen.

As an example of the friendly spirit which pervaded the much-married group, the Princess Irene cared for little Rebecca Welles all during the hubbub at L'Horizon. Princess Irene, who had virtually brought up Aly, still treated him as a son and he adored her. The Begum felt no apparent jealousy. The Aga beamed.

Aly's two sons, both charming young men with extensive worldly wisdom for their years, attended most of the functions. At one luncheon the young man who is now the Aga Khan served as my legman. He got me the list of guests, filled me in on those whom I did not know and offered some nuggets of news on his own.

When I met the Aga I tried my French, rusty from disuse. It didn't serve as a means of communication but the Aga quickly solved that by speaking in his beautiful, precise English. What I remember best about our conversation was that he regarded Americans and American newspapers as quite extraordinary in that they believed it worth while to send a reporter 6,000 miles to cover anything as ordinary as his son's wedding.

As I have already remarked, there was a difference in the manner in which the Aga and Aly regarded love and marriage and the manner in which we did.

The Aga spoke about Rita, saying he thought she was truly a beautiful woman. I got the impression he was really quite fond of her. He was my escort when we went to a screening of *Loves of Carmen* on the night before the wedding. Charles Vidor, who was one of Rita's favorite directors, and his wife Doris were the only other Americans at the screening.

The next morning I discovered that I had troubles which I had not foreseen. As long as the wedding had been scheduled to take place at L'Horizon, I was assured of my exclusive story. I had telephones at my disposal and no other reporters anywhere around. But now that the wedding site had been shifted to City Hall, I had to find a phone over which to dictate the story.

A quick survey revealed that while I had been getting news, the other reporters hadn't been wasting time. They had tied up every available telephone within a mile of City Hall. They had paid trades-men, shopkeepers and housewives, and in most instances had the lines open continually.

Then I had a brain storm. There had to be a telephone in the Mayor's office. I went there and again using my halting French, sought to make my predicament known to him. He was the first admitted Communist I had ever talked with but I found that he was not averse to capitalistic ideas. As soon as I mentioned money, he began to un-derstand me. And as I brought franc notes out of my purse, he un-derstood me better and better.

For a fee he agreed to permit me the exclusive use of his phone and I sealed the bargain by giving him half the agreed-upon sum at once, the rest to be paid immediately after the ceremony.

The wedding day was clear and beautiful. By 8 A.M., the bride was having her hair done and the bridegroom was busy supervising flower arrangements and the setting up of bars and buffets.

The town turned the day into a holiday. Thousands of persons gathered early and took up posts of vantage around the village square and in the balconies on the road from the château to town.

Prince Aly, in striped trousers and short morning jacket, arrived precisely at 11 A.M. By this time there were more than 10,000 cheer-ing spectators who were making it difficult for the 200 police on mo-torcycles and in jeeps to keep order. It was a sort of miniature Rose Bowl. Seven minutes later, Rita arrived and Aly led her into the freshly whitewashed City Hall.

I have known Rita a long time but I don't believe she will ever be

108

as serenely beautiful as she was that morning. Jacques Fath had created a masterpiece in ice-blue crepe, softly draped and with an intricately pleated skirt. The enormous cart-wheel hat which she wore made her look like a Degas model.

Our Communist Mayor forgot politics long enough to stare, open-mouthed, at Rita. He had to recover himself before he could begin the ten-minute ceremony that joined the daughter of an unknown dancer and the heir of an uncountable fortune—who was a spiritual leader of millions—in wedlock.

Rita and Aly were more composed than the Mayor or the small group of spectators. They answered his questions clearly and firmly. I make no pretense of knowing what is in anyone else's heart at any given time, but I believe that never were two people more clearly and deeply in love than Rita and Aly at that moment. It was love that gave her a special radiance and love that made him seem youthful.

The final words had hardly been spoken when I clambered over a high bench, skinning my knees in the process, and raced to the Mayor's private office and his precious phone. An attaché was guarding it, as the Mayor had promised, and Dottie May was on the other end of the line.

I promised a follow-up from the reception and started back toward the main room. At the doorway I was met by the Mayor whose hand was extended toward me. For a moment I thought he wanted to shake hands, then I realized that that wasn't what he intended at all. I quickly paid him the balance of what I had promised him and he bowed and *"merci'ed"* me back into the office.

I was given a pink-paper disc to distinguish me as a guest and member of the official party and then left the building. Aly and Rita were on the steps of the City Hall, receiving cheers and accepting a barrage of flowers. A few photographs were taken and we all piled into the waiting limousines and followed the Prince and his new Princess to the château for the wedding breakfast.

The swimming pool at L'Horizon was filled with flowers. Centered were two large bouquets, arranged to form the initials "M" (for Marguerita) and "A" (for Aly). The scent of the flowers filled the

109

garden and blended with the music being played by an orchestra in the background.

This was, literally, "princely." Everything about that day was princely. In all my life I have never seen so many beautifully dressed women. The gowns were extravagant, exciting and exotic. The jewels gleamed in the sunlight, throwing off all the colors of the spectrum.

East and West met in this garden and the representatives of the East, unself-conscious about colors or display, outshone the West. It was the Arabian Nights come to life and not even the biggest Hollywood production could have matched it. Some of the Ismaili women wore diamonds set into the left sides of their noses; diamonds about four times as large as what we would consider lavish engagement ring stones. But they were so natural, so completely themselves, that after a time I stopped thinking of them as strangely beautiful and thought of them only as beautiful.

Champagne flowed from fountains at both ends of the terrace. Food was piled high on buffet tables. There was dancing to the music that played continually. And gate crashing by newspaper people who forced their way into the party.

This created another crisis for me. Aly, angered but diplomatic, ordered that no one was to be allowed to use any of the telephones in the château. This order, I discovered, applied as much to me as to anyone else. And I had to find some way to evade it.

I suppose I could have asked Aly directly, but if he refused I would be in an untenable position. I would have abused my privileges as friend and guest and might well find myself cut off from the intimacy which I enjoyed. On the other hand, I was there as a reporter and it was my job to get my story to my newspapers just as fast as I could; and the more exclusive the better.

It was another guest, Dickie Gordon, who solved my problem. She said, "I'll tell Aly that I promised to get him and Rita to talk with Elsa Maxwell in London. After all, they owe that to her. She introduced them. When they're through, I'll ask if you can speak to Elsa from another extension. When you're through with Elsa, put in your own call and Aly will never know."

110

There was, I knew, a lack of ethics here, but I told myself that all was fair in love and newspaper warfare. I held my breath as Dickie spoke to Aly and Rita, saw them smile and rise. A moment later Dickie signaled me and I left the terrace and went into the house. And, after Rita and Aly had spoken to Elsa, and I had added a half-dozen choice words, I got through to Dottie May and dictated *sotto voce*. Of course the story scooped all the other newspapers and wire services.

Finally, after some six hours of celebration, of music and feasting, the guests began to depart, the newspapermen being ushered out first. That is how it happened that I got another exclusive story. At the end, when Rita slumped wearily into an easy chair, the still buoyant Prince dropped on one knee beside her and, with inbred gallantry, kissed her slipper.

It was a lovely gesture and the headline on the story carried by the Los Angeles *Examiner* read:

Aly Khan Kisses Rita's Foot, Climax To Fabulous Wedding

All during this period of excitement I had not only covered the Rita-Aly romance with special stories, written syndicate stories and features, but I had also done my usual radio show. This was done by means of a telephone hookup and it turned out to be one of my best shows because my old friend Maurice Chevalier had consented to sing a few songs.

Now, I was tired. I had used up so much mental and physical energy that it wearies me even to recall it. But Dottie May and I were to have a reward. Our assignment was finished; other Hearst reporters were taking over. We could go to Paris and have a ball.

We certainly deserved it. Our stories had been exclusive. We had sent them in fast. We had outwitted other reporters and had even found a method of coexistence with a Communist. It may be that coexistence can work if we pay a high enough price for it. Certainly it worked in the case of the telephone.

So it was with light hearts and much anticipation that Dottie May and I arrived in Paris. And were greeted at the plane by a cable from

111

Mr. Hearst himself. He wanted a series of fourteen articles about Rita. Her life story and all that had led up to her becoming a Princess.

My first reaction was to rebel. It just couldn't be done and, even if it could, why ask me to do it? I was in a strange city without files or records. There was no way for me to do any research or to check any facts.

But I had spent too many years as a reporter. The desk had given me an assignment and all I could do was my best to fulfill it. And I did have Dottie May, with a prodigious memory, to work with me.

We managed to hire two secretaries, and by working through the night into the early morning, we completed two articles and sent them off. With hardly a break to rest or eat we finished five more— half the series in the next two days. I had just corrected the seventh article when a cable arrived canceling the rest of the series.

There was no explanation. Just the blunt order.

My first reaction was one of relief. Now I could sleep. And sleep I did, more than fourteen hours.

When I awakened, a copy of the New York *Journal-American* of May 31, 1949, explained what had happened. Across the top of page 1 was a banner reading: CINDERELLA PRINCESS—THE LIFE STORY OF RITA HAYWORTH, By Louella O. Parsons. But also in headlines was: ALY CANES 3 HONEYMOON LENSERS.

I read the lead of that story:

"Aly Khan furiously punched and caned today three photographers who tried to take pictures of him and his wife leaving their villa on the first leg of their honeymoon. . . ."

That gave me the answer. Mr. Hearst had a tremendous pride in newspapering and newspapermen. He would not permit anyone— prince or no prince—to kick or beat a newspaperman. And for those who think that Mr. Hearst put profits above principle, let me say that the series had boosted circulation in every paper in which it appeared, yet Mr. Hearst did not hesitate an instant to cancel the series.

Dottie May and I were free now. We could have a vacation. So we went from Paris to London and from shop to shop. While in London I was able to read copies of various Hearst newspapers and in one there was an editorial which excoriated Aly, saying in part:

". . . Aly Khan's true colors are the usual colors of a spoiled Oriental prince, and may be demonstrated some day to the American girl he married. . . ."

I could agree in part with the editorial writer, but not completely. Aly had behaved like a spoiled prince. But the simple fact was that he *was* a spoiled prince. And he had behaved in a manner which had seemed right and proper to him. We were using our standards of behavior and he was using his.

These same standards applied, as the editorial writer had suggested, to Aly's relationship with Rita. He just couldn't or wouldn't adjust to marriage as editorial writers think it should be. He was hardly very different married to Rita than he was when married to her predecessor.

It was not long before an announcement was made that Rita was expecting a baby. After little Yasmin, their daughter, was born, Rita and Aly traveled about Europe and Asia and stories appeared that the marriage was not a happy one. Rita confirmed all these stories by returning to the United States with Yasmin.

Then began the long series of court battles between the two, with Yasmin the stake in a free-for-all tug of war. I talked with Rita many times during this period and found that she still remained the same type of woman she had been before. She could not bring herself to say anything harsh or bad about Aly. She could feel that he was wrong in seeking to get custody of their child, but she gave him credit for loving and wanting the child, just as she did.

Their divorce made no difference in his friendship with me. Every time I met him he seemed to go out of his way to be particularly courteous.

At a dinner dance given by Merle Oberon, he walked over to me, shook hands and said, "Why don't you ever call me when you come to New York? I would like to take you to the UN."

He danced with Rita, who was also a guest, and I couldn't help feeling when I saw light in her eyes, that there was still a spark. Certainly he was different from any man Marguerita Cansino had ever known.

At the time of his tragic death, Aly was Permanent Representative of Pakistan to the United Nations and was highly respected. He was no longer only a playboy. I never had a chance to accept his invitation. He was killed in an automobile accident.

A lot of years had passed since I had first met Rita but the changes which had taken place were surface changes. She was still insecure, uncertain; still seeking someone in whom she could place faith and trust. She was still looking for strength in someone else.

She had not found what she needed in Judson, in Orson Welles or in Aly. She was destined to fail again when she sought it with singer Dick Haymes.

She called me to tell me she was going to marry Haymes and asked me to go with the wedding party to Las Vegas. I thanked her and refused, saying that I was afraid I wasn't lucky for her. Her answer was, "It's not your luck, but mine, Louella. This time I hope it's better."

I couldn't say that I felt it wouldn't be. It was Rita's life and she had the right to live it her way.

That marriage was another fiasco.

And then she married again. Her fifth husband was writer-producer James Hill. It seemed to me that perhaps Rita's luck had changed. Jim is kind, considerate, literate without being pretentious about it. I had hoped he could give Rita the confidence, as a woman and a human being, that she has always lacked.

This little incident about him seems characteristic. When Aly Khan was so tragically killed in an automobile accident, Jim heard the news while Rita was off playing golf. Because he did not want little Yasmin to hear the news from a radio broadcast, he telephoned their home at once and explained to the servants, getting them to keep the children away from the radio and TV until their mother was able to get home. Then he raced out to the golf course and broke the news to Rita himself. Together, they returned to tell little Yasmin the desolating fact.

The Hill marriage unfortunately ended in divorce and Rita has found her consolation in Gary Merrill, ex-husband of Bette Davis. The once-elegant Princess Marguerita is a sort of feminine beatnik, appearing in cafés with Gary in her bare feet.

Rita Hayworth! From cabaret dancer to Princess to—I hope—

114

grown woman, in more than a score of years. Years that have seen her attain every success in a worldly fashion and so little happiness as a person.

I like her. She is my friend. I wish her happiness.

⇒ *Chapter 7*

THE CHIEF

LIKE him or not—and I revered and loved him—William Randolph Hearst was a great man.

No book of mine would tell much about me if there wasn't a section in it telling about him. I don't intend to write a biography of Mr. Hearst; just to tell some remembrances of him, both as a man and as my boss.

He was the best friend I have ever had. The proof of that lies in the fact that I am still here. I told in *The Gay Illiterate* how he was instrumental in my recovery from tuberculosis. How he "fired me with pay" until the sun and time and medical help could repair the ravages of that illness.

He was many things, but above all, he was a natural leader. He was a big man physically, but in so many ways he was bigger than his own life size. I worked for him a long time and familiarity bred only admiration. Admiration for Mr. Hearst as a man and as a newspaperman.

He was the hardest-working employee in the Hearst organization. He was, as so many have said, its top reporter and writer. I always found him a man of tact and refinement, quiet—almost gentle —in manner. Yet I always knew he was the boss.

John K. Winkler, one of his biographers, has written of Mr. Hearst: "He always seemed to hold something in reserve. Many knew a part, or phase of him, but not one—not even those in closest contact —ever felt he had penetrated completely the inner core of his strange, enigmatic personality."

I would not use the same words but I did draw the same conclusion. There was just too much of him for anyone who was not his peer to be able to see. And I have never known his peer.

He was kind. Like me, Jimmy Swinnerton, the famous cartoonist, became a victim of tuberculosis. Like me, Jimmy was "fired at full pay" while fighting his way back to health. Both of us went to the great California desert. I went to Hollywood, but Jimmy fell in love with the desert and remained there to paint some of the finest pictures of that part of the world that have ever been done.

A young actress was killed while being driven home from a party at San Simeon. A drunken driver plowed his car into the one in which she was riding. Mr. Hearst took it on himself to make certain that her family, who were in moderate circumstances, did not suffer a pecuniary loss because of the girl's death. He knew he could do little to alleviate the deep suffering the family had experienced, but he wanted to provide some softening for the blow.

Francis X. Bushman, once a matinee idol, ran into difficulties when his career ended. Wherever he tried to raise money, he failed. In desperation he wrote to Mr. Hearst to ask for a loan, offering the only collateral he possessed—some valuable dogs.

"The next day," Francis told me, "I received a letter from Mr. Hearst with a check for $10,000 enclosed. He said he hoped the money would tide me over and that no security was needed."

When, a long time afterward, I told Mr. Hearst that I knew of that loan, he said, "I'm sorry he told you. It was just something between us. I knew he really needed the money when he offered to give up his dogs. They were so important to him, both actually and symbolically. I could never have deprived him of them."

I saw repeated acts of kindness wherever he was; at San Simeon,

117

at Wyntoon or in Los Angeles or New York. I was his guest at all his homes; enjoyed both his hospitality and his generosity.

It was at San Simeon that I got my famous interview with George Bernard Shaw and found that Mr. Shaw, unlike Mr. Hearst, did not think my copy should be printed without editing. He virtually rewrote the interview.

I had happy times at the parties Mr. Hearst gave and sad moments when his life neared its end.

One of the happy times—as so many other happy times did—had to do with my marriage to Dr. Harry Martin. I wanted very much to marry Harry yet, when he asked me, instead of saying yes, I said, "I couldn't marry you unless Mr. Hearst approved."

"Other men," Harry said, "have to get a father's approval, but I have to be approved by the boss. Well, ask him, but don't be too long about it."

I knew this was no commonplace situation. I was a grown woman, mother of an almost-grown daughter. I had attained some success in the world. Yet I could not accept the man I loved without the approval of my boss. But, then, my boss was Mr. Hearst.

I made an unannounced visit to San Simeon and managed to see him alone. He looked quizzically at me. "What's the matter, Louella? Something wrong?"

"Mr. Hearst—" I could hardly get the words out—"Mr. Hearst, I'd like to get married." I was red-faced and stammering and felt like a fool.

"Oh, fine. Whom would you like to marry?"

"Harry Martin." I rushed on to remind him that he had met Harry a number of times.

"I like him. He's a fine man. And you're entitled to all the happiness you can get out of life." He paused a moment. "I sometimes think there isn't enough to go around for everyone."

Well, he helped me find much happiness in my life. And there was the joy he gave others too.

My husband died shortly before Mr. Hearst and he was never told of Harry's death. Bebe Daniels and I went to see the chief, who was very sick at the time. He was thin and wan, but his blue eyes were as

118

piercing as ever, as undimmed. A pad and pencils were on a bedside table and he was, as always, working.

He smiled his welcome and seemed glad to see us. As we visited, he appeared to gain vitality. Soon he was recalling happy moments we had shared through the years. He said to me, "Tell Dr. Martin I am expecting him to be toastmaster at my next party."

I had to fight to keep from breaking down and crying.

Bebe came quickly to my rescue. "Do you remember, Mr. Hearst, when Louella put her riding pants on backward and Jimmy Swinnerton drew that funny cartoon of her?"

Mr. Hearst smiled. "Why shouldn't she put her pants on backward? Louella never did anything like anyone else."

Those were the last words I ever heard him speak.

He left monuments of many kinds. There are his sons, who are keeping his work alive. William Randolph Hearst, Jr., was given the Pulitzer Prize for his fine reporting of the Russian situation. Wherever there has been trouble, Bill, Frank Conniff, and Bob Considine, the task force, are there for on-the-spot reporting. Randolph, one of the twins, is president of the Hearst Publishing Company and he works around the clock; David, the other twin, is an officer. George Hearst's son, George, Jr., is publisher of the *Herald-Express* and he has certainly inherited his grandfather's newspaper acumen.

But he left, too, remembrances. And I'd like to tell of them now.

It was Joe Willicombe, his secretary for so long and so close to Mr. Hearst, who originated the term "The Chief," for the boss. Soon the entire organization used it, but never to Mr. Hearst's face. No one took even that kind of liberty with him. Those of us closest to him called him "W.R."

Clarence Lindner, for many years publisher of the San Francisco *Examiner*, told me how he could tell where he stood with Mr. Hearst. "I could tell," he said, "from his greeting. If he said, 'Clarence, how are you?' I knew things were all right. If, however, he began with 'Mr. Lindner,' my blood froze.

"One morning I returned from a vacation and my first call was from the Chief. 'Mr. Lindner, how would you like to take a trip?'

"I said, 'A trip?'

" 'A trip, Mr. Lindner, to the composing room. Find out why we're getting such a bad printing job.'

"The next day he called me again. 'Clarence, how are you?' I was back in favor."

I had no such divining rod. And sometimes, as in the case of my story about Ivy Lowe, the Englishwoman who was Mrs. Maxim Litvinov, I learned a little late.

I had met Mrs. Litvinov during World War II when Russia and the United States were allies, and found her charming and interesting and warmly human. She showed me pictures of her children, talked of her home life and the adjustment required in being the wife of a Russian diplomat. It made a story that I wrote with great pleasure. Then I waited for the story to appear in print.

It didn't. Instead, the story came back with a note written by the Chief himself. "Confine yourself to writing about subjects you understand." *Ouch!*

But, on the other hand, he gave me credit for knowing much more than motion pictures. "You have a knack for getting stories," he said, "and we'll use it."

It was on his orders that I was assigned to cover the Hall-Mills trial in 1926; one of the most sensational murder trials of all time.

The Reverend Edward Wheeler Hall, rector of St. John's Church, New Brunswick, New Jersey, and Mrs. Eleanor Mills, a choir singer in the church, were the victims. Their bodies, bullet-riddled and knife-slashed, were found side by side in a cemetery. Some very indiscreet letters from Mrs. Mills to Rev. Hall were scattered about. And one of Rev. Hall's calling cards was propped up against his feet, like an identification card in a morgue.

Some time later it was charged that the calling card bore the fingerprints of Willie Stevens, brother of Mrs. Hall. The card had, somehow, come into the possession of the New York *Mirror,* the Hearst tabloid. And the *Mirror* also managed to obtain a copy of the minutes of the grand jury which had investigated the killings.

The *Mirror* printed the sensational testimony. Other newspapers began to play the story up. Local authorities were forced to take action and, as a result, Mrs. Hall, widow of the clergyman, her two brothers, Willie and Henry Stevens, and her cousin Henry Carpenter were charged with murder.

That was when I got a call from Mr. Hearst. "Go to New Brunswick and write a story about the trial." I went.

When I got off the train, I took a taxi to my hotel. I started to discuss the trial with the cab driver and he glanced around and looked at me. His next words made me glad that I was dressed as if I were going to visit a movie set.

"You don't look like a newspaper reporter," he said (a dubious compliment, but I accepted it). "I know something," he went on, "that those reporters would give a right arm to know."

I didn't say anything, just held my breath.

"Lady," he said, "Willie Stevens was never anywhere near the cemetery on the night the minister and his girl friend were killed."

I couldn't restrain myself. "How do you know?"

"Because I was with him. Nobody knows that and I'm keeping my mouth shut. I'm not going to get dragged into this case." Then he added, "Willie wouldn't even step on a flower; he's too gentle."

That was the lead on the first story I sent from New Brunswick. It was a line that became famous. It was quoted hundreds of times, in the courtroom and out.

That wasn't the first murder trial that I had ever reported. Over the years I have been caricatured and lampooned. I have been pictured as a journalistic hitchhiker, an accident. This has hurt because I have always felt that I was a newspaperwoman and a good one, that I have been a reporter who developed her own "beat" and has kept tight hold on it.

I wanted to be a reporter from the time I was a young girl. That was my first—and only—ambition. I was fifteen when I got my first job as church, social and sewing-circle reporter for the Dixon *Star* in my home town, Dixon, Illinois.

Shortly afterward, Dixon had a sensational trial. A young man from a good family in an adjoining town had killed a bartender. The man had refused to serve him a drink on the ground that the young man was already drunk.

I attended the trial. The judge, a friend of my family, halted the proceedings when he saw me in the court. "What are you doing here? This is no place for you."

I gathered all my courage and all my dignity. "I'm a reporter. I'm working for the *Star*."

"You'd be better off in school," the judge said.

The young man was found guilty and sentenced to a long term in the penitentiary. However, I had learned that he was engaged to a nineteen-year-old girl who wanted to marry him before he was taken to State prison.

I learned that there was no law against this and told the girl. We made all the arrangements quietly and when the ceremony took place I was the only outside witness. And the only bridesmaid.

I wrote the story for the *Star*. It was picked up by the wire services (without my by-line, however). I felt that I had reached the apex of my career at its very beginning.

A footnote: Some time later I wrote this story as fiction and sold it to the old Essanay Company in Chicago for twenty-five dollars. This was my first effort in the fiction field.

It was Mr. Hearst who assigned me to cover the first Jack Dempsey-Gene Tunney fight in 1926, when Dempsey was still champion.

Gene Fowler, that great writer and reporter who died only a short time ago, was told to indoctrinate me. He took me to Dempsey's training quarters in Atlantic City, New Jersey.

I must say that Jack seemed to be in wonderful physical shape. His muscles rippled and he knocked his sparring partners all over the ring.

A few days later I found it hard to believe that the same man was in the ring in Philadelphia, fighting Tunney. Jack looked drawn and sick. I was sure he had been poisoned and said so to Gene Fowler even before the first round began. Gene told me that there had been many rumors that the gamblers had put their money on Tunney to win and that some sinister underworld forces had passed this information on to Jack.

I am sure that anything that did happen was without Tunney's knowledge and I don't want to give any impression that he had anything to do with such a plot.

122

Some time later, I asked Jack if the whispers had been true. He changed the subject.

At any rate, I wrote what I believed in my stories and they caused a great deal of comment. My actual story of the fight caused even more comment. I had been asked to dictate a running story and the telegrapher working with me had done a literal job. My story was filled with "Oh, don't hit him so hard," "Be careful, Jack," "Get your face out of the way," and similar comments.

When the two men fought their return fight in Chicago, Mr. Hearst again assigned me.

My prefight stories were hardly impartial. I was for Jack and let everyone know it.

The night of the fight, I started to take a seat in the press box. This caused a near riot. There were 258 male reporters and a shout was raised that the press box was no place for a lone woman. Tex Rickard, the famous promoter, called for a vote and then decided that I had been voted the right to sit with the men. So there I was and there I stayed.

I will always believe that Jack won that fight. It seemed to me that that famous "long count" lasted twenty seconds longer than usual. And I'll never understand why Jack's manager and seconds didn't get him to a neutral corner.

When the fight ended, with Tunney given the decision, I sped from the press box and raced down the stadium passage. Gene Fowler called, "You damned fool, where do you think you're going?"

"To find Jack and tell him I didn't think it was fair."

I stood in the passage about five minutes. Then I saw Jack leaving his dressing room with his manager, Gene Normile. I ran to the defeated champion and tried to say something, but all I could do was cry.

Jack quieted me and the two of us went to the car that was waiting for him. As we drove to the Congress Hotel, where I was staying, I alternately wept and insisted that Jack had really won.

"Don't cry, honey," he said. "There'll be other fights."

"But how did it happen?"

"Oh," he smiled, "I guess I just forgot to duck."

I know that remark was supposed to have been made to Estelle Taylor, to whom he was then married, after the first Tunney fight, but it was really made to me and I'll take an oath on it.

I was wiping away the marks of my tears in my hotel room when the phone rang. It was the editor of our Chicago paper. "You're the only reporter Dempsey's seen tonight. Where's your story?"

I stopped mopping away the tears and started dictating a story. Half my heart was broken, but the other half was exhilarated. I'd beaten all the 258 male reporters at their own game.

Sure, it was another piece of Parsons' luck, but I had been at the right place at the right time.

The Chief sent his congratulations and I was on top of the world.

My next "outside" assignment was in 1928, when I was assigned to cover the Democratic national convention in Houston, Texas. I left from New York by train in a private car that had been loaned to Jimmy Walker.

Jimmy was publicly for Al Smith and he sincerely wanted Smith to get the nomination. At the same time, he disliked Smith personally and the feeling was, as the saying goes, mutual. They were men of completely opposite temperaments and personal philosophies and the only bond that joined them was that they were both Democrats.

Jimmy would make a speech for Smith each time the train stopped and afterward would come back into the car and take a drink to, as he said, "wash my mouth out."

But the real gossip I ran into concerned a difference between two of Smith's closest advisers, Belle Moskowitz and Elizabeth Marbury.

Mrs. Moskowitz had long been Smith's political mentor and she had devoted her life to working for him. Politics was her business. Elizabeth Marbury was one of the first important volunteer workers for Smith. She was probably the outstanding literary agent of her day, a woman who regarded taking part in politics as a public duty.

The two women were quarreling over what part Mrs. Smith should play.

Both women had a deep affection for Katie Smith, but Mrs. Moskowitz put aside her emotions and took a cold-blooded position. She felt that Mrs. Smith would be a liability. "There are too many newspapers against Al," she said, "and they'll use Katie and any interviews she might give to pillory Al."

Elizabeth Marbury came to me and said, "You're a newspaperwoman and they'll listen to you. Kate Smith is a charming woman. Her naïveté and sweet simplicity will make up for anything else she might lack. She's his wife, the mother of his children, and if he wants to get nominated for President, Katie better not be shoved into the background."

I asked, "What does the Governor think?"

"We haven't brought this to him."

Well, I could understand that. In a cat fight of this type, if he had been called on to make a decision, one of these two devoted women would have found herself on the outside looking in.

I had known and liked Al Smith for many years. I was aware that he and the Chief were long-time political enemies and that the breach between them was so deep it could not be healed. Now I was faced with a problem. If I wrote the story about Mrs. Smith it might well be harmful to the Governor and I would be accused of doing a hatchet job because I worked for Mr. Hearst. If I didn't write the story I would be failing as a reporter.

I decided to write the story and wait for the repercussions.

They came quickly—or so I thought.

At Houston, I immediately went to the hall where the convention was being held. It was stifling (this was long before good air conditioning) and felt like an inferno. I was sure it was an inferno when I was given a message as soon as I walked in.

I had been pulled off the assignment. I was to do no writing at all.

I was flabbergasted. I couldn't believe Mr. Hearst would do this to me because of the story. It just didn't fit in with his character as I knew it.

I called Joe Willicombe. "Why am I taken off the convention? Is it because of the Mrs. Smith story?"

"Oh, no. The Chief liked that story fine. It's because of your column. You carried a story in it about Anita Page that was completely untrue. She called the Chief and he's very upset about it."

That was when the Parsons temper did erupt. Before I left for the East, I had been assigned a new "assistant" at Mr. Hearst's request and it was she who had been doing legwork for the column while I was gone. Now I was being blamed for her stupidity and I didn't like it. I said so, quite forcefully.

"You have a point there," Joe said. "I'll talk to the Chief and call you back."

An hour later he returned the call. "Get to work, Louella, and when you get back to Hollywood, get yourself a new assistant."

Twenty years later, covering another convention, the Republican convention in 1948, I was involved in another feud between two women.

I suppose I should have known that there was no love lost between Clare Boothe Luce and the late Dorothy Thompson, but I didn't. I found myself talking to Miss Thompson and remarked that I had just been talking with Mrs. Luce. "Isn't Clare wonderful?" I asked.

Miss Thompson gave me a look that deepfroze me, snorted, rose and walked away.

The next day there was a reference in her column to the "Hollywood Mrs. Malaprop" who was covering the convention. Well, it was this same Mrs. Malaprop who came up with two of the best stories that came out of that convention. One of these was an exclusive interview with the nominee, Thomas E. Dewey. The other still has me baffled. Did I get a real "exclusive" or did I fall for a press-agent trick?

Near the end of the convention, my cousin Margaret Ettinger, one of the top public-relations experts in the country, came to me and asked, "Have you seen Gracie?"

I gave Maggie a hard look. "Gracie" was Gracie Allen, who was writing about the convention for a news service. Maggie knew how I felt about such "trained seals," whether her clients or not. I said, "No."

"Then she's lost," Maggie said desperately.

That was about as old a chestnut as ever there was. I said, "Too bad."

"It's true. Believe me," Maggie wailed. "No one has seen her for hours."

I was tired at the end of a long, long day. Cousinly love had its limits and I said so. Finally I said, "All right. I'll help you look for her, but I won't write a line about it."

"I don't want a line. I just want Gracie."

So we formed a two-woman posse and started searching for the missing comedienne. I quickly saw that Maggie's concern was deep and real.

Finally we found her. After looking everywhere, checking with police and hospitals, we went to the convention hall. The vast building was dark and littered and there was one person in it—Gracie. She was sound asleep in a chair.

Phony or real, it was too good a story to keep. I wrote it and the papers all carried it, many of them on the front page. I even got a note of congratulations from the Chief.

But I still wonder.

There were rough moments in my relationship with Mr. Hearst and some of them developed from that root of all evil—cold, hard cash.

When radio was at its zenith, I was offered my own show. The money was good and, as always, necessary. I asked Mr. Hearst's permission to do the show and he was reluctant. He felt radio competed with newspapers both for advertising and in the news field. Why give aid and comfort to the enemy?

Finally, however, I got his approval—provided I turned back one third of my salary to the Hearst organization.

I did not have much confidence in either myself or the show and I was quite surprised when millions of people tuned in to hear me say "Hello from Hollywood." I have long believed that I owe an assist to Walter Winchell for my success. I followed him on the air and Walter had just about the largest audience of all at that time.

While I was grateful to Walter for warming up my audience, he and I engaged in some hot verbal battles. I have always believed that he somehow managed to get a look at my copy before he went on the air. To this day I'm certain that he lifted my scoop on the elopement of Barbara Hutton and Cary Grant from my script.

Luckily, he used only a line and I went on with all the details, which had been called in to me after I had prepared my script.

127

All the years that I did my radio show, I turned over one third of my salary to the Hearst organization. Those were the depression years and, during them, a financial crisis developed in the Hearst empire.

Mr. Hearst, even with his vast fortune, found that economies were necessary. To that end, a group of financial advisers were called in and they took over control of the purse strings. However, Mr. Hearst continued as undisputed editorial boss. At the time I took a voluntary 10 per cent cut.

My contract expired a little later and when I received my new one, it called for the same salary I'd been getting. I felt I merited a raise and said so to Joe Connelly, head of International News Service, which syndicated the column.

"No raise," he said. "It's out of the question."

"No raise," I said, "no column."

"In that case we'll get Louis Sobol [Broadway columnist from the New York *Journal*] to go to Hollywood."

That was a jolt. The column was Louella Parsons and Louella Parsons was the column. No one could take it over. Still, I wondered if I hadn't issued one ultimatum too many. To check the wind, I called my old friend Bill Curley, managing editor of the *Journal*.

"I've heard the story," Bill told me, "but when Sobol told me about it, I advised him not to be in too much of a hurry to pack his bags. Just between us, though, I think you're wrong to ask for a raise these days."

It could be Bill was right, but I had taken my stand and I was stuck with it.

And then I got a call from San Simeon. I had not appealed to Mr. Hearst because this was strictly a financial matter and under the terms of his agreement with the financial advisers, he was precluded from taking any part in it.

"Louella," the Chief said, "you mustn't ever tell anyone I called you, but my advice is to hold out for that raise. You'll get it. Nobody else can do your job in Hollywood and Mr. Connelly and INS know it. Stay independent."

That bolstered my courage. I thanked the Chief and held out. But it wasn't easy.

128

The expiration date on my contract was coming up and the rumors about Sobol had traveled from coast to coast. Then the day before I was through—when I had begun to feel I had lost the biggest gamble of my life—Joe Connelly called. "You win," he said. "I never figured you'd hold out."

I never did tell Joe about the Chief's call and he died before I felt free to reveal it. The occasion when I did reveal it was a luncheon that the Hearst organization gave me when I received a Doctor of Letters degree from Quincy College. (I was the first woman so honored in the one hundred years of the college's existence. Me, the gay illiterate!)

William Randolph Hearst, Jr., Randolph Hearst, J. D. Gortatowsky, Kingsbury Smith, Harold Kern and other Hearst executives were my hosts. They presented me with a scroll, a gold typewriter, and a gold bracelet with charms depicting my life with the Hearst organization.

I started my "thank you" speech by saying, "I love the scroll, the gold typewriter and bracelet, but I hope this has no relation to the gold-watch routine which is usually accompanied by 'You've done a remarkable job and we accept your resignation with regret.' I don't ever intend to resign. I expect to die in harness. Now let me tell you a story that only the Chief and I knew until this moment."

That was when I told them of the Chief's kindness and consideration at a time when he was involved in so many troubles of his own.

Now, for a sequel. Six months before the next contract expired, INS sent me a new one, calling for a raise. I was delighted with it, but felt there was no rush to get it back to New York. A few weeks later a wire arrived, reading: IF CONTRACT IS NOT SATISFACTORY PLEASE LET US KNOW AND WE WILL DO WHAT WE CAN TO STRAIGHTEN IT OUT. JOE CONNELLY.

Well, something came up at the time and for some reason only a psychologist could explain, I didn't answer the wire. The next day there was a phone call from Joe Connelly. "Louella, what's the matter?"

"The matter? What do you mean?"

"The contract. You haven't signed it. My wire. You didn't answer it."

"Oh, that," I said. "I'm sorry. I've been too busy. I'll sign it and send it back to you tomorrow."

He let out a breath that sizzled the width of the continent. "Don't ever do anything like this again. It shortens my life."

Only once in all the years that I have worked for the Hearst organization did I consider leaving. Some years ago, the late William Hawkins, head of the United Press, and Monte Bourjaily, then syndicate head of the UP, visited me in New York.

Dr. Martin was with me when they made me an offer that called for a great deal more money than INS was paying me and would allow me to retain all my radio rights. I could not refuse it. It was agreed that the two would return the next day with the contract.

I couldn't fall asleep that night. I kept recalling all of Mr. Hearst's kindnesses, all the things he had done for me. For me as a person—as Louella Parsons—not for an employee. I remembered how much trust he had placed in me and his confidence in me as a newspaperwoman.

Finally, I got out of bed, went to the sitting room and sat there in the darkness. Moments later, Dr. Martin joined me. He said, "Louella, you never did intend to sign that contract, did you?"

"Of course I did. I'm going to."

He laughed in the darkness. "No," he said, "you won't. No matter whom you'd work for, you'd still be working in your heart for Mr. Hearst."

"But think of the money."

"Are you thinking of it?"

"No."

"Then go to sleep. When they come back tomorrow, I'll tell them you're staying where you are."

When Mr. Hawkins and Mr. Bourjaily returned in the morning, I insisted upon telling them my decision. I owed them that. "I'm sorry," I said, "for taking up your time, but I know I'd never be happy working for anyone but Mr. Hearst."

Mr. Hawkins gave me a "what can you expect from a woman?" look, and Mr. Bourjaily said "Good-by."

Some time later, when we were at San Simeon, Mr. Hearst said to me, "Why didn't you tell me about that UP offer?"

130

"I was afraid you'd fire me."

He laughed at my answer and dropped the subject. That Christmas he sent me a beautiful diamond pin and a note that said: "To the most loyal girl I know."

I've always valued the note more than the pin.

Throughout the years I have been accused of being vindictive, unforgiving and hardhearted. I've been called a witch, spelled with a "b." The charge has been made that I used my circulation and close relationship with Mr. Hearst as a weapon.

I don't claim that I haven't used the power of my circulation. All newspapermen do. But I maintain that I used it only to get news—to do my job—not as a blackjack. And I believe I have carried only one grudge for any length of time and that was against Orson Welles. I feel I was justified.

When Orson, characterized as the "boy genius," came to Hollywood, I was one of his biggest boosters. He was born in Grande Tour, Illinois, just six miles from Dixon, and I had known his family. I was delighted to give a boost to a local boy who had made good.

Then when I heard that the film he was making, *Citizen Kane,* was about Mr. Hearst, I called him to ask if this was so.

"Take my word for it," he said, "it isn't. It's about a completely fictional publisher."

I took his word, and so informed the Hearst editors who kept insisting that it did concern Mr. Hearst.

Then Orson pulled one of the classic double crosses of Hollywood. He arranged for Hedda Hopper to see parts of the picture. As soon as she left the projection room, Hedda called Mr. Hearst.

As the story was reported to me, she said, "Mr. Hearst, I don't know why Louella hasn't told you this picture is about you." Mr. Hearst thanked her.

Then Mr. Hearst called me and asked that arrangements be made for me and two of his lawyers to see *Citizen Kane.*

I must say now, so many years later, that I am still horrified by the picture. It was a cruel, dishonest caricature. It was done in the worst of taste. The boy genius certainly used all his talents just to do a hatchet job.

131

I walked from the projection room without saying a word to Orson. I have not spoken to him since.

When the lawyers and I talked with Mr. Hearst, the lawyers told him he had a foolproof libel suit and asked him to take it to court. "No," he said, "I don't believe in lawsuits. Besides, I have no desire to give the picture any more publicity."

Herman Mankiewicz, who wrote the screenplay, had once been an uninvited guest at San Simeon. He put telling touches, that stemmed from that visit, into the script. The zoo. The long drive from the gates to the castle.

Herman told me this much later. He was quite ill and had had, by that time, more than his fill of the boy genius. He said, "Louella, I'm sorry about the picture. I hope you'll forgive me for my part in it."

Of course I did.

And despite what some competitors might have wished or thought, the fact that I originally believed Welles did not lower me in the estimation of Mr. Hearst. He never had any affection for those who sought to curry favor with him by attacking any of his staff.

That was The Chief. A great man whether you liked him or not. Whether you agreed with him or not.

I think I have a right to quote Shakespeare here. Of Mr. Hearst, I can say, as Hamlet did of his father:

> "He was a man, take him all in all,
> "I shall not look upon his like again."

➤➤➤ *Chapter 8*

THE EX-MISS LE SUEUR

I HAVE known Joan Crawford for more than thirty-five years. I still don't know her at all.

She is as brilliant and many-faceted as a diamond.

Joan is unique in Hollywood in that she is the only star I know who manufactured herself. Others, men and women, have changed themselves and their personalities. Joan created herself and her personality. She drew up a blueprint for herself and outlined a beautiful package of skin, bones and character and then set about to put life into the outline.

She succeeded, and so Joan Crawford came into existence at the same time that an overweight Charleston dancer, born Lucille Le Sueur, disappeared from the world.

It took me a long time to realize this. I believed, for some time, that Lucille existed under the skin.

In all my relationships with Hollywood stars and personalities, none has been so impersonal as the one I have with Joan. She won't let anyone get to her. I never have, I know. So ours has been a relationship of convenience.

Joan Crawford is a news source, an acquaintance, a movie personality to me. And I think that she regards me as a newspaper-woman, a necessary nuisance who has to be tolerated.

This is fair enough, of course. As between us, we have set up rules by which to play. If both sides had observed the rules, I might like Joan better. But Joan has often sought to alter them in her favor. That's the basic reason why she and I have never been, and can't be, friends.

Before I go into that, I'd like to say I have a very real admiration for Joan. She was a great star and deservedly so. Even now she has stature in Hollywood. A lot of her contemporaries are long gone, but she remains; a reminder of Hollywood's greatest days.

This has not been easy. Almost a score of years ago a "smart" exhibitor labeled her "box-office poison." This should have marked her end as a star because most producers are willing to accept exhibitor judgment. But Joan believed in herself even when few others did.

She confounded her detractors and the fainthearted who listened to them by coming up with some of her biggest successes, and crowned her comeback by winning the Oscar for her performance in *Mildred Pierce*. She made her critics eat their words.

Joan has the confidence of success. She believes in herself completely. That's fine for Joan, but not so good for many who have had to deal with her. Certainly it has had a great deal to do with our own relationship. Our last encounter is typical.

Some two years ago, shortly after the death of her fourth husband, Alfred Steele, Joan returned to Hollywood and took a role in the picture, *The Best Things in Life,* at 20th Century-Fox. Since it was neither the leading part nor an especially glamorous one, there was a certain amount of talk about why she had taken the role. Finally the rumor came to me that she had taken it because she needed the money.

I found this hard to believe. Steele had been an important business executive and quite wealthy. In addition, few actresses had ever earned more money than Joan had during her career, much of which was before the present high tax rates. And Joan was never known for reckless spending. However, a news tip was a news tip and the only way to learn if it was true was to check it out. I put a call through to Joan and reached her in her dressing room.

I told her what I had heard and asked, "Is it true?"

"It's true," she answered. "I'm flat broke. I haven't a nickel. Only my jewels."

"But Alfred must have left you—"

She didn't let me finish. "Alfred left me up to my ears in debt, Louella. He expected his company to reimburse me for the half million dollars we spent on our New York apartment. They didn't." She then went on to tell me a sob story that would have brought tears to a glass eye. She ended by saying, "You know how hard Alfred's death hit me."

I did know how hard she had told me it hit her. A few weeks earlier we had talked to each other, immediately after Alfred Steele's death when she telephoned me from New York. She had sobbed out her heartbreak and found me a most sympathetic listener. I could understand the grief of a woman who had just lost the man she loved. I remembered the anguish I suffered when that happened to me. That was the only time, I think, that I believed that I was talking to the woman, not the star.

And now, speaking again to Joan, I felt that she was sincere and truthful. I had made it plain that I was calling to verify a news story and, talking to me, she did not once ask me not to print what she told me. Nor did she say that what she told me was in confidence.

Immediately after talking to her, I wrote the story. It was a news story that rated a headline and that was exactly what it got when it was printed. JOAN CRAWFORD FLAT BROKE.

But hardly had the story been printed before there came a denial from Joan. She gave a statement which said, in part, "I did not give the story to Louella Parsons. I have no idea where she got it, but it is utterly untrue."

Talk about being slapped in the face with a deceased mackerel!

Joan had given me the lie direct. And I was way out on a limb. Joan, herself, had been my source and now she denied ever having talked to me. I knew there was a lot of gloating in certain places, and it seemed there was nothing I could do about it.

But once again luck was on my side.

My phone rang and when I answered it I heard the cheery voice

135

of Harry Brand, head of publicity at 20th Century-Fox. "Nice little mix-up we have here," he chirped.

"I'm glad you think it's nice," I answered. "I'm burning. She gave me that story herself."

"I know she did. One of the men in my department was in her dressing room all the time she was talking to you."

Talk about heaven helping the working girl. Here was one time that had actually happened. "Repeat that," I said, "please."

"He heard everything she said," Harry told me. "She kept gesticulating and making faces all the time she was talking to you."

"Then why did she deny it?"

"Who knows why actors do anything?" Harry said, his voice weary.

"Thanks for telling me," I said. "I'm really grateful."

"Think nothing of it. In a case like this, I'm always on the side of the press."

I believe that Harry would always have acted in this manner, even in the old days. But I also know that one of the reasons he had no hesitation in calling me was because the stars are no longer studio properties but independent operators. Harry's first duty was to 20th Century-Fox.

The next day there was another story in the papers under my byline. It set the record straight on the basis of the call from Harry Brand. On of us hadn't told the truth, all right, but the person who had strayed from it was not Louella O. Parsons. Not even Joan had the gall to deny the denial of her denial.

I can be philosophical about Joan Crawford. I can even accept a mix-up like the one I've related without feeling bitterness. And that's because I know Joan is part of a world that is gone. The world in which stars, like the king, could do no wrong. She was part of that era when every effort was made to protect stars from themselves, from the press and from the world.

Hers was, and is, a world of make-believe in which lines are written, parts are played and the only reality is the reality of the moment. The fact that such a world no longer exists may be obvious to most people, but not to Joan.

She remains a star in the great tradition. And all the rest of us are her "public."

To that public she owes a certain debt—that she never step out of character. And I can think of no one who has observed this rule more completely.

I first saw her in 1925, a chubby girl who took part in the dancing contests that were held at the Cocoanut Grove each week. At that time this night club in the Ambassador Hotel was the after-dark hub of Hollywood. It was here that all the stars—and would-be stars —gathered.

Joan—at that time just beginning her acting career—kept winning the Charleston contests and she deserved to. It was remarkable to watch the abandon with which she threw herself into the dance. Her partner was young Michael Cudahy, heir to the Chicago meat-packing fortune. His mother, it was reported, was quite unhappy about this terpsichorean teaming.

In those days she was still Lucille Le Sueur, though most persons called her "Billie." She had just been signed by MGM and the studio decided that she ought to have a less theatrical name. An announcement was forthcoming from the studio publicity department telling of a contest to choose the new name.

The hokum rolled out of Culver City. The gist of the publicity releases was that "Miss Le Sueur was a popular subdeb in Kansas City and gave up a promising social career to further her acting ambitions."

What a distortion of the facts. I know that Joan, herself, resented this. After all, she has been the one who has set the record straight through the years. The truth was far different. She had experienced a childhood of grinding poverty. She had supposedly spent years in charity schools where she was more kitchen slavey than scholar. And a job in a five-and-ten was Joan's "promising social career" in Kansas City.

Yet, in a peculiar way, the hokum was the truth. The past belonged to Lucille Le Sueur; the future to Joan Crawford. And Joan, when she became Joan, could have been a Kansas City subdeb. As far as she was concerned, there was no longer—there might as well never have been—a dancing Billie in the Cocoanut Grove.

Joan believed completely in Joan Crawford. This was no Galatea who feared she might again become stone; no Liza Doolittle who feared that she might have trouble with her "h's."

Where other stars were slaves of fashion, she made fashions. It was Adrian, the late husband of Janet Gaynor, who designed her unforgettable screen wardrobe during the 30's and glorified her broad-shouldered, lean-hipped figure. Soon designers in this country and around the world were paying Joan tribute by copying the clothes she wore and merchandising them. Also exaggerating them, for there was a period when the best-dressed women looked like football players. But that, too, was a tribute to Joan Crawford.

Joan never let down her guard and I congratulate her for it. No one has ever seen her in slatternly pedal-pushers, hair in curlers, shopping at a supermarket.

That wasn't in character for Joan Crawford and so it never happened. Offscreen she played the same roles that she did on screen and that was because, I think, the actress was the woman.

Everything she has done publicly, she has done with verve. When she travels, she is accompanied by dozens of pieces of matched luggage. Her home is decorated, not furnished. The meals she serves are epicurean.

And she doesn't fear to wear colors that would terrify most women; mad pinks, off-greens, garish purples. These are not only effective, but most flattering.

But this was the same woman who could not attend the Oscar ceremonies when she was a nominee for her beautiful job of acting in *Mildred Pierce*. It was reported that she was ill and staying in bed on doctor's orders, but few in Hollywood believed this. The feeling was that Joan could not bear to be present, win or lose, when the name of the actress who would receive the Oscar was announced. Defeat would be unbearable; winning would be overwhelming.

Director Michael Curtiz accepted the Oscar in her behalf and took it to her at her home. He told me that she gave another Oscar performance, to an audience of one, when he handed it to her. The tears flowed.

But then, Joan could always give a performance, as so many people can attest. The actress is always just below the first layer of skin.

Her private life has had these same elements of flamboyance and has been, to a great extent, a continuation of her twenty-four-hour-a-day role as Joan Crawford.

Her first marriage was to Douglas Fairbanks, Jr., scion of Hollywood's ruling family. (More about that in a few minutes.) With it, she escaped from the last outside memories of Billie Le Sueur.

Next she married Franchot Tone, whose background was impeccable. Here was a further extension of the growing Joan Crawford. She had projected herself into a world of elegance, a world that was literate, a world that had its boundaries outside the theatrical world even though it encompassed a part of that world.

Only her third marriage failed to fit into the picture and yet it can be described as the union of a queen with a prince consort. Who but a queen could have dared public reaction to marry a younger man, a man who was a stranger to her world?

Her fourth marriage was, I think, the only really happy one. What a shame that it should have been so brief!

Alfred Steele was older than she, a mature man, whose background was in the world of finance and industry. He lived in an element where he was important and Joan was not. People in that world knew who she was, of course, but that did not set her apart or mark her important. It merely made her different. And she came to that world not at the height of her importance, but after she had passed that height.

I believe that it took great courage and maturity for Joan to accept all this. In this new world Alfred Steele held the center of the stage and she was usually in the wings.

It is much to her credit that she accepted this. Instead of the world revolving around her, as it had for so long, she became part of the world revolving about her husband. She placed his needs and desires before anything else. She catered to these. And so many who had believed that Joan could not adapt to living in such a way, and I was one of them, were pleased that they had been proven wrong.

She became chatelaine and dowager—though a far younger and lovelier dowager than the word connotes. For the first time she fitted the part of wife perfectly; appeared secure in it. How different from her first marriage.

It was an open secret that neither Douglas Fairbanks, Sr., nor his wife, Mary Pickford, were too happy about Doug, Jr., marrying Joan. In the Hollywood social scene, the Fairbanks family moved in a different circle from that of Miss Crawford. But they did their best to accept the new member.

However, as Mary told me, it was difficult. Joan was never at ease with her in-laws and they found it hard to be relaxed with her. There was always a barrier between them and it never came down during the period that Joan and Doug, Jr., were married.

Looking back, I think the one time that Joan was ever completely honest with me was when she and young Doug separated.

Normally, word that all is not well with an important Hollywood marriage spreads quickly. Often it is abetted by press agents, as willing to get their clients' names into print when they are unhappy as when they are happy. However, in the case of these two, there was never a sign that their marriage was on the rocks.

Then came a news story that the husband of an extra girl had filed a suit for alienation of affections against young Fairbanks.

The story broke on a Friday and Doctor Martin and I were packed to go away for a weekend.

When I heard about the suit, I started to write a story. I was going to say what is so often said about such a story, that the loyal wife was prepared to stand by her innocent husband. But, even as I wrote the first words, I felt that I had better check with Joan. I got her on the phone.

"Please don't print that story," she said. "It doesn't mean anything. I'll give you a better one in three days."

My news antennae started to quiver. "Why not give it to me now?"

"I can't give it to you now." And that was all that she would say.

After hanging up, I called Joan's lawyer. "What's this all about?"

"Hold your horses, Louella," he said. "Joan said she'd have a story for you in three days."

"A lot can happen in three days," I replied. "I'm going out to see Joan right now."

Doctor Martin was a little annoyed. The luggage was in the car, we were expected at Arrowhead and did three days make that much difference?

"They very well might," I said.

140

We got into the loaded car and drove out to see Joan.

When I faced her, she told me the truth. She and Douglas were going to get a divorce. When the decision was made she had given the story to a close friend, a magazine writer, exclusively. "The magazine will be on the stands in two days," she said. "Won't you wait until it's printed?"

"Of course not," I said. "By that time it will be everyone's story." It may be difficult to realize it now, but at that time it was a very important story. It was page 1 in every newspaper.

I borrowed a typewriter and sat down and wrote my story in Joan's home. I had Dr. Martin stand guard over the telephone until I could call my story in. Somehow Joan did get word to her studio publicity department and in a few minutes the house was swarming with publicity people.

But I had a one-edition beat and that was a triumph. The other papers were welcome to the story after that—and they took the leavings.

What was typical of Joan was that she could be so cold-blooded about the breaking up of her marriage. She could wait for all the long weeks between the time a story was written for a magazine and the time the magazine was printed, and continue to make a public show of a good marriage. I marveled then—I marvel now—that she could so completely keep her emotions under control, so completely act her part.

After she and Fairbanks were divorced she appeared in a number of pictures with Clark Gable and much was made by the MGM publicity department of a flaming romance between them. I reported it dutifully, of course, because they were being seen together a great deal but I couldn't take the prospects of this romance very seriously.

I was soon proven right.

Joan met and married Franchot Tone.

And, as I said earlier, this was in character. Franchot was urban, witty, intellectual. He had roots, family. If Joan married him, it would give roots and family background to the woman called Joan Crawford.

Joan threw herself into the new part, the new life. As Mrs. Franchot Tone, she became interested in good books, in classical music, in the fine arts. This was no pose. It was what the role demanded

141

and she could not help living the role, it was her life. This was what so many of us didn't realize at the time. We thought it was a pose.

(Peculiar, isn't it, how much this has been part of the lives of so many of our women stars? This drive, this need to propel themselves into an intellectual world?)

But this marriage also failed. I think that it was more because of Franchot than because of Joan. She had slipped into the part without effort, was living it without effort, simply, I think, because it was a part. But Franchot wasn't living a part; he was living his life. And, it turned out, he wasn't happy with it.

He didn't like the small, shallow parts he had to play in his make-believe world, the screen. He'd had enough of books and music and they didn't seem to exert the same spell on him that they did on Joan. I have a feeling that he got a little tired, a little bored with the whole thing.

If anyone wonders at my trying to understand and analyze this marriage, it's because it has always interested me and continues to interest me. In Hollywood, as in most places, I suppose, people are what they seem. But Joan was always different, has continued to be different. And so I've never been able to pigeonhole her. I keep trying.

I watched as that marriage ended. Their divorce was without bitterness. Joan did not cease being Mrs. Franchot Tone because she was divorced. How could she? As for Franchot, he went on to other ladies, several of whom made little or no effort to be intellectual. A ream of headlines and stories, some of which I wrote, attest to that.

Now Joan turned to another aspect of life, of completion. She became a "mother." She adopted two children, a boy and a girl, and threw herself into motherhood with all the power of her forceful personality. She rushed home to be with them, read to them, played with them, devoted almost all her time to them.

In a sense this was a good thing for her because her brilliant career appeared to be ending. A new world came into being after World War II and it was a world, it seemed, that didn't want Joan playing her parts in pictures like those she had been appearing in for so many years.

142

She was aware of it, I know, and sought to get the moguls at MGM to accept the fact that she was more than a type, that she was an actress. Or, to put it another way, that she was completely capable of changing her type. If they had been astute enough to check her private life, they would not have doubted this. However, they were not.

Just about this time, Joan married again. She had had no dearth of admirers after Franchot, but she did not seem to be serious about any of them. It was as if being a mother was more important to her than being a wife. It could be that she was not looking so much for a husband as for a father for the two children. The man she chose was not the most likely to fit the part.

He was a pleasant, handsome young actor, Philip Terry, younger than she and not established in his career.

Soon after their marriage, Joan won her release from MGM and went to Warner's. And then began a long wait for the right script.

For the first time in a score of years, Joan had time on her hands. She was not the great lady of the studio, but an actress who apparently had seen her best days. This thought must have been with her constantly. At the same time, there was another idle actor in the house, her husband. Having no one else to react upon, they reacted upon each other. And on the children.

It was hard on all four and must have left marks. I wonder how much this has had to do with the behavior of young Christopher who has turned out to be so difficult to control and whose escapades have caused his mother heartbreak, and brought him so much punishment. And how much it had to do with young Christina, who left home as soon as she could and is now trying desperately to become an actress.

I hear from her at intervals, little notes that always start, "Dear Aunt Louella."

Certainly the situation doomed the marriage of Joan to Terry. They were divorced in 1946.

One happy event did occur at this time. Joan was cast in *Mildred Pierce* and this role won her the Oscar. She has always given Jerry Wald credit for getting her the part because he had to battle the entire Warner Brothers' hierarchy. They just couldn't see her in the part and Jerry couldn't see anyone else.

It is typical of Hollywood, of course, that when Joan won the Oscar, everyone decided to get into the act and take the credit. But as far as Joan was concerned, only Jerry Wald was entitled to any. (I would like to say that no producer or anyone else is entitled to credit. Joan was. She gave a great performance and it was honored.)

For some time afterward good parts came Joan's way. In the late 40's, she adopted twin girls, the most beautiful pair of children I have ever seen. With the new children and her new career she seemed to become more relaxed.

It came as a surprise when, a few years later, she married Alfred Steele. It appeared to mark the end of Joan as a star; an acceptance by her that this part of her life was over. She would now really be a wife and mother. And when doubts about the success of the marriage disappeared, it seemed she had made the right choice.

It is sad to me that Joan should have been able to enjoy her hard-achieved happiness for so short a time. But at least she did have it—and I could name a dozen women in Hollywood who have never known what it is to love a man truly and be loved truly in return.

I don't know what the future holds for Joan Crawford. But one thing I do know. She will never cease being a star. For, if she did, she would cease being Joan Crawford.

❯❯❯ *Chapter 9*

DADDY-O!

On a spring night in 1954, Frank Sinatra was given a plaque that read:

DAD, WE'LL LOVE YOU FROM HERE TO ETERNITY.

A few hours later, he received the Academy Award for his depiction of the character of Maggio in *From Here to Eternity*.

Few ever knew about the plaque; the whole world knew of the Oscar. And that, I think, is an insight into Frank Sinatra.

He has been described in many ways and called many names. I've called him quite a number of names myself—in a polite, ladylike way, of course. But I don't believe that I've ever described him as a good father, one of the best I have ever known. The fact that he is a good father is news only because he's Frank Sinatra.

No book about Hollywood, no study of the amusement world in the last twenty years, would be complete without extensive treatment of the slim, fiery, mixed-up singer from Hudson County, New Jersey. Like him or not, he has been the epitome of show business. Like him or not, you can't ignore him.

I'm as confused about Sinatra as he seems to be about life. I like fighters, men who don't know when they're beaten, and keep coming back—and coming back—until they've either won or been destroyed. There is no quitter in Frank. And so I have to like him for his courage. But I don't like men who fight for the sake of fighting; who throw their weight around; who parade their private derelictions publicly. And so I am not entirely in favor of Frankie.

I suppose the answer is that Sinatra is not all of a piece. He's many things and most of them are self-contradictory.

My old friend Damon Runyon once told me that there is a species of human who can only be described as "cop fighters." He went on to explain that they are men who resent all authority, who prefer the law of the jungle, who can't conform. I suppose that no one I know better fits into this group than Sinatra.

Let's examine what he is in this year of Our Lord:

One of the top recording stars of all time.

A box-office magnet in motion pictures.

A guarantee of S.R.O. business in a night club.

A motion-picture producer.

A recording-company magnate.

A tireless chaser of beautiful "dolls."

An enemy of newspapermen, with a special phobia about photographers.

A "loner," who can't stand being alone.

And a father par excellence.

And if that sounds more like a holding company than one human, it's because Sinatra is much more than one human.

I suppose I stand high on Frank's "hate" list. (In his group, I understand, it is called "drop dead" list.) One reason stems, of course, from my profession. Another is more specific. I don't think he has any feeling of affection for me personally. This bothers me because, like Frank, I want to be liked. There is a touch of Willy Loman in all of us.

There was a time when things were different between Frank and me. That was when he first came to Hollywood from New York, a singer who was supposed to make teen-agers swoon and matrons dream. That was in 1943 and Frank was a different man then. I had talked to him on the telephone a few days before he left New York for Hollywood.

His close friend and adviser at that time was George Evans, now

146

dead, whose primary function was to act as Frank's press agent. I knew George and he called me and introduced me to Frank on the phone. And we arranged for me to see him when he arrived in Hollywood.

I'm afraid I'll have to use a word that Arthur Godfrey turned into a ridiculing cliché, to describe Frank's outstanding quality at that first meeting. He had—Noah Webster, forgive me—humility. He was warm, ingenuous, so anxious to please.

And a charmer. No getting around that. Either men have that quality of charm or they haven't. It has to be as natural as the color of their eyes. Frank had—has—it. A lot of women have learned that through the years.

As I write this I tell myself, "Take it easy." Frank Sinatra couldn't have been so boyish and unspoiled, so natural and considerate. But I have to admit he was. After I met him, I was enrolled in the Sinatra cheering squad. And I stayed in it a long, long time.

I recall one thing from our talk. He wanted very much to meet Bing Crosby. He told me he had admired Crosby for years. I assured him it wouldn't be hard to meet Bing but he shook his head and said, "I'm scared."

He didn't have to be. Bing took to him at once, introduced him all around town, went out of his way to show Frank that Hollywood might not be Hoboken, but it was a friendly town just the same. They have remained fast friends ever since. There is nothing Frank wouldn't do for Bing.

That means that Bing belongs in a select group—Frank's friends. They are not as numerous as many circles, but when Frank has decided on a friend, he acts upon the decision.

Ten years ago, he was a close friend of a fellow Italian, Patsy D'Amore, who started a restaurant in Hollywood. Because he couldn't get a liquor license—though his spaghetti and *pasta* were par excellence—the little place seemed about to go under.

Then Frank decided to help. Night after night, he plunked himself in the front booth at Patsy's, bringing along such pals as Humphrey Bogart and Lauren Bacall, Laraine Day and Leo Durocher, Dean Martin and anyone else he could round up to, as he phrased it, "dress the set."

Word soon got around if you wanted to see movie stars in the flesh, Patsy's was the place to go, cocktails or not. Success was soon Patsy's. Then he moved to larger quarters, gained the needed liquor permit, and now the Villa Capri is one of my favorite eating places.

Before he became such an international figure, he gave me a birthday party in the private room at Patsy's Villa Capri, and no one made a more charming speech.

Another instance of Frank's going all out for a friend was when Jimmy Van Heusen, a song-writing pal, hit a low spot both creatively and financially. Frank had just emerged from a slump of his own; he decided to do something to end Jimmy's slump. When he went to MGM to make *The Tender Trap* he insisted Jimmy be hired to write the songs; he was equally firm about the songs for his TV spectacular, *Our Town*. And Jimmy's "Love and Marriage," won the first Emmy Award ever given a song written expressly for TV.

Frank never forgets anyone who has ever done him a good turn. When his old-time friend, Charlie Morrison, owner of the Mocambo night club, died, he left his affairs in poor shape. Debts were piled so high the creditors were threatening to close down the place, forcing Morrison's widow into bankruptcy.

So what did Frank, the man of action, do? For ten days he appeared at the night club, singing his heart out—for free. At the end of his engagement, Mary Morrison had paid all her bills and had $75,000 in cash to boot.

Frank takes—and often deserves—a lot of raps. But there are many good things about him and, just to be different, I'm going to start with these.

I am much closer these days to Nancy, Frank's former wife, and their three children, than I am to Frank. Nancy, Frank, Jr. and Tina are among my favorite young people. Their happiness means a great deal to me. Young Nancy, who loves to ape her father's penchant for colorful language and mad nicknames, hails me with her own term of endearment: "Hi, little stinkie!" I assure you, no one else in this entire nation could get away with it!

It's been a long time since Nancy divorced Frank, but though they ceased being husband and wife, they have never stopped being mother and father to the children. Frank spends a lot of time with his family. He drops in for dinner or a visit often. He has the run of the house and knows he is always welcome.

Whenever Nancy has a problem with one of the children, she knows Frank is available for help, advice and—when the occasion calls for it—discipline. What's more, Frank has always revealed a maturity as a parent that he hasn't shown in so many other aspects of living. This has been especially true in relation to Frank, Jr., who is so much like his father. Headstrong, moody and gifted.

I'll leave it to the professional psychologists to explain Frank's continual, openhanded generosity toward those he likes when he likes them. However, I'd like to make the point that he is even more generous with his family. He remembers birthdays, saints' days and some—but not all—anniversaries. And give him any kind of reason for celebrating with his family and he will come laden with gifts.

This applies as much to Nancy as it does to the children. On a recent birthday he gave her an exceptionally beautiful mink coat that cost thousands and a diamond wrist watch. If she wants to take a trip and he hears about it, he arranges everything. Plane reservations, hotel reservations, dinner reservations.

All this on top of a divorce settlement which gives Nancy and the children one third of his annual income!

Now I'm going to stick in my two-cents' worth. I don't know another woman as completely in love with her ex-husband as Nancy Sinatra is with Frank. It's as if—having given him her heart when she was sixteen—she has never been able to take it back. Perhaps that's why she can understand other women falling in love with him—and they have.

If this home life of Frank Sinatra sounds unusual, it's because it is. He follows no patterns. He makes his own as he goes.

That's been true all through the years, from the time he first began to sing and made his first success with the Harry James band, and later with Tommy Dorsey.

It was back in those days that Nancy accepted the fact that Frank's world was different from hers and that she couldn't share in it completely even if she wanted to—which she didn't. She had her home, her love and her hopes and that was enough for her. It could be that from her Italian forebears she had inherited the concept that the man is the boss in the home; that his word is law. Hers not to question why, just to have supper on the table when he comes home.

Which was fine—as long as he came home.

I suppose a lot of people have placed the blame for the end of their marriage on Hollywood. That's ridiculous. It could have happened any place. If any outside source was the factor in destroying their marriage, it was success. Success that completely changed their lives and their world.

Frank had, of course, known success before he came to Hollywood for good in 1944. His records sold as fast as he could make them. Crowds lined the streets outside the theatres where he appeared, and teen-agers swooned inside those same theatres. But it was a success that could end almost overnight, as had happened to others who were a temporary "craze."

But his real success—a success with a solid foundation beneath it —came after he was in pictures, though not entirely from it.

In 1944 Frank signed a contract with MGM and began to work in his first musical, *Step Lively*. Nancy moved here and Frank, Jr., was born.

The next year was Frank's first "jackpot" year. He made his first million.

"I couldn't believe it," Nancy told me. "Only millionaires made millions. All I could think of was the time, six years before, when we had spaghetti without meat sauce because meat sauce was more expensive. And now Frank had made a million."

He made more than that in 1945, for he also made his first deep impact on Hollywood. He received a special Academy Award that year for the short, *The House I Live In*, that was a brilliant plea for tolerance.

When I have heard others say that Frank was a phony, that he was thinking in terms of publicity, not belief, when he came out for unpopular causes, I have always reminded them of this first award. I haven't always agreed with Frank, but I have always believed in his sincerity.

150

When he talks about injustices because of race or color or religion, he talks from deep inside himself. These are things he knows. He recalls his youth, as part of a minority. He recalls racial hatred and vindictiveness and how he fought it with his fists as a child. Now he fights it with other weapons.

Soon after the award, his stock as an actor—at least a box-office attraction—boomed. MGM was giving him the full value of its publicity department and his pictures were helping. *Anchors Aweigh*, still one of my all-time favorite musicals, moved him right up into the major star class.

And also left him wide open for attack. Because he was somebody in the Hollywood scene now. He was big. And, in Hollywood as elsewhere, the bigger they are, the more likely to be attacked. Not that Frank didn't have it coming to him. He did. It was the form of the attack that I resented.

I hate "blind items," those nasty paragraphs without names, but with just enough identification, that permit the printing of gossip, rumor and scandal without creating the possibility of a successful libel suit. Not only the guilty, but the innocent suffer. It recalls that old story of ten men receiving the same wire, ALL IS DISCOVERED, and all ten leaving town.

Well, it was in the form of "blind item" that Frank first began to feel the power of the press in his private life. One columnist wrote, "What blazing new swoon-crooner has been seen night-clubbing with a different starlet every night?" And another wrote, "Wonder if the wonder boy of hit records tells his wife where he goes after dark?"

The item, even the innuendo, had some basis in fact. Frank was on a tear and he was tearing about publicly. It was as if he were daring anyone to make something of it. And, of course, the dare was accepted. But that didn't keep Frank from continuing to parade about town with one glamor girl or another.

By this time I had come to know Nancy well. I liked her and sympathized with her. But I knew enough to keep my sympathy to myself. Just the same I was aware that she was deeply hurt. In a sense, I was almost relieved when I heard that she had separated from Frank.

The relief soon went. Talking to Nancy, I quickly knew that she didn't love Frank any less, that her pain wasn't quieted by the separation; only increased. And, like many others, I was happy when they reconciled.

Nancy bloomed, grew more radiant. Frank calmed down. And little Tina was born.

But this was the calm before the eye of the hurricane hit the Sinatras. Hurricane Ava. Ava Gardner.

When Frank met Ava, it was like atomic fusion. There was a terrific explosion, tremendous damage and long-lasting fallout.

The first effect was the end of the Sinatra marriage. Frank wasn't philandering now; he was deadly serious. A woman can, and has, been able to handle a dozen rivals, but I never knew a woman who could handle just one.

Few affairs involving a married principal have ever been carried on as openly as that between Ava and Frank. Here were two tempestuous people who believed in "going for broke" and didn't care who knew it. Both of them, for lack of a less polite word, were temperamental and didn't mind revealing it publicly.

Frank followed Ava to Mexico, to Las Vegas, to Houston, Texas. The press followed Frank. There was snarling, the hurling of insults, the issuance of threats. Frank, who had invited the public into his private life, was angered because he wasn't getting any privacy. It was childish—and typical. He put himself above and beyond any rules.

Ava went to Spain and Frank followed.

Nancy had reached the breaking point. As she had told me over the years, she loved Frank, loved him very deeply. However, she could not condone his public infidelity and keep her self-respect which, she admitted, was already badly bruised. However, there was a religious consideration that she had to deal with. At the end, she decided that much as it pained her to get a divorce, it would be far better for Frank, his children and his reputation if he were a free man.

Nancy got her divorce October 30, 1951. The grounds were extreme cruelty. She was awarded full custody of the three children and the substantial alimony I have already mentioned.

Frank was free. Eight days later he and Ava were married. The wedding was a day late, delayed by another of the violent quarrels that marked their relationship.

This chapter concerns itself with Frank Sinatra but no review of Frank's life and career, even one as limited as this, can merely mention Ava Gardner in passing.

I think she is one of the more tragic figures in recent Hollywood history. If she had never known Frank Sinatra, I think she still would have been one of the more tragic figures.

I think of her—this once beautiful woman—an expatriate in Spain, target of gossip, rude laughter, cheap remarks. I recall that she played Brett Ashley in the picture made of Hemingway's *The Sun Also Rises*, and it seems to me that nature outdid the writer's art.

A wise man once said, "You earn the face you have at sixty." He was saying that each of us mirrors his own life; and chose sixty as the date when the mirror was clearest. But there are those whose faces are mirrors long before they're sixty. And Ava is one.

I recall the excruciating beauty she had when she came to Hollywood from Smithfield, North Carolina; innocent, eager, excited. And I recall the last time I saw her. She had been as profligate of her beauty as she had of her talents. And how much she had of both!

It was soon after she married Frank that she reached the apex of her career. It was at the same time, right after their marriage, that Frank's career started downhill without any brakes being applied.

Frank's pictures had become routine. He was cast as the brash young man who sang songs in picture after picture and his audience was getting smaller all the time. Then came an opportunity for which he had tried very hard; the opportunity to play a straight role, the part of a priest, in *Miracle of the Bells*.

The picture wasn't good. Frank was worse than the picture. It was a blow to his ego and his reaction was to get tougher, meaner, harder to get along with. He needed something to bolster his self-esteem and he chose to throw his weight around. He found that it wasn't much greater figuratively than it was literally. In a short time it was announced that Frank and the studio had parted by "mutual agreement."

153

If luck had been prodigal in the beginning days, misfortune was also to come to him in heaping tablespoonfuls.

His voice began to fail. It had been his ace in the hole, his sure thing in a world where there were few sure things. He could always go into a studio and cut records that were sure to sell in the hundreds of thousands. He was the kingpin recording artist at Columbia Records and, as far as he was concerned, the kingpin could do as he pleased.

If he had a sudden whim to record at midnight, arrangements were made. Musicians and technicians were rounded up and what did it matter if they received overtime, double time, golden time? Anything Frankie wanted, Frankie got.

But now this too changed. The bearded Mitch Miller, a man well known for his strength of personality, took over at Columbia. Mitch had no patience with Sinatra's peculiar, and expensive, working habits. He let it be known that Frankie, like the other artists recording for Columbia, was expected to come into the studio on time—the studio's time, not his.

Once Frankie might have told Miller to "drop dead." But now he could not. His records weren't doing so well. In recording you're not much better than your last sales statement.

So Frankie reported for recording sessions in daylight. But that didn't help. His voice was obviously in bad shape. The word was whispered more, rather than less, gleefully that he was through. Now there are all sorts of magic that sound technicians can and have done to help a vocalist when his voice starts to go. If they like the singer, as has been proven a number of times, they can keep him going even when his voice is just about gone. But they didn't like Frank.

One of the technicians confided to a friend of mine, "He was one of the meanest —— we'd ever known. Nobody wanted to help him out."

Frank and Columbia Records parted by "mutual agreement."

This was the hardest part of his entire life. Of course he had a cushion. He would never be in need of money. And he was married to a beautiful, exciting woman.

But he didn't have the other trappings of success. The hit picture. The hit record.

154

And he didn't have his home and family. His wife—his new wife—was a star with a world of her own. And pretty much a life of her own.

And he missed the children. The court had awarded Nancy absolute custody and that meant she could prevent Frank from seeing the children if she wished. But she didn't wish that. He was their father. They loved him and wanted to see him. So, when he was in Hollywood, he had that at least.

Frankie, in the words of his own Broadway, started "to press." That meant he didn't think and reason things out, just tried everything. In 1951 and 1952 he was involved in two TV series and appeared in two pictures and all were failures.

The word was out. Sinatra was done. "Snake-bitten" is the term that the smart boys use. Frankie was snake-bitten. Stay away from him.

There is one phenomenon common to all branches of the entertainment world. More than a phenomenon, it might almost be called a commandment, and it runs, "Ride with a winner and rap a loser." When a star begins to fizzle, when someone at the top starts to slip, the anvil chorus always comes into play.

And the tune it played this time was, "Sinatra's done—finished—*kaput.*"

That's the moment when the hangers-on, the stooges and the parasites start looking for another host. That was the moment they deserted Frankie.

For a time it appeared as if even he believed them. For a time, he wasn't Frank Sinatra any more; he was Ava Gardner's husband. He even went along with her to Africa, where she filmed *Mogambo* with Clark Gable and Grace Kelly. When a man starts playing male maid for his wife, it is almost a sign that he has surrendered.

But a lot of us underestimated the skinny infighter from Hoboken. We didn't take into account that while we might believe he was beaten, he didn't think so. We didn't give him credit for a mile-wide streak of—well—guts.

A report came from Africa that Frank had packed up and left. Most people thought this was because of his public disagreements with Ava, disagreements that had caused many of the natives to report that Tarzan and his mate were back in the wilds. We couldn't imagine any other reason.

But he had another. He was going to see Henry Cohn, head of Columbia pictures, and try to persuade him that no one but he —Frank Sinatra—could play the part of Maggio in *From Here to Eternity*.

That wasn't too easy. Frank was a has-been. And even though the price was right—Frank was willing to accept $8,000 to play the role and had previously been getting $150,000 a picture—Cohn had his doubts. It took a superb job of acting on Frank's part to sell Cohn. He virtually played his first rehearsal before Cohn.

The rest is now a commonplace. Frank got the role. When the picture was released, he got the raves. When nominations were made for that year's Oscars, he got the nomination.

And the night of the Oscar awards, he got the plaque from his children.

"I guess we all cried," Nancy said.

And then, of course, he got the Oscar.

I recall that night so well. A peculiar thing happened and I can't explain it. I ran into person after person who said, "He's a so-and-so, but I hope he gets it. He was great." No one had to give the antecedent of the "he."

When anyone tells me the Oscar race is a popularity contest, I remind them of Sinatra's victory.

Something happened to Frank when he got that award. He told it best himself in an interview he gave writer Louis Larkin in 1959:

"The greatest change in my life began the night they gave me the Oscar. It's funny about that statue. You walk up on the stage like you're in a dream, and they hand you that little man, before twenty or thirty million people, and you have to fight to keep the tears back. It's a moment. Like your first girl or your first kiss. Like the first time you hit a guy and he went down. I've heard actors kid about the Academy Awards. Don't believe them. . . . I don't think any actor can experience something like that and not change."

Certainly Frank did change. Here he had been on an express elevator going down and, suddenly, the switch was reversed and he started up.

His voice came back along with his confidence. He moved over to Capitol Records and his new recordings sold as his old ones had in the days when he was everybody's No. 1 on the Hit Parade.

Producers started clamoring for him. Those who had shouted the loudest that he was snake-bitten now hoped that it was contagious.

Only his private life remained disturbed, unimproved. He and Ava did more fighting than the whole Foreign Legion and did it where it could be observed. After a time they started living apart. Everyone waited for the inevitable trip to Reno. Finally in October, 1953, it happened. Ava took up residence.

She stayed the requisite number of weeks and, ordinarily, this would be followed by the court putting two people asunder. But not so with this pair. Ava, her waiting period over, simply packed and left. Still married to Frank.

But if they weren't legally divorced, they certainly were and have been, in every other sense of the word. Ava's life has been filled with bullfighters in her beloved Spain. There she lives in her isolated home, waiting for twilight, I have been told, before she goes out.

And Frank—well, wasn't there a long-ago countryman of his named Casanova?

I said, far back in this chapter, that he had the charm that enthralled women. Apparently he has lost none of it with the loss of his hair and the passage of the years.

And he has received fairly extensive press coverage, although as one wag remarked, "You can't tell the girls without a score card."

But, and here again arises the contradictions within this man, he is also a family man. Hold that snicker!

At every opportunity he saw Nancy and the children. Whenever he was needed, he came. And all I can say is he is the most married bachelor I know. He has the full freedom of the home where Nancy and the children live. In every respect but one it's his. He not only seems to have his cake and eat it, but with icing.

In these past years he has been reported serious about only two women. One was Lauren Bacall, widow of Humphrey Bogart. He was a great friend of the Bogarts for a long period of time and very close to them during the period of Bogey's final illness. Afterward he and Lauren ("Betty" to her close friends) were almost continually together.

Unwittingly I caused their romance—if it was that—to break up. I had been told that the pair was serious about each other and, like any professional reporter, went to the source for verification. This happened at a party which Zsa Zsa Gabor gave for the son of the Dominican dictator Trujillo.

During the party, I found myself beside Lauren. With us, luckily for me, was her agent, Irving Paul Lazar. I asked her, "Are you going to marry Sinatra?"

"Yes," she answered. "We're going to get married before long."

She did not say this was a secret or off-record. She didn't ask me to hold up the story. I felt completely free to rush to my typewriter and pound out an exclusive.

From the moment the story appeared in print, Frank ceased seeing Lauren. Just like that!

Of course I was disturbed when I learned this. I hadn't wanted to hurt anyone and now, it seemed, I had done great hurt to Lauren Bacall. The only solace I had was that if my story could cause Frank to take off in all directions—except that one where Lauren was—then the romance could not have had any great depth or meaning for him.

And I must say this for Lauren: She never blamed me, never tried to deny the story or equivocate. What is more, she accepted the knowing leers with her head high. Now, happily, she is well over her unhappiness and in love with that fine actor, Jason Robards, Jr. I wish her well. She deserves it.

The second supposedly serious romance in which Frank has recently been involved had Juliet Prowse, a talented dancer from South Africa, as the party of the second part. Newspapers, including those in her native land, picked up the story and printed it. Her family assumed that an engagement announcement was only a matter of time. Juliet herself told me that her mother went to see *Can Can* every day that it ran in her home town because she wanted to see what her future son-in-law was like. (A Johannesburg newspaper even printed this story.)

158

Then Juliet's family came to Hollywood to meet Frank. He was the skinny man who wasn't there. He had a perfectly legitimate reason for being out of town. This was at the time when he was preparing the great pre-Inauguration show in Washington for President Kennedy. But, later, while Juliet's family was still in Hollywood, Frank was any place but.

When he finally did return, it was after they were gone. Gone or not, their memory must be lingering, for Frank and Juliet have not picked up their romance where it was dropped. Romeo has been a-wandering.

My own hunch is that he has developed an allergy to the word "marriage." Whenever it is mentioned, Frank gets an itch to run. And does.

I suppose this is really one of his most obvious habits—running. When he starred in the picture, *Some Came Running*, a friend remarked to me, "That's Frank, running all the time. Only, where is he running? And what is he running to?"

That's a good pair of questions and I wish that I had some idea of a good answer. I don't.

He has made the most tremendous comeback in the history of the amusement business. At this moment he is the champ. But this doesn't seem to have brought him either contentment or peace. Not if one can believe the stories one hears—or the things one sees.

He goes through life asking, "Where's the action?" and never stays content when he's found it. By now a mythology has grown up around him and his buddies. Their lingo demands an interpreter. When he says "ring-a-ding-ding," he means "action," and when he means "action," he means where the girls are. The habit of adding "ville" to words he began, starting out with "Dullsville," which is defined as boring beyond endurance. A "schmo" is a "square," and a "square" is anyone who isn't "hep"—and this means just about the entire population of the world, except Frank and his cronies. He is said to divide females into "dolls" and "dogs."

He seems to enjoy carrying on his feuds even when, as with me, the other party of the feud doesn't know how it came into being or why it continues.

As an example, in the split between Frank Sinatra—rugged individualist—and Frank Sinatra—father—there was the case of his
daughter Nancy's marriage to Tommy Sands.

Both Nancy and Tommy are part of my "young family"; those
kids whom I've watched grow, whose careers I have tried to help,
whose friendships I enjoy. When they decided to marry, as I reported earlier, I was "the first to know."

But when the wedding invitations went out, I wasn't on the list.
Frankly, I was hurt. It seemed to me that on this occasion her father
might have considered Nancy first. I think I have more in common
with Nancy and Tommy than Frank's side-kicks Dean Martin, Peter
Lawford, Sammy Davis, Jr. and Leo Durocher.

However, I suggested to the paper that a reporter and photographer be sent to the wedding. As always, Frank's backbone stiffened
when he saw them. But when the pair said that I was responsible
for their being assigned—that they were representing me—he immediately relented. "Louella," he said, "would never do anything
to hurt Nancy or Tommy."

And I close this piece as I began it. Whatever else he may or may
not be, Frank Sinatra is a good, loving father. And the one person in
the world from whom I've never heard a word against him has been
his first wife.

Not long ago, Nancy said to me, "There's nobody else in the world
as kind and good as he is."

How can you figure a man like that?

I can't.

→» *Chapter 10*

TRIAL BY TRAGEDY

FRITZI SCHEFF, a musical comedy and vaudeville star of some years ago, was best known for one song. Its refrain went:

> I want what I want when I want it,
> And I want what I want right away.

I have known just one woman who made those words her philosophy of life—to her sorrow.

That woman was Lana Turner.

Was, I say, because there is good evidence that Lana has changed. She may still want what she wants when she wants it, but she has matured enough to know that it may not always be good for her. Good not only in the personal sense, but in relation to the morality of the world and the other individuals who make it up.

It has taken a long time, filled with tragedy and heartbreak, for Lana to learn that it isn't necessarily right for her to get what she wants when she wants it. The fault, however, is not hers alone.

I remember one time, years ago, when she sat with me and said, "Maybe it's all been too easy. Maybe that's what's been wrong."

Yes, it was all easy—on the surface. High-school girl has soda in Schwab's drugstore. Movie producer sees her. High-school girl becomes star.

161

That was the way it happened to Lana. The story has been told a thousand times and has probably resulted in a million sodas being sold in that drugstore. Mervyn Leroy found her there and cast her in her first picture, *They Won't Forget*. A truly prophetic title.

She was—and remains—beautiful. Webster might have had her in mind when he defined "Glamor" as: "Magic; enchantment; magic spell or charm; seemingly mysterious and illusive fascination. . . . bewitching charm. . . ." She fits all the various nuances.

"Whenever I do something," she told me, "it seems so right. And turns out so wrong."

She was speaking, of course, of her personal life. Her career, except for one short period, has always been "right" in the sense that she was successful.

I have often wondered if she hasn't remained that same sixteen-year-old in all the years since she first went into pictures. If that wasn't the end of her growing up. For a long time I thought it was; now, I'm happily inclined to believe that it wasn't. But what a tragedy, what a nasty, unhappy tragedy had to occur to change Lana!

For so many years Lana was all heart and no head. She reacted emotionally and her emotions were subject to change with each day —or night.

Some years ago she was quoted in a magazine article as saying of her relations with men, "Let's be honest, the physical attracts me first. Then, if you get to know the man's mind and soul and heart, that's icing on the cake."

She acted that way for a long, long time. And paid for it. Repeatedly she fell in love, temporarily forever. And the love affair ended and she started all over again. Temporarily forever.

I did not know her when she first went into pictures. But I quickly knew about her. Soon after she got her start, she began to be seen with handsome Gregson Bautzer, a brilliant lawyer and, for many years, Hollywood's most determined bachelor. It was said she was in love with him but to most people it was simply a case of "puppy love," of a young girl idealizing an older man.

And then, suddenly, Lana eloped to Las Vegas. Not with Bautzer, who was to remain single for a long time afterward, but with musician Artie Shaw. These two had been in a picture together but Lana

162

had announced, while the picture was being made, that she didn't like Artie. And Lana's mother, who was with her constantly, added as a postscript, that she didn't like Artie either.

What, then, had happened?

This is what Lana told me. "I had a date with Greg and he called to say that he couldn't keep it. Some kind of legal business. I got mad and decided I'd go out anyway and I thought of someone who'd make Greg mad—and jealous. So I called Artie."

"Then what happened?"

"About midnight Artie said it would be nice if we got married. I said it would be nice too. The next thing I knew, we were on our way to Las Vegas."

She wired her mother from that city to say she was married, but did not mention to whom. Mrs. Turner called Bautzer and learned quite quickly that it wasn't he. She learned it was Artie Shaw in the next day's papers.

That marriage lasted five hectic months. Shaw has shown through the years that he can make beautiful music but not with his wives.

That marriage, however, was like so many that I can recall in Hollywood, some of which I have included in this book. Beautiful star marries intellectual man. Man decides to play Pygmalion. It doesn't work too well. Beautiful girl gets bored. Result: divorce. (It is interesting to note that the picture *Never on Sunday* comes so close to depicting just this.)

For five months Lana read thick books, listened to good music and went to art galleries. It turned out all wrong. She was bored.

"I know," she told me, "that I ought to be interested in those things. After all, I didn't have too much education. But, you know something, Louella, all they did was make me sleepy."

And it must have been hard for Lana to be a pliant Galatea. After all, she was famous. She was way up on the list of money-making stars and was accustomed to the treatment. At MGM, in those days, this included getting a star the moon if she expressed a desire for it. It was hard to adjust to reading Kant instead of the menu at Romanoff's.

Next came a period when Lana played the romantic field. Her name was linked with that of virtually every bachelor in Hollywood, ranging from Howard Hughes to Victor Mature, with Turhan Bey thrown in for good measure.

"I like men," she told me. "I can't help it."

But it wasn't any of these, but an unknown actor, Stephen Crane, who became husband No. 2 in 1943. This was after they had known each other a month and the publicity releases, in a highly original fashion, called it a "whirlwind courtship." "Hurricane" would have been more like it.

When I met Steve, I found that he was devoted to Lana. He was, of course, handsome and he was deeply in love with Lana, more, I always knew, than she with him. It quickly became evident that they were not the most happily married people in town. And then came a bombshell.

Crane had not been completely divorced from his first wife. He had believed the final papers had been processed at the time of his marriage to Lana. They hadn't.

So, amid a flurry of press releases from Lana's studio, her marriage was annulled.

Then came one of those ironies which have marked Lana's life. At the same time that she got her annulment, she discovered that she was pregnant!

And she wanted the baby.

Sometimes I think that the same script is written for so many stars when they're born; so many of the same characteristics are present in them. How many stars have told me how much they wanted children! And meant it with all their hearts as Lana did when she told me she was pregnant.

The powers that be went to work. Legal technicalities were cleared up. Crane was most happy to remarry Lana; he was still deeply in love with her. Perhaps having a child would remove many of the difficulties that had cropped up earlier.

When daughter Cheryl was born, she couldn't have been more legal. Nor could she have had a more precarious hold on life.

When Cheryl was born, far less was known about the RH negative factor in the blood than is known today. Chances of a child surviving when this occurred were very low. It took desperate meas-

164

ures, all the help medical science could provide, to keep Cheryl alive. The child needed transfusion after transfusion in order to get healthy blood to flow through her veins.

Her life was finally saved, but Cheryl was a weak and sickly child.

Lana told me: "I prayed and prayed and prayed. I had the feeling that with a child, I'd be more like other people."

That was something which had always troubled her. It was not only that she was a movie star, but went back into the years before she became a movie star. On the Christmas Eve when she was nine, her father had been waylaid by thugs, robbed and killed. It was a murder which has never been solved.

Somehow, from that time on, Lana said, she had always felt "different." Something had happened in her life which was unique and set her apart. Having a child was just the opposite. It meant that she was like other women.

But not enough like them to stay married. A year after Cheryl's birth, Lana and Steve Crane were divorced. Through the years, however, they have remained friendly and this affection was, a long time later, to be most important.

Again she was single, but it was a question from day to day if she would remain that way. I asked her about this and she said, "I have a compulsion to get married. Just let a man ask me and I start whistling the wedding march."

I really lectured her on how ridiculous this was. She kept agreeing with me. It was ridiculous, but what could she do about it? That was the way she was.

"I'll tell you what to do about it," I said. "Whenever a man proposes to you, you call me right away and we'll talk about it."

"I'll do that, Louella."

I always heard from Lana by the middle of the next afternoon. "You were right, Louella. How does it happen that something that makes so much sense in the moonlight doesn't make any sense at all in the sunlight?"

One time I did tell her that it wasn't something, it was Lana who needed daylight to see things in perspective. And as always, she agreed.

165

Then she became involved in a romance of which I approved. If wishes were horses, Lana and Tyrone Power would have ridden off together, hand in hand, into the sunset.

I think that this was probably the deepest emotional experience of Lana's life—her romance with Ty Power. I believe that for the first time she felt something that was more than glandular, that she didn't love just an aspect of a man, but the whole man.

They were such an unbelievably handsome pair. And they had so much to give each other. Ty, with his gentleness and his well-bred ways. Lana with her verve, her loveliness, her almost childlike sensuality.

And what a difference it would have made to Cheryl had Ty become a part of her life.

The end of their idyl came without warning. Ty was going off to make a picture in Rome and they gave a farewell party for him. The theme of the party was—love. The motif, the favors, the decorations all included hearts and flowers entwined. All the guests, including me, felt that this was an engagement party. That some time during that evening, when they were never farther than a handclasp apart, they would tell us that they were going to get married.

But there was no announcement.

And then came the shattering news, to Lana and her friends, that Ty was going to marry Linda Christian.

I recall Lana crying, without bitterness but with great hurt. She believed someone had poisoned Ty's mind about her. This could be part of the adolescent fantasy that was for so long a part of her life. It could be the truth. I don't believe she ever did learn the real reason.

Ty was a favorite of mine and it wasn't just because of Lana that I was unhappy when he married Linda Christian. I just didn't think she was right for him. I did know that when she set out to get a man, she was a huntress who would not be hindered. And set out to get Ty she did—and did.

If only—. But, like wishes, "if only's" have no part in a factual report.

After her experience with Ty, Lana was a long time recovering. Hurt, she stayed off by herself, waiting for the hurt or its outward

166

signs to go. I have always believed, however, that it was during this period that she developed a trend toward self-destruction. That she, possibly consciously, wanted to hurt herself.

Now came husband No. 3 in her life, rich playboy Henry J. (Bob) Topping. This certainly was a change of pace for Lana. He was hardly the perfect male animal and his entire background was as foreign from hers as any background could be. Except romantically.

About a year earlier I had written what I still consider a classic story about the marital entanglements of film people, café society and plain society. It was headlined:

ARLENE JUDGE, BOB TOPPING TO WED

In it, I remarked, "The complications resulting from Arlene Judge's becoming her ex-husband's sister-in-law, and of Bob Topping assuming the role of stepfather to his nephew, Dan Topping, Jr., is causing bewilderment and speculation. . . ."

I then went on to report that this would be Arlene's fifth marriage (her second was to Dan Topping) and that Bob Topping had two ex-es in his background; actress Jayne Shattuck and Gloria (Mimi) Baker, half sister of Alfred Gwynn Vanderbilt.

Had I continued to keep a marital score card on this group, I wouldn't have had time for much else in the next few years. But this story only concerns Lana and she did not stay married to Topping long.

During that marriage she had two dangerously difficult miscarriages, due to the RH factor in her blood, and some publicity about alleged physical damage. When she divorced Topping, she returned to pictures.

On my desk, before me as I write this, is a story I wrote about her in 1951. In it I remarked, "Lana Turner is a one-man woman now— one man at a time." And I reported that the man of the moment was actor Fernando Lamas, with whom she was appearing in *The Merry Widow*. I wrote, "They're playing their love scenes off the set as well as on." And then I made the point, so often glossed over, that she was still technically married to Topping.

What bothered me at that time, even more than Lana's trying to get what she wanted and get it right away, was young Cheryl. I had

167

seen Cheryl a number of times and it wasn't hard to sense that the young girl was having a trying time growing up, physically and emotionally.

Lana wanted to be a good mother, but in so many ways she was a child herself. She wanted the same affection that her daughter wanted and so she had to spend a part of her life looking for it.

Cheryl was unhappy and uncertain. She was growing too fast and seemed gawky. She was a child who hid in herself. And no wonder. After all, to whom could she turn?

Her mother? Of course, when Lana was available. Her grandmother, Mrs. Turner? There was too great an age gap. Her governess? Her real father, Steve Crane? Or to the stepfather of the moment?

No wonder the child felt lost.

And then, in 1955, Lana again married. Her fourth husband was Lex Barker, one of the handsome hunks of masculinity who have at various times played the role of "Tarzan."

That marriage did not start under the best of auspices.

Lana was a big star and Lex was a young man clawing his way up. They lived in her immense movie-star mansion. When they traveled, it was queen and consort. Such a life was bound to be hard on a man. And not too easy for his wife.

Yet for a time it appeared that all would be well. I recall interviewing Lana in 1956. She was happy because she was pregnant again. She talked a lot about this coming baby. (Poor girl. She lost that child too.) She laughed at the new trend of actresses who wanted to "look like the girl next door." She said, "That will drive the men out of the movie houses and to the back fence."

I asked about Cheryl and learned that she was attending a convent school. "The discipline is good for her," Lana told me.

It was a pleasant afternoon and it made me happy.

Then within a short period, whatever she had found became lost.

She had another miscarriage.

Cheryl ran away from the convent and black headlines reported the police search for her.

Lana's marriage broke up.

168

No wonder that, for a time, she lived a quiet, subdued life. She didn't appear in public. She tried to be with Cheryl more.

Perhaps, I thought again, this time it's for real. Lana was now thirty-six, had been in pictures twenty years and a star for almost all that time. It could be that she had made peace with life and herself.

Then came the rudest, most shattering shock of all. I had heard that Lana had a new interest; a man who was on the barest periphery of Hollywood and then only because of peculiar connections. His name, I was told, was Johnny Stompanato, an ex-Marine from Chicago. And he was, like so many of the men who had figured in Lana's life, the type whose likeness could well appear in *Physical Culture* magazine. A real mass of muscle. And quite handsome.

After a time I learned that these rumors were true. I also heard that Lana was going through an unbelievable period. Stompanato believed the way to handle a woman was to slap her down and he practiced what he believed. Lana had confided to friends that she had suffered numerous beatings at his hands.

When I asked why she didn't leave him, there were whispers that she was afraid, that Stompanato had underworld connections which Lana feared.

I was told by someone very close to Lana that at first she believed that Stompanato was really in love with her. He was attractive and she was lonely.

Then came the first inkling that it might be other than her beauty and glamour that attracted him. He said he was a little short on money and asked for a loan of $10,000, which she gave him. Months later, after she had been thoroughly frightened by him and they were in Europe, he asked her for $50,000.

When she told him that she didn't have that amount, he blackened her eye, beat her up, and threatened her life, even suggesting that he had friends "who would take care of her."

If Lana had only gone to the police when she returned home from Europe, all of the tragedy and sorrow might have been avoided.

We all knew that some day there would be a blowup, but none of us was prescient enough to imagine the tragic blowup that followed.

Then one day it was in the headlines:

169

There was the whole bitter, pitiful story. Cheryl, only fourteen, trying to protect her mother from Stompanato's fists, had stabbed him to death.

Lana's friends—especially Steve Crane—rallied around her. And the law and the press took their course.

The stories all reported the same set of facts and they added up to the fact that the real fault was Lana's. She did not attempt to deny it. Nor did she answer any of the editorials in which she was castigated and censured and damned.

The court finally brought in its judgment. No criminal charges against Cheryl, but she must be placed under a guardianship other than her mother's. The law did not believe that Lana was fit to care for her child.

And I know that Lana did not, at that moment, believe she was. But I am just as sure as I can ever be of anything that, at that moment, she made up her mind that she would be.

I think—and from what Lana has told me, it has become clear—that she knew that wanting what she wanted "right now" was at an end. She had betrayed her child and herself by her wilfulness. She could not change what had happened. She could only use every effort to atone for it.

Cheryl was placed in El Retiro Home for Girls, an institution for minors who needed correction. This wasn't what Lana desired, but she was aware that that was no longer what mattered. Then came another shock. Cheryl ran away from the school. More headlines. More sorrow. Cheryl was found and returned to El Retiro.

"I have to help Cheryl," she said. "Nothing else matters."

Nothing else did. I feel that it was during this period that Cheryl came to realize how much her mother loved her. She visited her to the limit allowed. When she was with her, she treated her as a daughter, a friend and an adult. She took her into her confidence, discussed plans with her.

It seemed as if Lana's career was at an end. When I remarked this to her, she answered, "If it is, it is. It's Cheryl, not my career, that's important to me now."

But then something happened to re-establish her career, even as she was re-establishing herself as a mother and human being. Producer Ross Hunter, at Universal-International, decided that only Lana could play the top role in his remake of *Imitation of Life*. And he brought the script to her and asked her to take the part and offered to give her a percentage of the picture.

His confidence in her was justified. The picture was a box-office smash. And so were the next pictures she made.

But she was through with the old life. One sign was her selling the large home that had been a hallmark of those years. She began to live more simply. "I'm not interested in things, in possessions, in show any more," she told me. "What did they ever get me?"

And then she fell in love again. But this time it was with a different kind of man in a different way. Gone was the helter-skelter, here-today-gone-tomorrow concept she had always had of relations with a man. "I've learned to love him," she told me. "Learned."

And who was "him?" Fred May, a businessman rancher, father of three children, solid and substantial. And handsome, but I could hardly hold that against Lana.

Late in August, 1960, she telephoned me. "Fred and I have taken out a marriage license but we're not going to use it right away."

This was a new twist. In the past, Lana had rushed to Nevada where license, ceremony and certificate all came in one package. The better to get it over with.

I asked, "How does Cheryl feel about Fred?"

"She likes him and respects him. And she's so happy for me." Her voice became more thoughtful. "Louella, I've learned one thing. Love—the real thing—isn't a wild passion. It's based on companionship and respect; on mutual interests and an admiration for the man in your life." Here was more of the new Lana.

"Does he like Cheryl?"

"Of course. And he has three children of his own to whom he's devoted and feels a sense of responsibility. That's one of the reasons I love him."

"Good for you, Lana. And good luck. You certainly deserve it."

"You can wish us well after we're married," she said. "You'll be the first to know."

171

I waited to hear from her, but didn't. Days passed. The license was due to expire in a few days. I wondered if I'd been wrong, if Lana had only given the appearance of change, but had not really changed. And then, three days before the license would have become invalid, she and Fred were quietly married in Santa Monica.

Cheryl was the proudest guest at the ceremony.

The first picture that Lana made after her marriage was *By Love Possessed*. I couldn't help thinking how often the titles of her pictures had mirrored her life. It came to me that this might be an omen. That, at last, Lana Turner was by love possessed.

➤➤ *Chapter 11*

THE MAN NOBODY "NO'S"

My phone rang one day and the voice at the other end said, "I'm married to Jean."

"What a story!" I shouted. "It'll make page one in every paper in the United States."

"Not page one. Either you'll handle it the way I tell you or there won't be any story."

"But—" That was as far as I got.

"Louella, I'm making a bargain with you. If you put the story on the front page, I'll deny it. Write it the way I want it and you can have it, not otherwise."

I wrote it the way he wanted it. Nobody that I know has ever been able to have his own way with Howard Hughes.

That was how it happened that my column, which carried the exclusive story of his marriage to Jean Peters, didn't even carry a banner line on the marriage while papers throughout the country picked it up and ran it on page 1; in the instance of one paper, the New York *Daily News*, giving credit for an exclusive story to my old friend Florabel Muir. About which more later.

Hollywood has long described Howard as fabulous, secretive and

173

a man of mystery. I suppose he does look that way to a town which parades its secrets and debunks its mysteries.

Not long ago *Fortune* magazine carried a story about the refinancing of his airline, TWA, and titled it, "The Bankers and the Spook." Howard was pictured as a man whom the bankers couldn't find while the $165,000,000 deal was being negotiated.

But I have never regarded him as mystery man or spook. I have known him since he was a boy of twenty-one and I realize that he is reticent, wary of strangers and secretive because that is the way he feels he can best protect himself and his interests. He is my friend. But oh, what an exasperating friend he can be for a newspaperwoman who wants to put everything she learns in print!

We have been friends a long time. I sometimes smile when I read that Howard can't be found, that he is incommunicado, that he has disapeared again. I think I can truthfully say that all though the years, Howard has rarely been farther away from me than the other end of the telephone.

In one respect that has not done me much good. My business is getting news about important people into the paper. Howard feels that there shouldn't be any news about him in any paper at any time. This has led to many an impasse.

Through the years we have worked out a way of handling stories concerning him. I have to put everything I write through a sieve. If Howard can find any way to keep his name out of print, he uses it. He once told me—as if he had to—that nothing would please him more than never to see his name in print.

One thing has come through quite clearly during the period of our relationship. He just doesn't trust people. He seeks to avoid close associations and, as time passes, he sees fewer and fewer people. And he has the power to drop out of sight when it suits his purpose. He wasn't always like this.

Before I ever met Howard, I knew his uncle Rupert Hughes, the late, well-known novelist. When Howard was still wearing knee pants, I bought a story from Rupert Hughes to be made into a one-reel movie by the old Essanay Company in Chicago. I was the company's story editor and I had strict orders not to pay more than twenty-five dollars for any story. However, because Rupert Hughes was well-known, I stretched my budget and paid him thirty-five dollars. Years afterward I apologized to him because I couldn't pay him more.

"Don't be sorry," he said, "you'll never know how much I needed that money at the time."

Howard Hughes has never known what it means to be pressed for ready cash. His problems have always been the result of his having money. It seems to me that one of the reasons he is suspicious of most people is that he feels that any interest or liking they show for him is because of his money and not for himself. I have heard that this is not uncommon among multimillionaires. This is something I'll have to take on hearsay, though.

When I first met Howard his personality was different. He was quite young; a tall, lean, good-looking man with a lopsided, ingenuous smile. He was more gregarious at that time too. I met him through my dear friend Ben Lyon.

When Ben married my closest friend, Bebe Daniels, I was matron of honor and Howard was best man. When Doctor Martin and I were married, Howard was among our wedding guests.

In those days he often went to parties, especially at the Lyons' beach house. And his wife, a soft-speaking Southern belle, sometimes came with him. I can't even remember when she ceased coming. She and Howard were divorced and she left the Hollywood scene. And Howard became Hollywood's richest, most eligible— and most elusive—bachelor.

He was to remain just that for three decades.

Through the years his name was linked with an album of beauties. Way, way back there was Billie Dove. And then came Jean Harlow, Katharine Hepburn, Ginger Rogers, Mitzi Gaynor, Susan Hayward, Elizabeth Taylor and Ava Gardner—among others.

There were rumors that he would marry this beauty or that. And whenever I checked with him, he gave me a forthright answer. "No."

No wonder, then, that I was thrilled and dismayed when he called to tell me that he and lovely Jean Peters were married but that I'd have to treat the story as just another column item. It didn't make any sense—newspaper sense, that is.

But it was the way he wanted it.

175

I asked some questions, among them, "How did Jean get you?"

"She doesn't care about my money. She thinks the way I do. We're interested in the same things."

"Can I print that?"

"No."

"What can I write?"

"That we're married."

After he hung up, I wrote the brief paragraph and called him back to read it to him.

"No good. It has too much information."

"But I can't just say that you and Jean are married."

"Why not?"

I rewrote the story until I got it in a shape of which he would approve. All the time I was giving myself the devil for not playing it for what it was worth. But there were a lot of reasons why I couldn't. One of them, of course, was my responsibility to a news source. In this case it went beyond that. Howard trusted me and had proven that trust over the years. I had called upon him for help in checking stories many times and he had given me that help when he could; and that was almost always.

However, I did resent his fifth call to me in which he asked, for the fifth time, "Was the story the way you read it to me?"

"Yes."

"Is it still going to run in the body of the column?"

"Yes." And finally I exploded. "Don't you dare call me again."

"Why are you so mad at me?" he asked with a touch of surprise in his high-pitched voice.

"I daren't tell you."

I learned later that Howard double checked on me. He called William Randolph Hearst, Jr., in New York, told him how he had insisted upon the story being written, and asked Bill to make sure that it would be handled that way.

I know the request must have galled as fine and astute a newspaperman as Bill. But he was a good friend and great admirer of Howard and, like me, he was being asked to respect a news source.

Now back to Florabel. She called me and told me that her paper had credited her with an exclusive story and said that was not her doing. "It was your story and I told them so," she said, "but why did you hide it in the column?"

"I wish I could tell you. I can't."

Howard's marriage surprised me. He and Jean had been seeing each other for ten years. She was a talented actress, lovely looking and ladylike. One of her infrequent screen roles was as the minister's wife in *A Man Called Peter* and it brought raves from the critics and the public. She could have had many more roles but even in the years before their marriage she was more interested in Howard than in her career.

They had been seeing each other for a number of years when Jean suddenly eloped with Stuart Kramer, III, a—as *Variety* puts it —nonprofessional. The general consensus, in which I joined, was that Jean had decided that there was no future in her relationship with Howard and had decided to make a complete break. However, Jean's marriage to Kramer did not last long. Soon they were divorced and Jean was back in Hollywood.

Then came the call. And my poor little story.

There is one touch of humor to that. The day after my column appeared, my good friend Hedda Hopper remarked with her usual milk of human kindness, "I'll believe they're married when Howard Hughes tells me himself."

Wonder if Hedda is still an unbeliever, after the Christmas cards of the past few years that have been signed, "Jean Hughes."

Yet, in a sense, there is a touch of mystery still about their marriage. No one has ever learned where it took place or when. I have always suspected that they were married in an airplane. And the couple has never gone out socially.

They live most quietly in a bungalow at the Beverly Hills Hotel and their passion for privacy is so great that the waiters and other help never enter their bungalow. Meals for the pair are left on trays outside the door.

If I have made Howard sound like a misanthrope, a man who is interested solely in himself, let me rectify that now. He has done many kind, generous things for many people. And done them with no intent except to help someone who needed help. When I've learned of these things, and even when I've been a party to them,

177

Howard has been as adamant against publicity as in all other instances.

There was, for example, the case of Mala Powers, a young actress who was on the RKO contract list when Howard owned that studio. She was taken critically ill with a blood disease which her doctors believed would prove incurable. For months she lay in St. Joseph's Hospital in Burbank.

Howard had never known her. She was just a name among a group of names at RKO. But when he heard of her sickness, he notified the hospital that he would be responsible for all her bills. In addition, he asked that no possible expense be spared. He sent his own doctor to care for her.

Some time later he learned that a group of boys returning from Korea, where they had been in that abortive war, had elected Mala "Queen Of The Homecoming Fleet." I suppose this was originally a publicity stunt, though done I'm sure with the hope that it would buoy Mala's spirits. And when Mala heard about it, the desired effect was achieved. She was thrilled and excited and grateful.

Word got back to Howard about this and he decided to cap it in a manner that was peculiar to him. He equipped a plane with a hospital bed and arranged for Mala, a nurse and me to be flown to San Diego.

I will never forget the gallantry of that girl, holding herself erect with superhuman courage, as she took the salute from these boys, returned it and welcomed them back home; back to life. At that time she knew that her own chance of life was far less than theirs had been on the battlefield.

And I'm pleased to report that this story has a really happy ending. Mala Powers won out in her fight for life. Now she is completely well and the mother of a child.

Never let anyone say a word against Howard to Mala. She feels she owes her life to him. This man she had never met.

And, right here, let me put the record straight on another item.

Some years ago Howard was almost killed in the crash of an experimental plane which he was flying. He was pulled from the flaming plane by a young marine. This undoubtedly saved his life.

Some time afterward snide stories appeared in a number of places to the effect that Howard, who could so well afford it, had never rewarded the young man. This canard is just that. A canard. I know how generously rewarded the boy was. But that was another story Howard would never let me write.

Of course my prime interest in Howard stems from the fact that he has been connected for so long with the motion-picture industry. It seems to me that the industry owes him a great deal more than it has ever recognized or acknowledged. He blazed movie-making trails. He broke precedents. In a town that prides itself on its showmanship, he has proven how effective showmanship can really be.

Because he has been a "loner," because he has made his own rules and lived by them, because he has had the hard cash to back up his opinions when they ran contrary to the current, he has been castigated. I don't think this has ever bothered him.

He never, of course, fitted any Hollywood pattern. He came to Hollywood rich, far richer than most Hollywood moguls. He came to the town already a success, though hardly more than a boy. He had talent, even genius, in fields that were foreign to the movie industry.

He has been a most successful inventor. He has created a financial empire. He has been one of our finest pilots. His life and triumphs should have made him a hero. Instead, he has long been a target for scandal and whispers (both of which he has ignored) and a so-called mystery man—a sinister figure. (I have a hunch that this has given him many laughs.)

I don't know the whole story of Howard Hughes, but I do know some facts and I'd like to tell them now. It seems to me that he deserves to be known for his services to his country and to the industry of which I am a part.

When Howard was eighteen, his father died, leaving him the major portion of the Hughes Tool Company. The elder Hughes had invented a rock drill for oil-drilling purposes and this was the foundation of the Hughes fortune. Howard's guardians and executors of the estate felt that he was too young to take over management of the company. He thought differently.

He went to court and sued for the right to run the company. He won the suit, borrowed enough money from the banks to buy out the other heirs and took over. In a few years he had boosted the company into a million-dollar-a-year profit position.

If I may digress for a moment, he has shown the same ability for high finance and organization in other fields. He created the world's largest airline, TWA. He built up an aircraft empire. And his ventures in Hollywood may have been costly, but they were also profitable in the long run.

But to return to the young Howard Hughes. He came to Hollywood when he was just about old enough to vote; already a success. He met many movie people and became intrigued with the industry.

Hollywood is a town of "promoters." There are always men with ideas that would make millions if only they had the few hundreds or thousands needed to put those ideas into operation. A lot of these people got a glint in their eyes when they saw the young Texas millionaire. Here was, to use an expression I have often heard, a "pigeon."

It may have been during this period that he began to develop the cynicism that is part of him now. He was no wide-eyed innocent and I'm sure that many who thought they were kidding him learned, much too late, that they were kidding only themselves. Certainly during that time Howard turned down proposition after proposition.

Finally he did go into picturemaking and his first venture, *Swell Hogan,* was a flop. Howard lost his entire investment.

And here another of Howard's basic character traits came into play. He doesn't like to lose. And he doesn't quit. He decided that next time he would be the boss. He made a second picture and this one made a profit of $75,000. He was on his way.

His third venture was *Two Arabian Knights* which won an Academy Award as the best comedy of the year. In three pictures Howard had reached the heights.

All this time he was deeply interested in aviation, and for his next picture he combined his two enthusiasms—aviation and the movies. He decided to make *Hell's Angels,* the first big picture about flying. He wasn't interested in what it would cost. Wise Hollywood snickered. One success didn't make a producer; one big failure could destroy him.

I remember watching this picture being made. Even I was appalled

180

at the way Howard was spending money. At one time he had twenty-four cameramen shooting battle scenes. Howard was creating his own war and it was almost as expensive as the real one.

Finally the picture, starring our mutual friend, Ben Lyon, was finished shooting. Howard was working on the final cut, preparing to arrange for release, when he saw *The Jazz Singer*, with Al Jolson, and recognized immediately that the day of the silent picture was over.

And here again he showed his courage. He scrapped the completed picture and started all over again! Before the picture was finally released, it had taken three years to make and remake and had cost $4,000,000. And this was at a time when a million was a million and that was more than most pictures cost, even the spectaculars.

In addition to making a picture, Howard also made a great star. Greta Nissen had appeared in the silent version but wasn't available for the sound film. Instead, Jean Harlow, introduced to Howard by Bebe Daniels, got the leading role. It has alwyas been a question which was the greater success—the picture or Jean.

When the picture was finished, Howard wasn't content to turn it over to someone else to exploit. Instead, he took on this job himself. He planned a tremendous première for *Hell's Angels* at Grauman's Chinese Theatre and then decided to redo the theatre for the première. He had it completely torn apart and redecorated. Workmen were still working on the day of the première.

On that day I realized that if I saw the picture at its première I wouldn't be able to make the deadline for the morning edition.

I called Howard and told him this. "If I can't see it earlier, I won't review it. I'll have someone else do it."

I was both a friend and his favorite reviewer. Also, and I say it only because it was so, at that time my reviews had more impact than anyone else's. I don't know which of these reasons brought his prompt, "If I let you see it early, you'll have to promise you'll never tell anyone. And you'll also have to come to the première or people will know something's wrong."

I gave my word that I would not tell, nor would I skip the première. Shortly afterward, my secretary and I slipped into the theatre. All work was called off and the workmen were told to return later.

181

Then, amid shavings and nails and vacuum cleaners, the picture was shown us.

It was an experience. *Hell's Angels* was truly a classic in flying pictures. And while my old friend Ben did a great job, it was a revelation to see Jean Harlow fill the screen, vibrant and sexy.

I rushed off and wrote the rave review that the picture deserved and then I went home to change for the gala show due to start only a little later. What a pleasure it was to sit in that theatre, all gussied up, and know that my review was already in type. This was one time I could really enjoy myself.

And a good thing it was that I had insisted upon seeing it earlier. Because the ceremonies and stage show took so much time, the picture did not go on until 10 P.M. I'd have missed my morning deadline, as my competitors did, if I had waited for this late, late show.

And now, for the first time, those competitors know how I happened to beat them on this review. I'm sure that enough time has elapsed so that the statute of limitations now applies to my promise to Howard.

Howard piled one big success on top of another. And with each sucess he also made new stars.

Scarface, still the classic of gangster movies, introduced Paul Muni and George Raft. *The Front Page* made a star of Pat O'Brien and depicted newspapermen realistically for the first and almost the only time. And in *The Outlaw* Howard presented Jane Russell.

Nothing in Hollywood annals matches his fight against censorship, by Hollywood, of *The Outlaw*.

Howard, as long as I have known him, has had an indomitable spirit. He won't be beaten. I remarked earlier how he had refused to quit when his first picture was a flop. Well, in this instance he stood up against the mores and powers of Hollywood and fought them both until he won.

He had produced *The Outlaw* with two unknowns, Jane Russell and Jack Beutel, in the leading parts. He spent millions to make the picture and, as was his custom, a fortune to publicize it. Then, just when it was about to be released, the Hays Office, Hollywood's self-censorship bureau, notified him it would not pass the film. No seal of approval would be forthcoming unless Howard made 136 cuts of shots which were termed "objectionable."

The Hays Office had come into being as a result of protests, some years before, about Hollywood. (How innocent those pictures were compared to so much of the "Sick Sex" that fills our screens in the form of many foreign imports and a few of our own products today.) Until Howard challenged the Hays Office, its word had been absolute. And it was agreed that if Howard won his fight then the whole concept, as well as the methods, of the Hays Office would have to be re-evaluated.

Now Howard was challenging the power of that office. And in the process was also challenging Hollywood. I know how many efforts were made to get him to back down, to compromise, to help save face for all concerned. But his feeling was that he was in the right. If so, why compromise?

The objections to the picture were not based on content but on shots of Jane Russell which revealed her—shall we say?—pulchritude. There was too much of too much of Jane Russell on the screen.

Howard didn't base his fight on any constitutional ground. He wasn't really fighting censorship. He was fighting censorship of his picture. And he fought on the grounds that he was not doing anything more than other producers had done and still received Hays Office approval.

He hired experts and had thousands of enlargements made of shots from other (approved) films. Then he put experts with slide rules to work to measure the exposed areas of flesh. When this was done, he hired other experts to prepare charts and analyses.

This was, of course, tremendous publicity and would pay off when the picture was released—provided it was released. Everybody knew about *The Outlaw*. The question was, would anybody see it?

It took thirty-six months of persistent, unremitting effort, but Howard carried his point. Some three years after the fight began, the picture was passed by the Hays Office—without a single cut.

From the first days when *The Outlaw* went before the cameras, Jane Russell has been Howard's most loyal champion. She likes and

183

respects him, as he does her. And that is as far as it goes. This may be hard for the whisperers and rumormongers to accept. They like scandal and dirt. But it is all in their minds.

Certainly Jane is grateful to Howard. She had done no acting before she was cast in *The Outlaw*. During the three-year wait for the picture's release, Howard hired one of Hollywood's highest-priced press agents to promote her name. Long before the public ever saw her on the screen, she had been sold as a star.

When the picture was finally released, she was credited with having a beautiful face and an outstanding figure. Only a few realized that she was also an expert comedienne and that she would become a good actress. But in later pictures she proved she had ability, and really scored in a big way in *Son of Paleface* with Bob Hope. She had a great deal to do with "Buttons and Bows" (from that picture) being chosen as the Academy Award song that year.

Of course it has been commonplace for years to encounter smirks and leers whenever Howard puts an unknown into a picture. It could be that is one of the reasons why he hates publicity.

In 1946 I heard that Howard was negotiating to buy RKO studios from Floyd Odlum and called him to ask if it was true.

"I've already bought the studio."

And that was how the news broke that one of Hollywood's most famous studios was now the property of Hollywood's mystery man. And added to the legend that he was a mystery man.

There is one quirk to Howard's personality that has not been examined. He is a night person. It seems as if he doesn't really start to function until that "evening sun goes down." And, since he is the boss, that means that everyone who works for him has to forget about time, about normal schedules. I suppose it has worked for Howard in such enterprises as his tool company, his airline and his aviation company, but somehow it didn't work with RKO.

I happen to have a deep affection for that studio. Many of my friends worked there. Many fine pictures were made there. My daughter, Harriet, was a producer there for twelve years. RKO was a big, profitable enterprise at one time, giving employment to hundreds. And I'm sorry that under Howard it became a shell which he ultimately sold.

184

Here, I suppose, is another aspect of Howard's character. Buying RKO was a business deal and the human elements never entered into it. Past history, movie tradition and jobs were none of his concern. He had bought a piece of property.

The studio, of course, went downhill during Howard's period of ownership. Jerry Wald was hired to run it but, like so many others, found it impossible to work out any arrangement with Howard which would allow him or the studio to function. Howard's nocturnal habits were probably not as important to Jerry as they were to others for I believe that Jerry never sleeps.

But the working departments were on a daytime schedule and they were stopped cold. Executives learned that there was no way for them to reach the boss. All they could do was wait and hope that he would call them. And while they waited, production ground to a halt.

I have asked many persons, but none has ever been able to prove to me that Howard ever set foot on the RKO lot during the period when he owned the studo. Well, pictures can't be made on a remote-control basis.

Among the many tales about Howard is that he has no office but works entirely on the move. That isn't true. I know of various offices he has had during the years; one on the Goldwyn lot, another in an office building on Romaine Avenue in Hollywood. But reaching him at any office he might be occupying is a different matter. It depends upon whether he wants to be reached.

Certainly he never worked out of any office on the RKO lot. He had one, but never occupied it. After a time it took on an eerie quality and so did the rest of the studio.

Finally Howard sold the ghost town that had been RKO. It is both ironic and typical that when he finally liquidated his RKO holdings, he showed a profit. Them as has, gets. Them as hasn't, gets it in the neck.

Today the studio is back in operation, but no longer a movie lot. Instead, it is the headquarters of Desilu, prime TV producers. I'm happy for the sake of my old friends Desi and Lucy, but unhappy for the business I love. I wish that more great movies were being made on that lot today, rather than time killers for the one-eyed monster.

185

In all that I have written so far, I haven't told Howard's history in aviation. That certainly deserves mentioning for there are many, including me, who think that he is second only to Charles A. Lindbergh as an aviator. (Howard won't like my saying that. He shies off from praise even more than he does from criticism.)

In 1935 Howard set the world's record for a landplane by flying at a speed of 352 miles an hour. That same year he won the Harmon Trophy, an Academy Award for fliers. During the next three years, he established a number of other records for solo flights.

In 1938 he broke the round-the-world solo-flight record and on his return to New York received that city's traditional salute, a ticker-tape parade that many said was greater than Lindbergh's. That was the year in which Howard received the Collier Trophy; as far as aviation was concerned, the equivalent of a Nobel Prize.

In 1939 he was awarded the Congressional Medal of Honor for flying. In 1940 he received the Chanute Award.

I'll always remember the chuckle I got from a report that came back from Russia after his world flight in 1938, this time with a crew of four. Howard had become increasingly careless of his clothes and appearance during the years. He affected battered hats, well-worn suits and beat-up sneakers. When the Russians saw him, they refused to believe he was a millionaire. They felt that they were the victims of a gigantic hoax.

Howard's flights were made for more than glory or thrills. He used them to provide him with information on how to improve aircraft. He has always sought to do this and he was in an experimental plane when he crashed and was almost killed. Hughes Aircraft has long been dedicated to just such experimental work and even now is involved in it.

Experts in the field have told me that he was responsible for many of the improvements that have taken place in commercial flying as well. Much that has been done to increase comfort, speed and efficiency has resulted from his planning and designing.

Howard's capacity for fighting for himself and his rights has been as much in evidence in aviation as it was in pictures. In 1947 he took on a Senate Investigating Committee which was checking one of his contracts.

186

As his opening gun, Howard charged that Republican Senator Owen Brewster, of Maine, chairman of the committee, was secretly in the pay of a rival airline and that Brewster had offered to call off the investigation if Howard would be "co-operative." Howard then went to Washington and personally led the attack. Against the advice of his lawyers, he handled his own cross-examination. When Howard left the hearing chambers, he was applauded.

Senator Brewster was not re-elected to the Senate.

A strange man, indeed, is my old friend Howard Hughes. He has changed with the years, grown into more of a recluse. At one time he would drop in on me unexpectedly in the late-evening or early-morning hours and stay on after everyone had left. And it was not unusual, in the old days, for him to phone in the early hours of the morning.

I think the telephone is the most important invention of man in Howard's mind. Certainly he does all his business on it. Some time ago he got into the habit of dropping into an all-night café in an out-of-the-way part of town and having a hamburger and coffee. Then he would go into the one phone booth the café boasted, with an enormous amount of change, and spend hours in it, preventing anyone else's using it.

Finally the annoyed proprietor got to the end of his patience. "Mister," he told Howard, "this has got to stop. People try to call me to order hamburgers-to-go and they can't get through. I'm losing business."

Howard took out a roll of bills, peeled off $500 and handed the money to the man. "This ought to pay for the use of your phone," he said. Then he went into the booth.

But he never returned to that café again.

Even now, when the phone rings in the early morning, my first reaction is that it is Howard.

I recall all the years I have known him and that other people have known him. I have heard him described as a combination of Dracula, Bluebeard and Satan. I have heard stories told about him that I know are completely untrue and read others equally false.

And yet I know that I do not know the truth, the whole truth and nothing but the truth about him. I'm not sure that anyone does. He

187

is so complex that there must be times when he is a stranger even to himself.

I wonder what life is like for that pair of people in the bungalow on the palm-fringed grounds of the Beverly Hills Hotel. I hope they bring in the trays on which they get their food before the food grows cold.

→» Chapter 12

HER SERENE HIGHNESS

HOLLYWOOD cast patrician Grace Kelly to be a movie Queen. But Mother Nature type-cast her to be a Princess. She was born to be the legendary Princess of storybook enchantment—and Mother Nature won out.

Grace Kelly, the Irish beauty, has been Her Serene Highness, Princess Grace of Monaco, since April of 1956.

I grew to know her quite well during her short reign in the realm of movietown. The Princess of Monaco, however, is almost a stranger to me. It is therefore natural that I think of her more easily and recall her more vividly as Miss Kelly of Hollywood, than I do as Her Highness, Serene or otherwise.

I first met Grace when she appeared on my radio show shortly after she finished working in *High Noon* opposite Gary Cooper. At this time the movie was still unreleased and Grace agreed to appear on my radio show to help exploit it.

Her beauty literally lit up our broadcasting studio. There are some women who are beautiful on the screen but lose a part of that loveliness off it. Not Grace.

In preparing the material for our "aired" interview, I noticed that she found it difficult to talk about herself. She particularly shunned

189

discussing her background which was, in simple language—Grace was the adored daughter of the extremely wealthy Jack Kellys of Philadelphia.

Her father, brawny, handsome, Irish through and through, was a fascinating "story" in himself. Starting out as a bricklayer, he had come up the success-and-money ladder so fast he frequently admitted the ascent had left him dizzy. You'd never have guessed it. His level-headed astuteness was foremost in everything he undertook from his success in the construction field, and later in politics and athletics. As a young man he had won the Olympic sculling championship.

Jack Kelly married a woman as handsome as himself and together they produced a physically beautiful clan of young Kellys—all of determined mind and strong personality.

But back to our radio interview. If she did not care to talk about her prominent background—how did she feel about this career she had chosen, an unusual one for a girl of great wealth?

"I came here to act" she said, "and to learn." (Not exactly burning radio interview copy.)

Would she compare Broadway, where she got her start, with Hollywood?

"Wouldn't that be silly? I'm not an authority on either—and I'm in love with both."

We settled on the neutral ground of discussing the part she had just played. Grace spoke of her sincere admiration for Gary Cooper and her respect for Fred Zinnemann who had directed *High Noon*. Frankly, the "material" I got from Grace was far from being my most scintillating radio interview!

It was some time before I again talked with her. In the meantime she had gone to Nairobi, in Africa, to star with Clark Gable and Ava Gardner in *Mogambo*. While this trio was in Africa, reports wafted home that Gable, the King, was more than slightly interested in Grace. This was during the interlude when Clark was divorced from Lady Sylvia Ashley and not yet married to Kay Williams.

When the MGM company returned, I asked Clark if there was any truth in the gossip that he had "flipped" for his blond co-star.

Clark chuckled. "Why, Louella—she's just a kid." Then he added, "And what a nice kid."

Frankly, Clark, who was very much a man of the world despite all his down-to-earth he-man type publicity, was a bit amazed that Grace's family had permitted her to take the trip to Africa unchaperoned. Not that she was in moral danger—but it was a difficult location, primitive in part, dangerous. "How she was permitted to go there alone, a girl like Grace, is something I'll never understand."

I was amused that Clark felt it was so unseemly for Grace to be unchaperoned in the wilderness and expressed no such sentiment about Ava! But I was to learn that, among other reactions, Grace had the knack of arousing protectiveness in the male breast.

From my woman's point of view, I always felt that Miss Kelly was big enough—five feet seven inches, plus the "Kelly" in her make-up—to take care of herself. Time, I think, has proved me right.

What was it, I asked Clark, that had impressed him most about Grace?

"She's the kind of a girl you can have fun with," he said enthusiastically. "She used to get up early in the morning to go big-game hunting with me. It wasn't easy, and my God, the smells! But she never complained."

After *Mogambo* was released it was obvious that Grace had "bagged" stardom. An actress and a beauty, she became an outstanding box office bet. Plus becoming one of the most publicized girls in town, especially in the romance department.

Her name was linked with practically every male she said hello to; unfairly, I thought. I suppose the gossips felt a man just couldn't be around Grace without falling for her—and few of them disputed the talk whether it was true or false.

And then came into being a romance which never should have been. Grace went into Alfred Hitchcock's *Dial M for Murder* with Ray Milland!

Ray had been a quiet, dependable, talented part of the Hollywood scene for almost as many years as Grace had been alive. He was a good actor, an important one, and for many years had been contentedly married to lovely Mal Milland, the mother of his two children.

It is true Ray and Mal had weathered some stormy moments in the early years of their marriage, once even going so far as to separate. But that had been many years ago. At the time *Dial M for Murder*

191

started, the Millands had long presented a happy marital front to the world—and to Hollywood.

Almost from the beginning there was talk that Ray seemed to have lapsed into a "daze" about Grace. I didn't pay too much attention to the gossip which reached my ears. Whether it is right or wrong, the propinquity of picture-making, attractive people being thrown together day after day in the most romantic love scenes, frequently sparks these "set" flirtations. When the picture is finished, so—often— is the infatuation. No harm done, as a rule.

But when Ray unexpectedly moved out of the family home and took up residence in an apartment in Hollywood, the talk flamed into the open.

A deplorable situation seemed in the making.

About the time the rumors were really beginning to catch fire about Grace and Milland, Grace paid me a visit. The "serenity" she was later to acquire was missing. Instead, it was a nervous and troubled girl who came to my home one cocktail hour.

At first she talked about this and that—nothing important. But it was obvious she had real trouble on her mind. I had never seen the cool Miss Kelly so perturbed, so lacking in poise. She wasn't actually twisting her hands—but she might as well have been.

And suddenly, the pent-up storm burst forth.

She was, she felt, deeply in love with Milland. On meeting him, she had found him charming. Working with him, her first reaction had been respect for his ability as an actor. Then she had grown infatuated with him. And he was a married man.

Grace was hurt—and horrified by the situation. Because she is a very religious Roman Catholic, marriage is a holy sacrament to her. Now she found herself torn between the teachings of her religion and her feelings and emotions.

A Catholic myself, I pointed out that she had known from the start that Ray was a married man.

"But, I thought, separated from his wife. I thought they had been separated for some time," she explained desperately. I told her I knew this wasn't true. I had talked with Mal.

I tried as best I could to advise her. The conflict she was experi-

192

encing was personal and the ultimate decision would have to be hers. I did say that her whole religious training was a part of her from which she could not escape even if she wanted to—and obviously she did not want to.

We sat together a long time and I learned during that time what a basically warm, sincere girl operated behind the seemingly cold beauty. I was never again to see Grace Kelly as she was that afternoon: alone, and a little frightened. And very appealing.

When she left, I was still not sure whether or not my words had been of any help.

I found out a few days later. I received a gift I have always treasured. It was a gold bracelet, a chain with a crystal ball dangling from it. Inside the crystal was a mustard seed. Along with the gift came a message in Grace's handwriting, a quotation from St. Matthew:

"If ye have faith as a grain of mustard seed, ye shall say unto the mountain, Remove hence to yonder place; and it shall remove, and nothing shall be impossible to you."

Never again did we mention Ray Milland to each other. I got the "message"!

I feel that Ray did fall in love with Grace—and out of it. There is no question in my mind but that she had that effect on men. I've been told so often enough. I also feel, and have felt, that Ray gave Grace the wrong impression about his estrangement from Mal. But what man has ever found it possible to tell only the truth, and the whole truth, when he was hit by such an infatuation as Ray felt for Grace?

Some time afterward he came to me and discussed this experience. "I don't know what hit me," he said. "Deep in my heart I loved Mal and always have." Then he went on to say how much he was missing his wife and children. They were still separated.

Later Mal and Ray reconciled and I have always been happy that they were able to accept Ray's behavior for what it was—a sudden but honest infatuation; nothing more.

Grace, too, made a quick recovery.

She went on to appear in new pictures, all of them successful, and always with Hollywood's top stars. I kept hearing that some of these stars had crushes on Grace—and vice versa—but somehow I had the feeling that nothing would come of these. There were just too many of them.

Then in 1954 Grace went to Europe to the Cannes Film Festival. At that time she was being seen quite often with Jean-Pierre Aumont, the French star, whose wife Maria Montez had died so suddenly.

Also at Cannes were Olivia De Haviland and her French husband, Pierre Galante, editor of the magazine *Paris-Match*. Galante wanted to do a story on Grace but, lovely as she was—important star that she was—she was also notoriously "bad" copy. Grace was always the lady; restrained in manner, careful of what she said and certainly no prospect for that stand-by of picture magazines—leg pictures.

Galante came up with the idea of a story and layout based on the meeting of Hollywood "royalty" and Monacan royalty, Prince Rainier. It would require co-operation from both Grace and the Prince, and it was Olivia who managed to get the promise of this. The meeting was arranged and Grace went to call on the Prince, accompanied by a battery of photographers.

Some time later, Grace told her mother that Rainier was "extremely charming, although I did think he seemed extremely shy, for a Prince."

Soon afterward Grace came home, still unattached, and Jean-Pierre passed out of her life as Clark Gable, Ray Milland and some others had.

A few months later, after a series of rumors most of which were dismissed, came the announcement that Grace was engaged to marry Prince Rainier.

And, as I have remarked, with that announcement Grace became a Princess and felt that she could no longer indulge in such talks as we had had and which had led to her sending me the bracelet. However, the story of the engagement and how it came about was not to remain a state secret. It was to be revealed in a ten-part series of articles by a nonprofessional writer but one who certainly had access to the facts: Mrs. John B. Kelly, Grace's mother.

This was a most interesting, if ingenuous, series and was by-lined, "By Mrs. John B. Kelly, as told to Richard Gehman." Above each

194

article there was a note that "Mrs. Kelly's royalties from these articles are being sent in their entirety to the Women's Medical College of Philadelphia." This college, the only medical college exclusively for women in the United States, was Mrs. Kelly's favorite charity.

The articles were most enlightening, with Mrs. Kelly beginning by saying that the very last thing that had ever entered her mind was the possibility that Grace might become a "real-life, honest-to-goodness Princess."

Mrs. Kelly also wrote that, over the years, "Grace had had a number of affairs of the heart; some rather serious, some rather trifling." Mrs. Kelly said she had approved of some of them, had disapproved of others, but had never interfered.

In another installment, Mrs. Kelly said that when Grace became a star, "gossip columnists, hard up for material" had linked Grace's name with everyone she dated and that, in the case of Ray Milland, "this was blown up beyond all proportion."

I thought, reading the articles, that Mrs. Kelly had rather approved of Oleg Cassini, the dress designer who had been married to lovely, unhappy Gene Tierney and who, in recent years, was much publicized as Mrs. Jack Kennedy's *coutourier*.

But it was when detailing just how Grace and Rainier III ultimately became engaged that Mrs. Kelly did her best job of reporting.

It had all started innocently enough. Some friends of the Kellys —Mr. and Mrs. Russell Austin, of Margate, New Jersey—were visiting at Monte Carlo and found they could not get a table at the casino. Recalling that Grace knew Prince Rainier, Mrs. Kelly reported, "Mr. Austin, a forthright kind of man, called the palace and explained he was a friend of Grace's."

The explanation, for some reason—possibly because he was an American—was given to the Prince's spiritual adviser and chaplain, Father Francis Tucker. Father Tucker not only arranged for the Austins to get a fine table, but also invited them to the palace the next day, where they met Prince Rainier.

When the Austins returned to the United States, they told the elder Kellys that the Prince had talked of nothing but Grace.

Then, in the early winter of 1955, Prince Rainier came to the United States for a physical checkup. He accepted an invitation to spend Christmas with the Austins. By coincidence, Grace was home that Christmas. And the Austins asked the Kellys if they might bring their royal visitor to the Kellys' home for a visit. Just a nice, homely, friendly, democratic group.

The Kellys would be delighted.

The Austins, the Prince, Father Tucker and Dr. Donat, the Prince's personal physician, came to dinner. The Prince, Mrs. Kelly said, "was simple and democratic." He monopolized Grace all during the meal.

Afterward, the elder Kelly drove Father Tucker to the railroad station to catch a train. The Prince just stayed on and Mrs. Kelly reported, "He was reluctant to leave . . . and I knew, by glancing at my daughter, that she didn't want him to go. Impulsively, I suggested that perhaps the Prince and Dr. Donat would like to stay at our house overnight. . . . The Prince agreed so rapidly that I knew, then and there, that his intentions were not just those of a smitten young man. There was purpose in his every word and movement."

Later, Grace took the Prince to visit her married sister. During their absence, Father Kelly informed Mother Kelly that, while driving Father Tucker to the train, he had been informed by Father Tucker that the Prince wanted to marry Grace. Father Tucker had been empowered to say so as the Prince's representative. So very Old World. So very European.

Then began a series of engagements in which Grace and the Prince took part. (Engagements, not "dates," and even Clark Gable would have been unable to protest that Grace was unchaperoned or unprotected. They were always accompanied by Father Tucker, Dr. Donat or some of the various Kellys.)

And thus real-life romance came to the girl from Philadelphia. Mrs. Kelly closed the articles with the wish that these "two wonderful young people be permitted their privilege of privacy so they can live happy, normal lives and assume their responsibilities with comfort and happiness."

It was as the fiancée of Prince Rainier that Grace returned to make her last picture, *High Society*, with Frank Sinatra, Bing Crosby and Louis Armstrong.

196

And, as I have said, she was changed. Cooler. More reserved. More distant. But for all that she was a real woman. She had the biggest engagement ring and when I went out to visit the set of *High Society* she took time off to show it to me.

"I even sleep with it," she told me, "I hate to take it off. It's the most beautiful piece of jewelry I've ever owned."

I have since thought that she was going through a trying period of self-doubt. Her courtship had been so quick—and so well policed. She was an American girl, brought up in a world where freedom was personal as well as general, and where she could go off to Nairobi by herself. Her values were normal Irish-American values and it was only by these that she could make judgments. And I suppose she must have been recalling other times when she had believed herself in love.

As a devout Catholic, she was entering marriage with a knowledge of its finality, and it might have been that very knowledge which made her withdraw into herself.

All this, of course, is nothing but conjecture on my part. Perhaps I have read too many scripts over the years. It could well have been that none of these thoughts ever occurred to her, and that she kept aloof from those whom she had known so well in Hollywood because she wanted to, and that was that.

I saw Grace at the huge engagement party which MGM gave in her honor and she again showed me her beautiful ring.

And then, on April 19, 1956, Grace Kelly became the wife of Prince Rainier; became a Princess, Her Serene Highness. It was quite a ceremony, with more than 1500 reporters and photographers present to report and photograph the pomp and circumstance. As you probably recall, things got slightly out of hand and it was necessary for the Prince to ask the French to provide a riot squad to restore normality to the principality of Monaco.

Hollywood's main representative at the wedding was Ava Gardner. These two had been close friends ever since *Mogambo*. There were many hurt feelings when Grace ignored directors, producers and actors who had helped build her career.

Like so many others out here, I clung to the belief that Grace would be coming back to Hollywood. I suppose it was wishful thinking. Somehow, even now, I get the feeling that being Princess of Monaco isn't a life to Grace, but a part. A wonderfully tailored part.

She has not seen much of her Hollywood friends since her marriage. She has borne two children; Caroline, the older, and Albert, Prince and heir to the throne. And what cheers greeted Albert's birth! The subjects of the Prince and Princess really celebrated. After all, if there had been no male heir, Monaco would have reverted to French rule—and French taxation.

I have heard from Grace several times since she left us. Not so long ago I received a photograph of Grace, the Prince and their two children, warmly inscribed to me.

When Grace's father died, I wrote to express my sympathy. Grace answered in a letter with much of the warmth that I recalled from our first meetings. And later she telephoned me. She and the Prince took separate planes to return home after the funeral and there were reports that they had quarreled. I asked about this.

"It's silly. We just don't like to fly together, Louella. If anything were to happen, the children would lose both parents at once. Take my word for it. All's well with us."

I'm glad that all is well with them. I suspect it is as difficult for two persons in their kind of fairytale world to have an always untroubled life as it is for those of us who live in more mundane worlds. Whatever our world, we have our human weaknesses, our moments of stress.

Recently, when Grace and Prince Rainier III celebrated their fifth wedding anniversary, a great deal was written about them. It was interesting to me to read that Grace had gone out of her way to discuss two quite personal matters. The first had to do with the "dowry" her father was supposed to have given Prince Rainier at the time of the marriage.

He gave no dowry, Grace said.

The second had to do with the fact that Prince Rainier had been left no bequest in John B. Kelly's will.

Why should he have been? Grace asked. Her father had not given any bequests to any of his sons-in-law. Instead, he had named his wife and his children.

And, as a postscript, Grace remarked that her husband had no

198

need of dowry or inheritance. He had plenty of money of his own.

There were some lovely pictures of Grace accompanying the article. She is now in her very early thirties, a little heavier than when she was in films and had to be not just thin, but almost skinny. The few extra pounds add to her beauty.

It was bound to happen, of course. That Hollywood should produce a star who would not only look like a reigning Princess, but be one.

It couldn't have happened to anyone more fitting.

➤➤➤ *Chapter 13*

THE NEW FRONTIER

SOMEONE remarked, when the stars became their own producers, "The inmates are now running the asylum."

This wasn't as crazy as it sounds.

With the advent of TV, the lessening of productions at the major studios and the curtailing of contract lists, there was a rush of acting, writing and directing talent anxious to cross the starting line into the New Frontier, and stake out homesteads in the wide-open spaces vacated by the studios which had had pretty much of a monopoly on picturemaking until then.

Of the stars, Jimmy Stewart was the first to form his own producing company along with director Frank Capra. Later, Jimmy was also the first actor to make a deal that gave him a percentage of the gross and a share of the profits; the bounty to be found in this New Frontier where they were prospecting for gold in the form of cold hard cash and capital gains.

In time, Burt Lancaster, John Wayne, Frank Sinatra, Marlon Brando, Richard Widmark, Gregory Peck, William Holden, Van Heflin, Kirk Douglas, Dean Martin, Doris Day and Jerry Lewis doubled in brass as producer-stars.

Just as nothing is new under the Hollywood sun or in its movie scripts, stars producing their own pictures weren't completely original. Long before John Wayne produced, starred in, directed and defended *The Alamo*, Charles Chaplin, Mary Pickford, Douglas Fairbanks and exhibitor Joseph Schenck formed United Artists to release pictures in which they starred. They emerged millionaires in those comparatively tax-free days. In time, United Artists, without the box-office draw of the Fairbanks, Pickfords and Chaplins, went into the red; and little more than ten years ago, a new United Artists was formed by an enterprising, far-seeing group of businessmen headed by Chairman of the Board Robert S. Benjamin and President Arthur B. Krim.

This new setup released and helped finance many of the independent productions of the stars themselves as well as the product of other independent producers; among them the Mirisch Brothers, Harold and Walter, former film distributors.

The impact and effectiveness of the new independents was dramatically demonstrated the night of the 1961 Academy Awards. Every major award but one went to an independent film. *The Apartment*, made by the Mirisch Brothers and released through UA, won five awards—best picture, best direction, best original screenplay, best black-and-white art direction and best film editing.

The Mirisch Brothers are so forward in their thinking, with freedom and independence for all—especially the creative talent of Hollywood—that they permitted Billy Wilder to produce as well as direct this highly decorated *Apartment*. He also collaborated on the screenplay with I. A. L. Diamond.

Yes sir, the last Academy Awards were really a tribute to Hollywood's own Declaration of Independence.

Producer-actor Burt Lancaster won the best acting plum with his incisive portrayal of the title role in *Elmer Gantry*. His coproducer, writer-director (and now producer) Richard Brooks, got a gold statuette all his own for the screenplay he wrote, based on material from another medium—the Sinclair Lewis novel. And to top off honors, Shirley Jones annexed the best-supporting-actress award for her performance of a tart in the same picture.

Kirk Douglas' Bryna Productions, Inc., which releases through

Universal-International, saw one of its players—Peter Ustinov—win the best supporting actor award for *Spartacus*.

The only major studio to grab a big award was Metro-Goldwyn-Mayer. After four successive nominations, Elizabeth Taylor finally won her Oscar for *Butterfield 8*.

The New Frontier has one new producer who stands out like a beacon of hope to the motion-picture industry; Joseph E. Levine, President of Embassy Pictures Corp. He's a born gambler and takes chances much as Sam Goldwyn did in the earlier days. In fact Joe, whom I know very well, said to me, "You can do a big favor for me." I knew he didn't want to borrow money because he talks in millions. "I want to meet Sam Goldwyn," he said, "I have admired him for a long time."

Now Sam has earned the right to be a little hard to get to if he chooses, and I wasn't sure what he would say when I telephoned him at the Sherry-Netherlands where he was staying. I mentioned that Joe had a bum leg.

"Well, that's easy," said Sam. "I'll go to his office. I want to meet him, too."

I first heard about Joe when one of my editors suggested I write a story about him. Born in Boston, he had descended upon New York like a cyclone. Joe never does things halfway. He had been an exhibitor in New England and if ever there was an Horatio Alger story, Joe can claim title to it.

Like myself, he's lucky. With a $35,000 nest egg, he paid down on *Hercules*, starring one Steve Reeves, an unknown. The picture wasn't good, but so great was Joe's advertising prowess that it made millions and made a star out of Steve Reeves, who received $10,000 for *Hercules* but who now commands $200,000 a picture. This 200-pound muscleman now figures his muscles are worth $1,000 per pound. He's one fellow who'd better not diet.

Joe Levine spends a fortune in exploiting his pictures; and his very talented and artistic wife Rosalie designs all the promotional gadgets which her husband gives away to get word-of-mouth advertising.

To give a concrete example of Joe's good luck, he saw a picture in Italy, *Two Women*, starring Sophia Loren. He bought the American distribution rights. Shortly afterward, Sophia won the Cannes Film Festival Award for her performance. Joe leaves no stone unturned in his efforts to make the most of any opportunity. He brought Sophia to New York concurrently with the picture's opening, and for ten days launched a typical Herculean campaign. Sophia, all the green-eyed voluptuous beauty of her, willingly appeared on TV, radio and interviews to plug her picture which she told me she thought was the best she had ever made.

After the first story I wrote about Joe, he and I became good friends. Then started an avalanche of stories, even in *Time* magazine. He gives me credit for discovering him; as if you had to discover Joseph Levine.

Much of Joe's revenue has come from buying pictures already produced. He's been decorated by the Italian government, but now he has gone into producing his own pictures with such stars as Kim Novak, James Garner, Gig Young, Tony Randall and Donald O'Connor. Whether he will do as well with his own productions remains to be seen, but MGM and Warner Brothers vie to release the films he buys abroad with his shrewd instinct for what will bring people to the box office. We need more showmen like Joe Levine who isn't afraid to take a chance and is willing to spend money to make money.

I have always felt that creative people should be able to keep as much of the money they earn as they legally can. Frequently, their years of great earning power are limited. How well I know. The Motion Picture Country Home is filled with disillusioned folk whose fame and fortunes ran out at the same time.

The capital-gains approach to taxes was the best solution Hollywood found to eke extra revenue from its earnings. In time the government quickly stepped in with "cross-collateralization," which in plain words meant that the actors couldn't make separate deals for each of their pictures, but had to make deals covering a number of pictures and profits. This way losses of the entire group of pictures were balanced against each other. One failure could wipe out the profits of two or three successes and often did.

Many actors discovered they were actually making less money by operating their own companies than they would have made by either straight salaries or a percentage of the profits. Marilyn Monroe, who's anything but a dumb blonde, earned over a million dollars for her profit-participation deal in *Some Like It Hot*.

I think Burt Lancaster's success story is the most fantastic of all, and I might add, financially as well as artistically. His private life, like his tax ledgers, can withstand the closest scrutiny.

Bronx-born, Burt quit Manhattan's New York University where he had an athletic scholarship, to form a trapeze act with a friend. For ten years he worked in small circuses. Then the war came and he went into the service. While performing in a camp show, he met his wife Norma, a member of a USO troupe.

After the war, Burt's rise to stardom began funnily enough in an elevator where a theatrical producer spotted the long, lean, handsome veteran and signed him to play a top sergeant in *The Sound of Hunting*. The play ran long enough for Burt to get some movie offers and an agent, Harold Hecht. All of the big agencies were after Burt but he turned them down for the lesser-known Hecht.

"I'm a gambler," Burt told me later, "and Hecht said that someday we would produce our own pictures together. That was the biggest gamble I'd ever heard of so I signed." Hal Wallis put Burt under contract and loaned him out to Mark Hellinger for *The Killers* which made Burt a star.

Later he was cast in a picture with an actress who liked to collect men as a hobby and wanted to add Burt to her collection. He dampened her ardor very quickly and succinctly, by inviting her to his home to meet his wife and their first baby, Jim.

In 1953 the Hecht-Hill-Lancaster Company was formed. The third partner was James Hill, who later was to marry Rita Hayworth. The trio hit the jackpot in their production, *Marty*. Burt didn't even appear in the picture which was offbeat from the word go. The hero was a butcher—an ungainly, unprepossessing man—magnificently portrayed by Ernest Borgnine. The now historic *Marty* took the 1955 awards for best picture, best actor and best director. It also won the Grand Prix at the Cannes Motion Picture Festival; the first American picture to win this prize since World War II.

Not all their pictures made money. Later the producing trio broke

204

up and Burt formed his alliance with Richard Brooks for *Elmer Gantry.*

Star-producer Kirk Douglas, a strong-jawed young man in both looks and actions, came from a poor family in upstate New York. "I was trying to work my way through college doing janitor work," Kirk told me. "One night I got into a poker game and lost my eating money. I had to go home to get fed.

" 'What a fool you are,' my mother said to me when I explained what had happened. 'You bet money on cards. What do the cards care about you? If you want to bet, bet on yourself. Your chances are better' . . . I've tried to follow that advice ever since," Kirk admitted.

In both *The Vikings* and *Spartacus,* which he produced, Kirk went for broke. He insisted upon making the pictures the way he wanted to without regard to cost. "I started from the bottom before, so if I lose everything I'll just start from the bottom again," Kirk told me.

To each his own. I personally prefer a little security.

Another he-man who struck out on his own—one of the screen's most virile men—is a former college-football star who was born with the sissy monicker of "Marion" Morrison. Movie fans know him as John Wayne, but he's "Duke" to all his friends. Duke's Batjac company has been successful. His most recent production, *The Alamo,* was nominated for an Academy Award. Its box-office success has been especially gratifying to the producer-director-star because he feels it's a justification of his deep, unswerving patriotism. This picture, he told me, with its theme of American history, would be a weapon in the war against Communism.

Not long ago I was talking to Duke and he said, in his famous drawl, "You know, Louella, you're a good girl and I'm fond of you."

"Go on," I teased, "you're only saying that because I write nice things about you."

"Not at all," he protested. "I think you're a good American and I like people who are good Americans."

A simple sentiment that comes from John Wayne's heart; but then, he's not a complex man and makes no pretense that he is.

205

Simplicity has paid off for him. He's been one of the biggest money-making stars since 1949, when the boundaries of the New Frontier widened in Hollywood.

At first glance, for Jerry Lewis to cast himself in the role of his own producer would seem to be offbeat casting for this zany comedian who never stops trying to be funny. Yet beneath that crew cut is one of the shrewdest heads in Hollywood.

Before Jerry and Dean Martin broke up the million-dollar partnership, Paramount Pictures, seeking to protect its interest in the team (which was feuding off-stage) put $5,000,000 into the boys' independent company, York Productions. But nothing could hold these two together once they stopped thinking the other wasn't very funny. To prove himself, after the split, Jerry began directing his own pictures as well as producing them. No matter what grownups may think about the farfetched characters Jerry inevitably portrays, the kids love him and his pictures clean up.

Dean, who has a beautiful singing voice and is a handsome Italian, went on to bigger things. He became one of the most popular male stars on the screen and had every company bidding for him.

I am much closer to Dean than I am to Jerry. I know him better. He is fun loving, but as he says, "I have to work, with seven children to support"—four by his first wife and three by his beautiful second wife, Jeanne, the former Jeanne Biggers.

Dean threw in his lot with Frank Sinatra, Peter Lawford, Joey Bishop and Sammy Davis, Jr. If I have any criticism of Dean, it's the fact that he pretends to be unable to utter one word without a glass in his hand. It has given Dean the reputation of being a real drunk. This isn't true.

Dean too has his own company. He and Shirley MacLaine recently made a picture, *All in a Night's Work,* for his own company, released through Paramount.

Probably the biggest money-maker for herself and for the people for whom she works, is my neighbor in Beverly Hills, Miss Doris Day—she of the provocative freckles, the sweet singing voice and the fresh well-scrubbed "girl-next-door" look. Doris' husband, Marty Melcher, acts as executive producer on all her movies. This duo turns out one hit after another, both on film and records. Doris has so many gold discs for her hit recordings that she could panel a room with them.

There is another type of actor-businessman today, but this breed stands in danger of becoming extinct if the federal law is passed whereby Americans living out of the country for eighteen months still have to fork over to Uncle Sam the high percentage of income that we other Americans are content to pay for the privilege of being Americans.

William Holden is a prime example of this. He has chosen to take up residence in Switzerland and profit from the tax laws of both that country and the United States' eighteen-months-abroad clause.

Bill had to die on the screen to really come alive at the box office. That was when he played the part of the screen writer, in *Sunset Boulevard*, whose body opened and closed the picture as it floated in the immense swimming pool of the faded Hollywood star, played by Gloria Swanson.

Ava Gardner has chosen Spain as a place to live and stay; if not untaxed, less overtaxed, let's say. Jack Palance is making his pictures overseas. Carl Foreman, the writer and producer, has been living in Europe and getting all the advantages allowed him under the tax laws.

Fortunately for all of us who live and work in Hollywood, the industry is making more money than ever before. We are making fewer feature films, it's true, but the ones turned out by the major studios as well as by the independent producers, are really bigger and better —and frequently longer—than ever.

Television, and the production of films for that product-consuming medium, has taken up the slack. Many of the stars formed their own television producing units.

Dick Powell, who heads Four Star Productions, has become a millionaire since he crossed the TV frontier. Everyone knows the fabulous success story of Desilu Productions, wherein Lucille Ball and her then husband, Desi Arnaz—out of the millions they made producing *I Love Lucy* and other TV shows—actually bought the RKO studios where they first met and worked together in pictures.

The studios are humming with activity and that is a sweet sound indeed to anyone like myself who has seen Hollywood through its depressions, its recessions, its ups and downs.

One of the outstanding Frontiersmen is a young man I have a special interest in. He is William Orr, recently appointed by Jack Warner as head of the studio; not only in charge of TV film production but the regular product as well. Warner Brothers, under Bill Orr's supervision, turns out eight hours of filmed TV fare a week; the equivalent of making nearly a feature film a day. *Cheyenne, 77 Sunset Strip, Maverick, Hawaiian Eye*—all of which Bill Orr created, among others—not only clicked financially, but unearthed valuable stars in Efrem Zimbalist, Jr. and James Garner.

My interest in Bill Orr dates back to 1939 and '40 when I took a troupe of young Hollywood stars on a nation-wide tour, the first road show of this kind. I chose the most promising young players from each studio, among them Jane Wyman, Ronald Reagan, Susan Hayward, Robert Stack. Orr came to my attention when I saw him on the stage in *Meet The People*. Bill was a brash young man—he's only forty-two now—who had the courage of his convictions even then. No one impressed him and that's a pretty important asset for a producer. Bill defied me every chance he had and rewrote my act every day, needless to say making his own part bigger—and bigger. Many were the battles we had. He did an imitation of both Franklin Delano and Eleanor Roosevelt in the act and every performance he gave got longer and longer.

Robert Stack was known then, not as the star of TV's *The Untouchables*, but as the rich society boy in real life who gave Deanna Durbin her first screen kiss. His blond, curly hair and serious manner gave young Bill Orr a brilliant idea—or so he thought. One day, unbeknownst to me, Bill went out on the stage and spoke to the audience. "When Bob Stack comes out," he said, "don't give him any applause, just sit perfectly still and silent. It's a joke. We'll explain later." The audience entered into the game and you can imagine the surprise on Bob's bewildered face when not one sound came from the audience. Bill sneaked up to a box to watch the effect.

As soon as I learned what was going on, I went out and explained that the joke was over and they could applaud to their hearts' content.

Then twenty years later, when Bill became studio head, I wrote about him because I've always been extremely fond of him.

He sent me flowers, thanked me and said, "When do we hit the road again?"

⇝ *Chapter 14*

DOUBTING CINDERELLA

To me, Marilyn Monroe is a Cinderella who is certain that twelve o'clock is going to strike any minute of the day or night. She doesn't believe in fairy godmothers.

That is why I believe she will never realize her full potential. It isn't so much that she believes failure is personal, but that she believes failure is inevitable in life, in love and in work. The fault, she insists, is in our stars.

Don't think I'm downgrading Marilyn. Let me go on record right now as saying that she is the most exciting movie personality of this generation. She possesses the star quality that has to be natural; that can't be manufactured. And the femaleness—the right word because femininity is something else—that makes every man a satyr in his own mind.

No one has ever described this quality better than Clara Bow in a letter she wrote me last Christmas. She said:

"Not to [Elizabeth] Taylor, not to [Brigitte] Bardot, but to Monroe did I mentally bestow the 'It Girl' tag some time ago. She and Jean Harlow are the only women I've ever seen who possessed the flesh impact that people said I had on the screen. What do you think, Louella?"

210

That term—"flesh impact"—is the most apt I have ever heard. It does describe Marilyn's effect. And, for the record, let me add that Marilyn has the advantage of being a good actress. She has exhibited a wonderful sense of timing in handling comedy and an ability to "feel" a dramatic part even when she couldn't define that feeling in words.

With these advantages, Marilyn should be capable of conquering all cinematic worlds. But so far, despite her success, she has not. Her potential, revealed in picture after picture, has never been fully reached. Instead of being the great star she should be, she still remains only a most striking personality.

To put it bluntly, Marilyn Monroe is bigger in the news than she is on the screen, large as she looms on film.

Marilyn was made for printer's ink and printer's ink was made for her. She captures the imagination. That's been true of her as long as I've known her. It goes back all the years to the times when I used to see her at Joseph Schenck's home where I so often dined.

Joe and I have been friends for a long, long time. We met when I was working in Chicago and he was just entering the motion-picture business.

In those beginning days, when I first got to know Marilyn, Joe was still active and powerful at 20th Century-Fox. It should have been quite easy for him to get her career into high gear at that studio. It wasn't.

The reason was Darryl Zanuck, then head of production at Fox.

No matter what Joe tried to tell him about Marilyn, Zanuck insisted that she was not the material of which stars were made. He admitted that she was beautiful. Nothing more. He felt that at best she would be a "starlet," an all-encompassing term that meant little, and someone who looked attractive posing for cheesecake art for promotion purposes. He maintained that she could not act and that he didn't believe she would ever learn.

And, despite Joe's importance and prestige, Zanuck would not be budged.

Joe, however, felt that Darryl was wrong. He continued to push for Marilyn, told her that despite Zanuck she would someday be a star. He called her his "Number 3 girl," and put her just behind me, whom he had long before dubbed his "Number 2 girl," and both of us behind some anonymous "Number 1 girl."

Yet, even in those days Marilyn hoped, but she did not believe. She was grateful for everything Joe did for her, but when so little came of it she was not surprised. "He was very kind to me," she said, "always treated me like a lady and gave me excellent advice."

To which Joe added, when I told him this, "Advice which she never took."

I had heard about Marilyn long before I met her. It was Ben Lyon, married to my oldest friend, Bebe Daniels, who first talked to me about her. During the 1940's, Ben and Bebe came back to the United States from England, their adopted home. Ben shortly afterward became head talent scout for Fox.

One day an agent called Ben and said she had a new client whom Ben ought to meet. "Her name is Norma Jean Daugherty. She's been modeling and now Howard Hughes wants to have her tested."

It seemed that Howard, then in the hospital as the result of his almost fatal crack-up in an experimental plane, had seen some pictures of "Norma Jean Daugherty" in a magazine. They had revealed a lot of Norma Jean but not whether she could act.

As soon as Ben heard that Howard was interested, he was also interested. After all, Howard's batting average in picking female film personalities was better than that of Ty Cobb in baseball. He arranged to meet Norma Jean immediately.

Ben liked what he saw. "She had a good face," he told me. "You can tell with some faces—the way the flesh sits on the bones; the planes and angles—that they'll photograph well. And she was real blond, a rarity. In addition, there was the way she moved." He might have been the first to notice that movement but he certainly was not the last.

He told the agent he would like to test Norma Jean but that it would require Zanuck's approval. (Remember, all this came before Joe Schenck became interested in Norma Jean—Marilyn.) At that time, everything that took place at the studio required Zanuck's approval, and why not? He was the boss.

The agent, however, was aware that in Hollywood you didn't wait until tomorrow to press the advantage you had today. It might be gone by tomorrow. "I'll give you two days," the agent said. "Don't forget, Howard Hughes is interested."

Ben didn't forget. He tried to get through to Zanuck before the deadline but found it impossible. He decided to take a gamble—to make the test without Zanuck's okay. To do this required almost as much mystery and suspense as a Hitchcock picture. Anything as important as a test without Zanuck's approval was like getting a story in *Pravda* without Khrushchev's permission.

As few people as possible had to be involved. The fewer those concerned, the less chance that word would get around the studio. So Ben decided to test Norma Jean by himself. He persuaded Leon Shamroy, one of Fox's top cameramen, to shoot it. He personally spirited a solid-sequined evening dress out of the wardrobe department.

When Norma Jean had been poured into the gown and her face been properly made up, Ben gave her a few small pieces of "business." Then he told her, "I just want you to walk across the stage. I want you to project sex the same way you do in the still pictures."

She did just that. When Ben saw the test on the screen, he just gaped. "It was incredible," he told me. "She was all fire."

Zanuck apparently agreed. Despite the fact that the test had been made without his knowledge or authorization, he raised no fuss. Instead he ordered that Norma Jean be signed to a contract.

Next it was decided that her name be changed. Because she so reminded Ben of Marilyn Miller, that ill-fated sprite of the Broadway theatre, he suggested she take that first name. And the second name, "Monroe," was chosen for a number of reasons, depending upon who tells the story. It has been said that it was a family name of Marilyn's mother and that Marilyn chose it because President James Monroe was one of her ancestors. Or it might have been that it sounded good and the stories came later. It still doesn't matter. What does matter is that Norma Jean Daugherty became Marilyn Monroe and Marilyn Monroe has become part of the folk history of our times.

If beauty is in the eye of the beholder, as has been reported, I must add that sin is in his mind. I have learned through the years that people are not only willing to think the worst of others, but having invented the thought they quickly decide that it's fact. And much of Marilyn's public reputation, I feel, is based on just this.

I know that immediately after it was reported that Fox had signed Marilyn, rumors started that Ben had a personal interest in her success. The fact that Ben was then, had been (and still is) a happily married man didn't bother the rumormongers. What was a reputation or two to them?

I don't pretend to know all the details of Marilyn's personal life. She has a right to it and is responsible only to herself and to God. But I would like to go on record as saying that in my relations with her I have seen that she is ridden by a sense of sin. Not guilt, but a sense of sin in the Puritan meaning. Her concepts are like those of the revivalist preachers only she takes them more seriously than the Elmer Gantrys of the world.

Marilyn may give the impression of being a Circe, a siren, a temptress incarnate but that is only what she looks like. I believe that the appearance has been taken for the reality.

If I were asked to choose one adjective with which to describe Marilyn, I would choose "frightened." That was the way Ben Lyon described her to me not long after her screen test. "I want you to see for yourself," he said.

So I viewed the test and there it was—fright, sheer fright. It came out of her eyes and created a feeling of compassion in me that I have never lost. I think she has always known this and it explains why she has turned to me, confided in me often during some of her unhappiest moments. And, poor darling, she has known so many of them.

The story of her illegitimate birth and her harried, frustrated, insecure childhood has been told and retold. A lot of people have made a monetary profit out of just this retelling; not caring what effect it might have on Marilyn and caring, in some instances, even less if what they told was truth.

I have no doubt that Marilyn has been responsible for some of the distortions, but not out of malice. It was not a childhood that held many pleasant memories, and being shuttled back and forth among foster parents—some good and some not so good—did nothing to give rose colors to that childhood. She has, I know, long been torn

214

between telling the truth and creating fantasies. By now, I suppose, it is almost impossible for her to separate the one from the other.

Her story—and her life—began in the fortresslike confines of the huge Los Angeles General Hospital on June 1, 1926. The hospital records note the entrance into this world of one "Norma Jean Mortensen." The name that she was known by, however, until she was sixteen, was "Norma Jean Baker."

Her father was killed in an accident when the child was three; she never knew him.

Her mother worked as a film cutter and was hopelessly moviestruck, as was her mother's closest friend, Grace McKee. When other children played with dolls and building blocks, the infant child was given movie magazines. She was taken by the two women to the arc-lit premières of movies and stood behind the rope barriers, crying as the crowd applauded and cheered for the movie personalities who drove up to the theatres.

The lives of these two women were dedicated to movies. It was what they read about, what they talked about, what they dreamed about. And by the time the child was three she had already been told a thousand times, by each of these two women, that she was destined to be a movie star.

Her mother had a mental breakdown. "Aunt Grace" took the child into her own care but that proved no solution. Grace had to work and found that she could not give enough attention to Norma Jean. (She was made the child's legal guardian when Norma Jean's mother was ruled incompetent.) But she had to turn the child over to the authorities to care for and thus began that long round of foster homes.

A number of years ago a reporter asked Marilyn what she would miss most in her life if she were poor again. She gave an answer which, at first glance, appeared ridiculous to me. Now I know better. That's because I know Marilyn better. What she said was:

"It wouldn't be diamonds because I don't care for jewelry. Or furs or clothes or automobiles because I can get along without these very well. I guess the thing I would miss most would be a great big, comfortable bed. When I was poor, I always had to sleep with a female relative in a bed too small and too uncomfortable."

215

Thus spoke, not Marilyn, but Norma Jean.

She must have been thinking of the period when she was in an orphan asylum in the center of Hollywood. It was located near both Paramount and RKO and, at night, the RKO sign flashed interminably into the room which she shared with so many other unfortunates.

After the orphanage she had her first normal home in a long time. Aunt Grace had married a man named Goddard and Marilyn went to live with them in Van Nuys. This is a part of Los Angeles located in the San Fernando Valley. Now, for a time, she had a home. She could live as other girls her age did and go to school as other girls her age did.

Only Marilyn wasn't like other girls. Not then and not since. At fourteen she was fully matured. And her youth, which had taught her to be self-contained, self-assertive and always self-protective, had brought with it a brashness that was too often taken for hardness.

Of course I didn't know her then but all her biographers seem to agree on one point about this period in her life. She was "sexy" but, at the same time, unknowing and innocent.

One thing is certain—and this Marilyn has told me—she had a fierce desire to be loved. Having known so little of love, she was anxious to have visible signs that someone cared for her. In addition she had spent her life almost entirely with women and girls. And now, for the first time, she was part of a world that included boys.

There is no question but that in her immature way, she was a high-school flirt. She delighted in making the other girls jealous and she flaunted the fact that she was a queen bee. This wasn't really too difficult, for so many of her "rivals" were still scrawny and flat chested.

Then, at seventeen, she married.

The Goddards were moving East and Mr. Goddard did not want to take Norma Jean with them. A family named Daugherty were their neighbors and friends and they had a son, James, who was twenty-one. Young Daugherty had dated Norma Jean a number of times and the two families decided that it would be a wonderful

216

thing if the youngsters married. After all, young Jim had a job at an airplane plant and was making enough money to care for a wife.

From all that Marilyn has said to me about this marriage, I have concluded that she married—as so many others have—for security. "I kept thinking of all the years in the orphan asylum and in the foster homes. Of all that time when I was afraid of what the next day might bring. I knew, if I married, that I wouldn't have to worry about that. You don't send married women to foster homes."

There is another facet here of Marilyn's character. She was almost passive in this decision, which was so important. She wasn't acting, but being acted upon. Even then there was that touch of fatalism which was to mark her life.

I don't know many of the facts of that marriage except that it lasted about four years. Others have written what may be fact or what may be fiction. I have to admit that I don't know. Only that at the end of those four years, Daugherty went into the Merchant Marine and, to all intents and purposes, out of the life of Marilyn.

Now Norma Jean went back to her daydreams. She could—and still can—recall those times in her childhood when she had been told by her mother and Aunt Grace, "When you grow up, you're going to be a movie star." It still seemed a wonderful idea. Another girl might have taken some positive step toward this end. With her, however, such action was impossible.

But circumstances acted for her.

An army photographer, assigned to take some pictures in an airplane factory where she was working, saw her. He took some shots of her in black and white and some in color. Two weeks later he telephoned her. He had shown these pictures to Potter Hueth, a commercial photographer, who thought he might be able to use her as a model. Would she talk to Hueth? She most certainly would.

It is interesting to note that she arrived for the appointment with Hueth ahead of time.

Hueth asked if she would pose for him on "spec." He would gamble his time, his work and his film if she would also gamble her time. Well, she had plenty of that.

The results were even better than Hueth had hoped. Norma Jean

217

and the camera were meant for each other. She posed easily and naturally and the pictures brought out all her latent sensuality. But her abilities were just that—latent. They had to be developed, for there is more to being a model than assuming a pose and watching the birdie. And, again, things happened to her.

Hueth showed the pictures to Emaline Snively who ran a modeling agency and school. Miss Snively then talked with Norma Jean and offered to train her. Norma Jean pointed out that training would cost money and she had none.

This was no handicap. Miss Snively was willing to gamble. She would train Norma Jean and would get paid when Norma Jean went to work. This, again, was all right with Norma Jean.

And, for the record, all the time that Norma Jean was studying with Miss Snively and in the period afterward when she started getting assignments, she appeared on time.

It was obvious from the beginning that Norma Jean was not destined to be a fashion model. That called for the lean-and-hungry type, the straight-up-and-down figure. But she was a natural for the "pin-up" type of magazine and soon her face and figure were being seen on covers and inside such publications.

Early in her career, an assignment called for a blonde. After much persuasion, Norma Jean consented to bleach her hair the platinum shade that it still is. (I recalled this at one time to Ben Lyon who had told me of her natural "blondness." His answer was, "She *is* a natural blonde. I didn't make the mistake. Nature did.")

In those days Marilyn loved to dress up and pose before mirrors. She would pout and smile and practice allure. It was both real and a game to her. And the pay-off came, of course, when Howard Hughes saw her picture and the agent rushed her to Ben Lyon.

Now comes the baffling period of Marilyn's life. She had made a most successful test. Ben and Joe Schenck were always pushing for her. There was no question but that she had an atomic impact upon males. Yet she was just another starlet at the studio; just another contract player.

She accepted this as she had everything else. And took advantage of it. She was sent on publicity jaunts and used for publicity pictures. It was suggested that she should take lessons in acting, diction

218

and dancing and she enrolled in every class that was open to her. She worked hard. Finally she was given a small part in a picture—and the part was cut from the film.

This was the period when I first got to know her. She was shy, quiet, attentive—and flattering. She told me she thought she had learned to read from my column. That it had been her primer. Her mother and Aunt Grace read it aloud to her, pointed out items to her and then gave her the column. I can't, at this late date, see any natural progression from the column to *Crime and Punishment.*

Call me gullible, call me soft, but I felt then that this was an innocent woman. She knew the facts of life, of course, but she also had a wide-eyed view of the world in which she lived. At the same time, as she told me, that wide-eyed view was being sharpened by the parade of "wolves" who were beating a path to her locked and bolted door.

She certainly was leading an exemplary life. When so many other contract players were making the rounds of night clubs and night spots, smiling into the cameras of publicity men, she was working in the Actors Lab, behind Schwab's drugstore on Sunset Boulevard. And working was the word.

But no matter how hard she worked, no matter how many people tried to help her, she was still up against the fact that Darryl Zanuck just couldn't see her as box-office bait. And the studio dropped her contract.

She was out of work for eight months; a grim period. She had saved very little money and that went fairly quickly. She did occasional modeling jobs. Then she was signed by Columbia.

Here, too, she had a booster. This time it was Natasha Lytess, the drama coach. I suppose that Marilyn has always sought substitutes for the parents she never had. This is hardly uncommon. To my mind it explains her relationship through the years with so many older men and women.

But, at Columbia, she did more than find a mother substitute. She also fell in love.

She was cast in a routine "B" musical, *Ladies Of The Chorus,* and had to sing two songs. Freddie Karger, then head of the Columbia music department, was asked to coach her.

219

Freddie was older than she, a handsome, likable young man. He was kind and sympathetic and worked like the devil with her. Marilyn fell head over heels in love with him. Karger just wasn't in love with her. He told her he liked her a great deal and he proved that liking by the efforts he made to help her.

I am inclined to think that Marilyn's devotion to "culture" stems from this unhappy love of hers. Karger was, and is, a fine musician who likes the classics as well as popular music. He is well read. He has an appreciation of the arts. And it may be that Marilyn has always felt that the reason he never fell in love with her was because of her background.

I don't think that, at that time, Marilyn had ever head of Dostoevski or Freud. I don't believe she knew the difference between Berlioz and Berlitz. And, being with Freddie, meeting his friends, listening to them talking, she must have become aware of that lack in her. And decided that somehow she would remedy it.

Columbia dropped Marilyn after a short time and again she was out of work. And again she was broke. So she returned to modeling. A photographer named Tom Kelley had once offered her fifty dollars to pose for some nude photos and she had refused. But now she needed fifty dollars and she called Kelley.

He said the offer was still open and arranged for the "sitting." While the pictures were taken, Mrs. Kelley was with them. It was most proper and Kelley assured her that he would light the pictures in such a way that her face would not be recognized. And fifty dollars was fifty dollars.

At the time, it seemed like a good break. And was soon forgotten by her.

She took other modeling jobs and got a bit part in the Marx Brothers film, *Love Crazy*. But it seemed there weren't going to be any fairy godmothers—or godfathers—coming along to help her. Then one did. His name was Johnny Hyde.

Everyone knows the story. There were a lot of laughs in Hollywood about them. "Beauty and the Beast" was what they were called.

Johnny Hyde was in his fifties, one of the most important men in the William Morris Agency. He was a small, slight man who, even then, was known to be quite ill. He had suffered a severe heart attack a short time earlier. I had known Johnny for many years and knew of his ability as an agent. He had done much for many aspiring young actresses (with never a hint of scandal) and he was determined to do even more for Marilyn.

His reason was the most basic in the world. He fell in love with her.

Now it was the Karger situation in reverse. Marilyn was very fond of Johnny and made no secret of it. But she didn't love him. She told him so and he accepted it and kept right on working, day and night, to further her career.

He wanted to marry her and told me so. "Of course I do, Louella," he said. "I guess that's no secret, but she says she doesn't love me enough to marry me. I'll keep asking her, though."

And when I talked to her about Johnny, she said, "I love him but I'm not *in* love with him."

She had, of course, found that long-gone father.

It was Johnny who got her the part in MGM's *Asphalt Jungle* that was the turning point in her career. If there was irony in the relationship she had with Louis Calhern in that picture, when one thinks of her relationship with Johnny, it was unintentional. John Huston thought she was right for the part and there certainly was no intentional cruelty.

I know Johnny anticipated that her bombshell effect in the picture would get her an MGM contract, but it did not. At that time MGM had one outstanding blonde under contract and, in most studios, there just isn't room for two. And, good as Marilyn was, no one then felt that she could replace Lana Turner.

Marilyn accepted this philosophically, but Johnny wouldn't give up. He found her a part in another picture, *All About Eve*, which Joseph Mankiewicz made at Fox. She had only one scene in this film but, again, she burst right out of the screen.

And the result was that she got a six-months' deal back at Fox.

Then Johnny died.

Marilyn wept her heart out to me. "Was I wrong, Louella? Should I have married him even if I didn't love him? He was so good to me. Do you think, maybe—" She couldn't continue, could only sob.

221

I did my best to console her. She poured out her loneliness, her regrets, her shadowy feeling of guilt. I was able to get her to cease weeping. I said that if she wanted to show how she felt about Johnny, the best way was to prove that he had been right. That she was the stuff of which stars are made.

I know that was trite. But what would you have told her?

She tried to take the advice I had given her but neither she nor I had reckoned with Zanuck. He was still head of the studio and still had little regard for her capabilities. There were no parts for her.

But if she couldn't get her face on Fox's moving pictures, she was made to order for their still cameras. The publicity department was delighted to have her back.

Whatever she was asked, she did. She was available for pictures at any time and co-operative all during the long hours of the sittings. The publicity department took full advantage. They made series after series of pictures and started inundating newspapers, syndicates and magazines with shots of Marilyn Monroe. And the great American public became aware of her.

She appeared in no pictures, yet her fan mail started to grow. In a short time it was greater than that of some of Fox's "big names." Mr. Zanuck, though he was unaware of it, was being outvoted by the only group more powerful than he—the people who buy tickets.

Then she got her reward. Exhibitors from all over the country were coming to the studio for a meeting. Fox's stars, near stars and starlets were to be put on exhibition. Her pals in the publicity department told her that this was her chance. "Knock them dead," they told her. When she asked how she was to accomplish this, they showed her some of her more sexy pictures. She caught on quickly.

She went to the wardrobe department and, since this was "company business," she was allowed to take her choice of the myriad gowns there. She picked one that kept few secrets from an inquiring —or admiring—eye.

When she walked into that party it was like dropping a magnet amid iron filings. These were exhibitors and they unanimously agreed that she was the prize exhibit. They surrounded her, demanding to know what pictures she had appeared in, what pictures she was scheduled to do.

222

Sweetly, demurely, she gave them all the same answer. "You'll have to ask Mr. Zanuck about that."

Present at this meeting, and observing what was going on, was Spyros Skouros, head of the New York office of the film company. He watched as the exhibitors ignored long-established stars and gave all their attention to Marilyn. He asked some of the studio people who this girl was, and made some notes. Then he joined the group, offered Marilyn his arm and led her to the head table where she sat beside him all during the dinner.

This was the booster shot that really launched Marilyn in pictures. Even Zanuck had to admit that Marilyn had "something," though she might not have it for him. Her next option was picked up and she received a salary raise.

Now the publicity about Marilyn changed. Instead of it all being based on the "sexy" girl, it began to tell the harrowing story (edited, censored, chopped and varied) of her youth.

My daughter Harriet was producing *Clash By Night* at RKO at that time. The picture starred Barbara Stanwyck, Paul Douglas and Robert Ryan, and there was a smaller—but very important—role still to be cast. Harriet arranged to borrow Marilyn from Fox. She had heard me talk about Marilyn and had, of course, heard of her impact on the exhibitors, but she wasn't quite prepared for her.

"She's bringing thick philosophy books on the stage with her," Harriet told me, "and spends all her spare time reading them. I thought it was a pose until I talked with her. I'm not sure how much she's getting out of those books, but she takes them deathly seriously. And I thought she was just another sexy blonde."

There were a number of other changes in Marilyn that occurred while this picture was being made. She began that habit of tardiness which has since become constant. It was only a matter of minutes at this time; nothing like what developed later. (I have heard that she reported on the lot while *Some Like It Hot* was being made at 6 P.M. to answer a 10 A.M. call.) And she insisted upon her own dramatic coach, Natasha Lytess, to give her direction. There were times too when she asked for retakes though everyone else was satisfied with a scene.

It was, as Harriet told me, more annoying than anything else. But

223

it was a sign that deep, deep changes were taking place and an omen of what the future held in store.

However, all was forgiven when the picture was released. Marilyn, the relative newcomer in the small part, overshadowed the three other stars. The reviews were raves—for Marilyn. The child who had watched the flashing RKO sign from her orphanage bed had become a star on the RKO lot.

Then, out of the blue, came the "calendar scandal."

One of those nude pictures for which Marilyn had posed some four years earlier was being used on a commercial calendar. The same picture had been used some years before without attracting attention, but now it did. Four years had made a public personality of Marilyn. While the model was not identified, there was no question about who she was. However, the news services wanted verification from the source. They called her to ask if she had posed for the pictures.

Now, every Hollywood contract contains a "morals clause." This permits the studio to cancel a contract if the individual under contract does anything that can be construed as embarrassing the studio. Under this clause Fox could, if it wished, cancel Marilyn's contract.

She called to tell me of this development. I asked, "How are you going to handle it?"

"I'm going to tell the truth."

And she did. She said she had posed for the pictures because she needed the money. "It paid my rent," she said. Then she added, "What's so terrible about posing for an artistic picture?"

The public, it was quickly revealed, didn't think there was anything terrible about it. It cheered for her, wrote her more fan letters and rushed to see *Clash By Night*, then in release. There was also, of course, a rush on the Marilyn Monroe calendars.

A few months later there was another rash of Monroe publicity. Her official biography had stated that her mother was dead. A reporter had learned that her mother was still alive, quite ill, and that Marilyn was paying her hospital bills. This reporter made considerable fuss about this "discovery," but it, too, helped Marilyn. She received thousands of letters of sympathy.

And now we come to Marilyn Monroe, star.

224

She was famous. Her pay check was continually growing. Studios were begging to borrow her and Fox, at last, was convinced that she represented a fortune at the box office. If ever an individual should have grown more secure, it was Marilyn. But, instead, it seemed that she was more insecure.

It showed itself in her work. Where once she had walked out on the stage and done what her director told her, now she insisted upon special coaching by her own coach. And there were times when she fumbled and lost her sense of continuity and had to turn frightened, uncertain eyes on her personal dramatic coach for confidence.

And the tardiness became chronic. It was as if she couldn't bring herself to her place before the camera. She would be late getting to the studio. Then she would delay, for every conceivable and some inconceivable reason, the moment when she went before the camera.

There were physical manifestations of her fear. She appeared on my radio show a number of times and, each time, got violently sick to her stomach.

In the years since, Marilyn has been ill time after time, both before and during the periods when she was making a picture. At all other times she has had normal health.

The only time she ever reacted impatiently to me was when I said to her in an interview, "A psychologist has written that the reason for your illness is that you really don't want to begin or finish a movie. Is that so?"

"You know how much I want to be a star," she said. "Any psychologist who said anything like that was just looking for headlines. It isn't true." And she would not discuss it any further.

Marilyn, of course, had read all about psychological illness. She was reading the thickest books ever at that period. But it was also the period when she started seeing baseball star Joe Di Maggio. And here was a contradiction.

She had always had a penchant for older men whose interests were, at least in part, intellectual. Joe was certainly older and while he was a nice guy and an all-round sports hero, he hardly qualified as an egghead. The thought came to me that perhaps Marilyn, now established as a star, might have decided to leave the books to the libraries.

225

Joe's courtship was different from the usual Hollywood romancing. He took her on long drives. He spent evenings with her watching TV. They avoided night clubs and public places. They were the despair of press agents. It seemed that these two people, both so famous, wanted—of all things—privacy.

That was, of course, hard to attain. Wherever they went they were bound to be recognized and surrounded by either movie or baseball fans, and very often both. Anonymity was impossible. The newspapers and the columnists, L.O.P. among these latter, knew that this pair was news and so whenever an item came to me that I could use, I used it. And, at the same time, found myself thinking that it wasn't really fair to them. But it wouldn't be fair to my bosses, my readers and me if I didn't write about them.

Marilyn made news in other ways. She was chosen by *Photoplay*, a leading fan magazine, as "Best New Star" and was to be given an award at the dinner which featured the magazine's annual awards.

Marilyn arrived two hours late!

But it wasn't her lateness, it was her attire which caused a sensation.

Marilyn wore a dress of gold lamé—that cloth of gold which was so popular in the long-ago era when vamps were vamps and Theda Bara was a star. But it wasn't the fabric, but the way it was put together and what it concealed—and revealed—that resulted in long-drawn-out gasps.

This dress was so form-fitting, the skirt so narrow, that Marilyn could hardly walk in it. And it was clear that she had nothing under it but skin.

After the gasp, there was a hush. And after the hush, a mixture of whistles, applause and catcalls. The reaction, then and later, was loud. And not all of it anonymous. Joan Crawford took it upon herself to speak out and said:

"It was like a burlesque show. The audience yelled and shouted, but most of us in the industry just shuddered. . . . Miss Monroe should be told that the public likes provocative feminine personalities, but it also likes to know that, underneath it all, the actresses are ladies. . . ."

I suppose that I could give Joan an argument on her last point.

226

Underneath it all not all actresses are, or have been, ladies and I'm not sure that the public really cares.

The criticism struck Marilyn hard. (She doesn't have the resiliency, say, of an Eva Marie Saint.) She hid out in her apartment for a time. Word also came that Di Maggio had been terribly upset by the reports of her appearance. He had not been present, so his knowledge was word of mouth.

It seemed to me that Marilyn should have a chance to say her piece and so I called her and asked her to let me tell the public her side of the story.

She grasped the opportunity.

It was a frightened, distrait Marilyn who opened her wounded heart to me. "I didn't mean to do anything that the industry wouldn't like. I just thought that I was expected to look alluring. Maybe my choice was bad, but my intention wasn't. And the way so many people jumped on me—as if I'd committed a crime. Especially Joan Crawford."

And then she added something that seemed out of context, but was quite revealing. "I've always admired her for being such a wonderful mother. For taking four children and giving them such a wonderful home."

Here was Norma Jean again, shuttled about from home to home, lost and forlorn, wishing—deep down in her heart—for someone like a Joan Crawford who would "take" her and be a "wonderful mother."

Like most publicity, this died down and was soon forgotten except insofar as it became part of the Monroe legend.

Her career moved steadily forward. She proved, in a number of pictures, that she was an expert in comedy, could handle herself with the most accomplished performers and look good in the process. The studio announced that she had been cast in *The Girl In Pink Tights*.

Marilyn issued an announcement of her own. She hated the script. She had no intention of wiggling her hips in pink tights. And, to prove she meant it, she left town.

The studio in turn did what studios normally do with recalcitrant actors. It put her on suspension. "No work. No pay check."

But the days were long past when a missed pay check meant disaster to Marilyn. Now, Uncle Sam suffered more than she did.

Her whereabouts did not long remain unknown. I got a call from San Francisco, a special message to me from Marilyn. "Marilyn and Joe are being married right now in the office of a justice of the peace. She wanted you to be the first to know. That's why I'm calling."

I sent her my best wishes and pounded out the story for my paper and syndicate.

She and Joe went to Japan on their honeymoon. There Marilyn contracted a terrible cold that she still had when she returned to the United States and appeared with me on my radio show. It seemed she had caught it when she went to entertain some troops in freezing weather.

"I knew they wanted to see me," she said, "so I couldn't very well wear an overcoat."

The same Marilyn; so anxious to please, to be loved.

Stories had been printed quoting Joe as saying they wanted a large family. I asked her about this. "We do," she said. "I want babies of my own. Lots of babies."

But the next months found Marilyn back at work and, almost at once, there were reports that she and Joe were having their problems.

Joe didn't change with marriage. He still sought to avoid crowds, still liked long, quiet drives, still thought that the way to spend a wonderful evening was to watch TV. And he had an active, often expressed, dislike of the social side of Hollywood. There was no Toots Shor's where he could meet with people whose interests were the same as his.

Marilyn tried to adapt to this but she could do only so much. As a star, there were certain public functions that she had to perform, certain places where she had to go. She found that she had to do these unescorted.

I recall one night when my friend Jimmy McHugh opened at the Ambassador Hotel and a group of Hollywood's most important stars were there to catch him in his new act and be introduced. Marilyn was one of this group, but she came alone. Late in the evening a waiter came to our table with a message for her. Joe was outside in the car waiting for her. He wouldn't even come in long enough to exchange greetings.

The real break came when she had to leave town for a considerable stretch of time while on location making *Seven Year Itch*. When she returned, Joe gave her an ultimatum. Either she live with him in San Francisco and be Mrs. Di Maggio, or she could stay in Hollywood, be a star and be Marilyn Monroe.

She chose to be Marilyn Monroe. Her final divorce, on the grounds of mental cruelty, was picked up in October, 1955.

And now she entered a new phase but, to me, it was only a continuation of an old, old one. She found someone else upon whom to be dependent. In this instance it was Milton Greene, a photographer, with whom she formed an independent company. Lots of actors were doing this, but in Marilyn's case there was one difficulty. She was still under contract to Fox and the contract had three years to run. The studio informed her firmly that if she was going to make any pictures, she was going to make them for Fox.

Her decision was not to make any pictures. Instead, she went to New York with Greene, his wife and entourage and decided to study acting!

Here was Cinderella in her coach but she didn't trust either the coach or the footmen. She knew they weren't real.

In addition to the Greenes, Marilyn had other substitute parents. These were Lee Strasberg, the well-known dramatic coach, and his wife Paula. Strasberg teaches "The Method," a form of acting based upon the theories of Stanislavsky. And Marilyn, exuberant, sexy, extroverted in her earlier film roles, was now going to be taught to act from the inside out.

I saw her a number of times during this period and she was ecstatic about her schooling. "It's the greatest thrill of my life," she said, "to study with Mr. and Mrs. Strasberg."

Paula Strasberg was equally ecstatic. She told me, "Lee feels she has phenomenal talent as an actress. He has a solution for her nervousness. He says nervousness indicates sensitivity and Marilyn has great sensitivity. She is still frightened but she is getting over it. Show me an actress who isn't nervous and frightened and I'll say she won't go far. Marilyn has a talent that is a combination of Jeanne

Eagels and Pauline Lord and, like them, she is greatly misunderstood.

"She tries to achieve perfection and it's almost impossible. She constantly seeks it even at the expense of her health and peace of mind."

Obviously Marilyn felt that the Strasbergs were the answer to many of her doubts and fears. It was not long before Paula Strasberg had replaced Natasha Lytess as dramatic coach.

While she was "learning" to act in New York, exhibitors were clamoring for her to appear in pictures. And so were stockholders of 20th Century-Fox. It is possible that no compromise between Marilyn and the studio would have been effected except that Darryl Zanuck had resigned as production chief, to produce his own pictures, and had been replaced by Buddy Adler. With Adler it wasn't a case of pride, but one of pressures. Marilyn, even on her own terms, was needed.

A new contract was written and she agreed to appear in the movie version of the stage play, *Bus Stop*, which would be directed by Joshua Logan, an ardent advocate of The Method.

When she returned to Hollywood, it was as if a Joan of Arc had returned to Rouen. However, she wasn't burned at the stake, just the victim of flashlight heat.

She made the picture and, when it was released, the critics agreed that she had proved she could act. Most of them, of course, had felt that way before.

Now came a new-old twist in Marilyn's life. She fell in love again. This time with Arthur Miller, one of America's leading playwrights and authors.

Miller, like both her other husbands, was older than she. In all other respects, however, he was different from Daugherty and Di Maggio. Here, truly, was an egghead, a nonconformist, a figure in the world of letters.

When I asked her about Miller, she said, "He attracted me because he is brilliant. His mind is better than that of any other man I've ever known. And he understands and approves my wanting to improve myself."

Miller had long been married and had two children. I don't know whether or not his marriage was happy. I am inclined to believe that Marilyn did not break up the marriage because I don't believe any third person really breaks up a marriage. However, it may be that she accelerated the breakup.

Certainly these two—the screen's outstanding exemplar of female sex and the nation's intellectual top playwright—hardly seemed made for each other. But they disagreed.

I recall seeing Miller, tall, slightly stooped, peering out through his horn-rimmed glasses, trying to smile as photographers flashed pictures and reporters threw questions at him. He tried so hard to be co-operative but it was obvious that he wished to the good Lord that he were a million miles away.

Soon after the marriage, the couple went to England where they combined their honeymoon with Marilyn playing in the film, *The Prince and the Show Girl*, with Sir Laurence Olivier.

If ever she should have been over all fear, all uncertainty, all insecurity, this was the moment. Her husband was a man who represented her ideal. Old enough to give her a feeling of confidence. Intellectual enough to allow her to disregard those who called her own attempt to be intellectual a pose. After all, if Arthur regarded her as at least a possible intellectual, who were they to cast the first doubt?

And, in addition, she was going to play opposite one of the admitted greats of the acting profession. If she could co-star with Olivier who could question that she was an actress?

To use a colloquialism of the day, it appeared that she "had it made."

And yet—. And yet—.

I recall being at a party in London at that time, given by Vivien Leigh—then still married to Olivier—at Terence Rattigan's beautiful home. I saw Marilyn holding court, surrounded by such theatrical notables as Dame Sybil Thorndyke. Still, at moments, her eyes went to Miller for assurance and reassurance. Still, at moments, she appeared just a little uncertain; as if wondering what the slavey of the myriad foster homes was doing in this elegant atmosphere.

And, professionally, she showed no fresh, new confidence. She was always late and played havoc with shooting schedules and the budget. On the set, she asserted herself repeatedly over minor

231

items, as if testing to see if she was really the co-star. She behaved like a child asking to be spanked.

I have heard that Sir Laurence would have been delighted to have granted that request. After all, he was both director and co-star and his was a reputation that far transcended hers. But, instead of spanking, he shot whenever she was available and finally finished the picture.

It didn't impress the critics as a great work of art. What did impress them, however, was Marilyn's performance. It was almost unanimously agreed that she had stolen the picture from Olivier. I think that is one of the reasons that he has never joined a Marilyn Monroe fan club.

Afterward the Millers returned to New York and it was there that I next interviewed her. Her lines had changed slightly since their marriage.

"I'm in love with the man, not his mind," she said. "When I first met him, I didn't know that he was the famous writer. The Arthur Miller who attracted me was a man of warmth and friendliness with a charming personality."

"In every marriage," I said, "one partner appears to dominate. Who is the boss in yours?"

"I suppose," she answered, "that when we're in New York Arthur is the boss, and when I'm working everything centers about me." Then she added quickly, "Please don't misunderstand. I am a wife in every sense of the term. Arthur has helped me adjust myself. I'm easily frightened. You know I've always been unsure of myself. Well, Arthur has helped me overcome this feeling."

Then she went on to talk about their life together. They had a home in Connecticut and she had learned to cook and often did the cooking. Miller's two sons visited them frequently and she told me how much she enjoyed their being there. And then she added, "More than anything, I want a baby. Lots of babies."

At least, in this respect, she was consistent. I know how deeply she has wanted children and what a shock, both physical and emotional, it was when she twice lost children she was bearing. The second time it was most serious and she was, for a period, in grave danger.

232

That happened after she finished *Some Like It Hot,* probably her biggest money-making film. She took a long time recuperating before she returned to play in *Let's Make Love.*

Always before, when she was in Hollywood, she had called me immediately on her return and we had seen each other. This time weeks elapsed and I didn't hear from her. Even worse, I was unable to reach her. Finally I got annoyed and informed the press agents who were working on the film that I was no longer interested in Monroe. I didn't want to see her. I know this was childish but I was quite burned up. If I couldn't get anything else from Marilyn, I certainly deserved politeness.

Then came word that Marilyn was giving a big press party. L.O.P. chose that night to stay home. I was in my dressing room, having my hair set, when Marilyn burst in. She had left her own party when, asking for me, she had been told that I wasn't coming.

I must say that I had never seen her look prettier. She was wearing a dress of pale beige that blended with her hair. And her eyes, her whole face, seemed alight with a strange, new happiness.

"Please forgive me," she said. "I can't explain why I haven't been in touch with you, but I just couldn't. It isn't because I don't still think of you as one of my oldest and best friends."

And it is a sign of how Parsons has mellowed through the years that I did forgive her. Not that I was ever really adamant, but in the old days I would have insisted upon at least a little coaxing.

"Visit me at the studio, please," she said. "I want you to hear me sing 'My Heart Belongs To Daddy' and see me dance. Please come."

A week later I did go. Not only to watch her but so that I could get to know Yves Montand, one of her two leading men. He had made a terrific impact on Hollywood and the word was spreading that a lot of female hearts, including some that shouldn't, were going "flip-flop" over him. I wanted a close-up view of this actor who was, though few knew it, Italian by birth. He is regarded as 100 per cent French but he left his native Italy when a young child and the French is both adopted and adapted.

I found him a dynamic personality, charming, vital and Gallic. Marilyn described him to me as "all male." That made my eyes blink.

Midway during the filming of the picture, the actors went on strike. This stopped production and Yves decided to go to Paris, rather than wait in Hollywood for a settlement. Marilyn also went East.

Then came a story from New York. Marilyn had been at the airport to see Yves off. French newspapers picked this up and always on the alert to exploit French charm, reported in their largest type that Yves Montand had come between Marilyn and Miller.

The fact that Yves was married to Simone Signoret apparently cut no ice. It would have been a blot on the French amorous escutcheon even to suggest that Marilyn might have broken up the idyll of Yves and Simone.

I, of course, don't know Yves and Simone as well as I do American actors and actresses. I think one of the few times I ever saw them together was just prior to, and at, the 1959 Academy Awards program. It was then that Simone received the Oscar for her performance in *Room At The Top*. It seemed to me that she was terribly in love with him. She found it hard to keep her hands off him—after eleven years of marriage!

I wondered if this was a French technique, if this was the way French women held their husbands.

From my un-French point of view, it didn't seem like the best possible technique. I've always believed that no woman should ever make a man feel 100 per cent sure of his hold on her. The male animal has a tendency to seek what he shouldn't have, or thinks he can't have. I find it hard to believe that Montand is an exception.

The rumor pot was a-boiling. It had been some time since Hollywood had had a "scandal" involving big names, and everyone latched on to this one. Word came that Simone was desperately unhappy and everybody reported it. Arthur Miller said nothing and everyone reported that. Marilyn and Yves expressed shock that anyone could take something as innocent as a "bon voyage" and blow it up out of all proportion.

We printed that.

The flurry died down. The picture was finally completed, but there was no hard news, no fact that could be used to bolster the idea of a romance between Yves and Marilyn.

234

Then Arthur Miller started to produce *The Misfits*, a picture he had written himself in Reno especially for Marilyn. And, at about the same time, Yves was back in Hollywood. Up popped the rumors again.

In the middle of *The Misfits* Marilyn became ill. The diagnosis was "exhaustion." Marilyn was rushed to a Los Angeles hospital for treatment. While it was news that she was ill, it was part of her pattern. The question in everyone's mind was not would Marilyn get sick, but when would she get sick? That it coincided with Montand's being in Hollywood came as no surprise.

I decided that I would find out for myself what this situation was. I called Yves and asked him to come to my house. He arrived at eleven in the morning and we shared a coffee break. It was remarkable how much his English had improved since last we had talked. I asked him what was what.

"I more than *like* Marilyn," he said quite candidly. "I tell you this because I trust you, Madame. She is an enchanting child. And I won't say that had I been free, I wouldn't have fallen in love with her. But for eleven years I have been married to a wonderful, understanding woman. Simone and I have been very happy. There will be no divorce."

That seemed to be that, but then he went on to put some more icing on the cake; to create a piece of French pastry. "I have," he said, "told Simone *everything*. Marilyn is a pure, fine girl and it's awful the insinuations that have been printed."

"If you told her *everything*," I said, "then there must have been something to tell. What was it?"

"Nothing, I assure you. Nothing. The matter of the visit at the airport, which has been so misunderstood. She brought a bottle of chilled champagne and we sat in a car and drank it and talked. It was very innocent. The French reporters made it into an *affaire*. How ridiculous."

"Of course," I said. "Of course. Still it was quite a tidbit that Marilyn Monroe should spend such a long time in a car with a man who is supposed to have more sex appeal than any male since Rudolph Valentino."

"Madame, we only sat in a car."

235

That was all he had to say about that episode. We talked of Marilyn's illness and he said that he wished he might go and see her but obviously he couldn't.

Making an attempt at humor, I said, "Why don't you go in disguise? Dress up as a woman or put on a false face."

His answer rather threw me. "I'm sure," he said, "some of the nurses would recognize me and I can't risk upsetting Simone." (Maybe there is something to her technique?)

I decided that American and Gallic senses of humor didn't mesh and decided not to continue along this line. Shortly afterward he left to return to the studio.

I long ago learned that there is quite a difference between the attitude European men have toward love, marriage and sex and those held by Americans. Maybe this explains why the Montand-Signoret marriage is still unbroken, while the Miller-Monroe marriage is now a thing of the past.

It was immediately after *The Misfits* was released that the Millers parted.

And, almost at once, she started seeing Joe Di Maggio again. Maybe, with two baseball teams now located in Los Angeles, they have more in common than they used to have.

This is the Marilyn Monroe story up to now—but it's not guaranteed to stay that way past publication date. Marilyn continues searching for something that has evaded her all her life. In the process, she has married three times, been devoted to a number of older men and women. It seems as if she will always need that crutch, that support.

I would like to quote from Maurice Zolotow who has written what I think is a most perceptive study of Marilyn. Mr. Zolotow said:

"This woman casts a powerful spell over every man in her orbit. She did over me, I know, during a series of meetings we had several years ago. It was almost like a hypnotic spell. But there is a paradox that lies, almost like a sickness, in Monroe's relations with men she comes to love and who become enraptured by her. The paradox is that a man can be a father to her, or husband or even both, but he can never completely fulfill her own standards of what the father image must be.

236

"As he loves her more and more, as he surrenders his own pride and personal achievement to the demands of her insatiable ego, as he gives her what she needs and cries for she little by little loses respect for him and suddenly does not want him any more.

"As Arthur Miller knows—now."

My own diagnosis is different and I don't claim that it is more correct. I just feel that Marilyn can't place complete trust and confidence and belief in anyone because she can't place that belief and trust and confidence in herself.

She reaches a moment when she is disappointed that the people about her are unaware of what truly ails her. And then, of course, she turns from them.

And what is true of people is true about her career. She has the ability to reach the heights. She has the personality, the "flesh impact," as poor Clara Bow said, to dominate the screen. But she has not completely succeeded. I keep wondering if she ever will.

But, no matter what, one thing I do know. Marilyn will make news for a long, long time. I hope, for her sake, that it will be happy news.

Perhaps, sometime, someone will slip the shoe on her foot and she will realize that it's real, not make-believe.

➤➤➤ *Chapter 15*

THE METHOD THAT WALKS LIKE A MAN

AN irate young woman stepped up to me at a party one day and said, "You don't like Marlon Brando, do you?"

"Don't like him," I said, "I don't even know him."

And I'm afraid that I'll have to repeat the confession. Louella Parsons, who sees all, hears all and knows all about Hollywood doesn't know Marlon Brando. But, I'd like to ask, who does?

There have been enigmatic personalities in Hollywood before. Men and women who were "loners," and kept themselves apart. There have been "characters" in Hollywood before; men and women who did everything from eating flower petals to riding to hounds in Model T's. Brando is neither the first loner nor the first character, though he may be the first combination of the two; which is like mating an owl and a cockatoo.

I've interviewed him and talked with him and there was one night when I thought he was going to kiss me. Yes, me. That was the night when he received the Academy Award for his performance in *On The Waterfront.*

As is customary, I went backstage after the Awards ceremonies to talk to the winners. There, among the group, was a changed Brando.

238

He was talking with reporters, a happy smile, instead of a stormcloud, on his face. A smile on the Brando face!

He was exuberant, bursting with joy. When he saw me he rushed up to me as if we were old, dear friends. He reached out as if he was going to embrace me. And that was the moment when I thought it was going to happen.

But it didn't. He stopped just short of it. He shook my hand.

But on this night he loved everyone, including reporters. And some of us remarked that perhaps we had had him all wrong. Maybe there was this nice, human quality beneath the surface of the method that walked like a man.

Maybe there is. We never since really had an opportunity to find out.

From the day that Marlon Brando hit Hollywood, he has been one of the things that the guides on the rubberneck buses point out. And he has also been a walking, loving—but not talking—example of "The Method."

For those who don't know, The Method is a naturalistic school of acting that is credited (sic) to Stanislavsky, the great (White) Russian who taught acting and whose theories are "the law, as interpreted by Lee and Paula Strasberg at their New York school of acting."

And its Hollywood prophet is Brando.

The hallmark of The Method is "identification." The actor must cease being himself and become something else.

You either love The Method or you hate it. Marilyn Monroe is a devotee. So, too, is that fine director Elia Kazan. Tony Curtis expressed his feelings about The Method some time ago. He was discussing Method actors.

"These people," Tony said, "have taken the idiosyncrasies and genius of Marlon Brando and built a way of life about him. Confront them with a role that asks them to perform a simple action or speak a simple line and they're completely tied up. They want nice, wholesome stories like 'I Hate My Mother,' or 'My Sister's a Prostitute,' or 'I Smoke Marijuana.' It's got to be all involved and complex."

I use the quotation for two reasons. The first, to show that there are some who do not hold The Method in high regard. The second, to reveal that Brando's fellow actors regard him as a "genius."

239

As for me, I'll go on record at once as stating that with or without The Method, Brando would have been a great star. His is a personality that dominates the screen. In fact, I'll go further. I feel that he is a star despite, not because of, The Method. Can you imagine a Brando who talked instead of mumbled?

I've met and talked with Marlon Brando, Sr., a charming, outgoing gentleman who speaks distinctly and well. It's my daring guess that son Marlon once spoke equally distinctly before he found himself involved with The Method.

Further, I think that it is his addiction to this approach to acting which has caused so many to say that he plays every role in the same way. And I have heard Texans complain that his Texas accent in *Sayonara* wasn't Texan and Germans say that his German accent in *The Young Lions* wasn't German. It was just Brando.

But nothing can take away his effectiveness on the screen. He has carved a special niche for himself in my town, at the same time that he has sought, so very, very carefully, to set himself apart from Hollywood.

I'd heard about him as a result of his performance in *Streetcar Named Desire* which made a star of him. It has been interesting to me that this man, who has always decried Hollywood, came here just as fast as he could. The moment he had the chance, he packed his black boots and leather jacket and headed West. That was where the big money was.

His first part in Hollywood was in Stanley Kramer's *The Men,* a story of paraplegic ex-soldiers. From the day Brando hit Hollywood, he went around flaunting his individuality. Hollywood wasn't going to change him. Success wasn't going to change him. They weren't going to make him change his sweat shirt and blue jeans for a sports shirt and slacks. You couldn't do that to Stanley Kowalski— beg pardon—to Marlon Brando.

The first reaction to him was amusement and the second annoyance. Even the characters in town found him difficult to take and it was they who first called him, because of his attire, "The Slob."

I heard stories about him and his serious approach to acting, if not to anything else. Preparing for his role in *The Men,* Brando spent a great deal of time in veterans' hospitals. He accustomed himself to

240

going about in a wheel chair, to the point where he would roll himself around in public in order to get "the feel" of the part.

A number of times Marlon caused a fair amount of consternation with this latter tactic. He would be wheeling himself along, accepting sympathetic looks and words, and then leap from the chair and, at times, shout, "I've been cured. I've been cured."

It is antics such as these that have always made me feel that Brando has a large streak of charlatan. It seems to me that he isn't the true, brooding, self-destructive type that Hollywood has known at different times. There is in him none of that self-corrosion which marked John Garfield and James Dean and, to a lesser extent, marks Montgomery Clift.

In other words, I think Brando acts as much, if not more, off the screen than he does on it. He's all ham and six feet tall.

However, there are many who disagree with me. His friends have assured me that he is in pictures only as a means to an end. He will make his pile and then go off and lead the life that means something to him. Travel. Study.

My answer is that the record shows this isn't true. What is his latest ambition? Not to go off into the wilds or visit the lamaseries of Tibet. He is now going to direct pictures.

"Ah," they tell me, "you don't understand him." He is truly "humble." (That word again.) He identifies himself with the underdogs of the world. The poor and the unfortunate. And they point out that he can't pass a beggar without emptying his pockets of every cent.

And I point out that this can't cost him much because his father keeps him on a very short cash allowance indeed. If he wants to be profligate with a beggar, he'll have to lend him his credit card.

And yet he can be truly generous in an entirely different way. This is well-illustrated by a story that that fine actor, Karl Malden, told me.

Karl is, admittedly, one of the ablest supporting actors in pictures. He had a nice role in *Streetcar,* with his biggest scene the poker game. But, when they began to shoot this sequence, Marlon began "horsing around." In the process he was taking all of Karl's effectiveness out of the script. He was stepping on all his lines.

241

"He was the star," Karl said, "and he could get away with it. But I also knew that he was a nice guy and was probably not thinking of what he was doing to my part. I put it to him straight. I said, 'You've got fifty sides and can toss them away and still register. If I lose one of mine, I've got nothing.' He understood right away. 'I never thought of it that way,' he said to me. And when that sequence was shot, I got more than was coming to me.

"That's Marlon. He's a great actor and a great guy."

If a poll were taken of actors, I feel that Brando would not only rate near the top in ability, but in being a "great guy." So many actors have told me of his thoughtfulness and his insistence that others in the cast get all the breaks to which they're entitled. Over the years, I haven't heard this about too many actors.

On one score, however, I am grateful to Brando. He makes news. And one of the ways in which he makes it is in his personal life. He has a very obvious penchant for exotic women. He likes his women to be beautiful, dark-haired, tawny-skinned. Oriental and Latin women seem to head his list.

Anna Kashfi, whom he married, appeared to meet all his requirements. There was, of course, the later story that the Oriental background may not be quite authentic, but she certainly looks the part.

It was a sudden marriage, taking place in October, 1957, and a relatively short one. However, the memory and the court battles, especially over their small son Christian Devi, linger on. We'll return to these shortly.

Marlon has hardly proven a good-luck charm for the women whose names have been linked with his. Take France Nuyen, as an example. She pined so for Marlon that she lost the wonderful role of the lead in *The World Of Suzie Wong*.

In one respect, France added a new dimension to pining. In the old days, pining away also resulted in wasting away. In France's case, it was just the opposite. The more she pined, the more she ate. And the more she ate, the less willowy her figure became. As a result, France was replaced by Nancy Kwan in *Suzie Wong*.

(Recently I asked Nancy if *she* had ever met Marlon. Her answer was quick and to the point. "No. And I'm not interested in ever meet-

242

ing him." Well, in that respect Nancy is different from most women with whom I've talked.)

Marlon is not the kind of bachelor who plays the field, as the saying goes. He's not flighty, preferring to be a one-woman man over a long period of time and—as has been reported—returning to old loves after a temporary new one. But that doesn't mean that he likes the word "marriage" any better than some of his less constant fellow bachelors.

There was, for example, the French fascinator, Josanne Mariana-Berenger. She was the daughter of a fisherman and her father took it upon himself, after Marlon and Josanne had been seeing a great deal of each other, to announce that she had made a prize catch—a Marlon.

Brando, always the perfect gentleman in such circumstances, had no public statement; only a smile. However, from that time onward, the *"Affaire* Josanne" took on the quality of that famous Cheshire Cat in *Alice In Wonderland*. It just started fading away until, at the end, not even a trace of Josanne or her smile remained in the public sight.

And then, of course, there is the instance of the beautiful Porto Rican actress, Rita Moreno, with whom Marlon has had an on-again, off-again romance for so long. Only a short time ago she took an overdose of sleeping pills and then, accompanied by a friend, drove to Brando's home. Luckily he wasn't there. An ambulance arrived before Brando and headlines followed.

And now, to return to Anna Kashfi. She and Marlon have a running court battle in relation to both custody of their son and visiting rights. Even absence does not put an end to this fight, for very recently Marlon hailed Anna into court, even though he was in far away Tahiti filming *Mutiny On The Bounty*.

Anna not only had a denial of all the charges Marlon was making, but a sensation of her own. She said that Marlon had telephoned her from Tahiti to say that he was now married to Movita, also known as Maria Castaneda, who had played the part of a Tahitian beauty in the 1935 version of *Mutiny On The Bounty*.

"He told me they had been married in Mexico," Miss Kashfi told a group of reporters, "and that they had a son—I don't remember his name—and that divorce proceedings were underway in Mexico."

Now that came close to a complete story with a beginning, a middle and an end—but Anna had more. "Marlon," she said, "wants to establish a close relationship between his two sons. He thinks our child and this child should get together. My answer was that the children should be left out of it completely. This child of Movita's is his own problem and what he does about him is his business."

And, unfortunately, the public's.

As I remarked earlier, Marlon now talks of leaving acting and becoming a director. He has already directed one picture, *One-Eyed Jacks,* a western in the traditional mold. He made this picture for his own company, under a deal he had with Paramount. Originally it was intended as a moderately budgeted picture with a normal shooting schedule.

Marlon changed this. As director, he insisted upon perfection and that meant shooting take after take. As producer, he insisted that the story be "perfect" and, to some extent, that meant longer.

As actor, he directed himself and, as he later remarked, didn't have as much success as he had hoped.

Before he was done the picture was two years in the making, some millions over budget and some minutes overlong.

With a tremendous investment in the picture and his own reputation at stake, it would be presumed that he would go out of his way to build up both the picture and himself. But not Marlon. He gave an interview to a *Newsweek* reporter who quoted him as calling the picture "a pot boiler," and added, "My career as an actor is coming to an end."

In his candid estimation, the picture "was not an artistic success," and he elaborated further, "Any pretension I've sometimes had of being artistic is now just a long, chilly hope."

I thought the picture was too long and that Brando was too fat. (Could it be that he was pining away while it was shot?) But I also felt that it was a slick, commercial job of movie-making. Most other critics have agreed with me, with some of them a great deal more enthusiastic.

But Marlon continued to disagree. "I took a long time making it,"

244

he said. "After a time I got an attachment to it. It's like spending two years building a chicken coop. When you're finished you want to feel you've done something with your time."

This certainly sounds like madness coming from a producer. But perhaps Marlon knows what he is doing. There could be a definite madness to his Method.

⇒ *Chapter 16*

FEMME—VERY FATALE

BYRON's phrase, "The fatal gift of beauty," could have been written for Elizabeth Taylor, who combines the *femme fatale* qualities of Helen of Troy, Cleopatra and Madame Du Barry.

She has always been beautiful and from that beauty has come all she has suffered and all she is. She has been both blessed and damned by it.

Without it, she could never, of course, have achieved stardom. Nor would she have been subjected to the vilification, the scorn and the anger that have been her lot. I would say that, for a time, Elizabeth Taylor was probably the most disliked—even hated—woman in America.

Never did I receive as much mail as I did during the time when it first became public knowledge that Eddie Fisher was leaving Debbie Reynolds for Elizabeth Taylor.

My mail has always been heavy. It comes from those who read my column wherever it appears in the world. And through it, I have been able to discern trends in the motion-picture industry that did not become facts until some time later. But, even more, that mail has been an index of the popularity—or unpopularity—of different actors and

246

actresses. It has helped me guess which actors were headed for the top and which were beginning to slide.

And no star has ever caused the letter writers to work overtime as has Elizabeth Taylor. This goes back to the time when she appeared in her first picture, and has continued to today. There have been letters of praise, of advice. There have been attacks. Some of the letters have been so vicious, so unprintable, that I have blushed reading them. And, in the same mail, there would be a dozen letters—and these would be signed—repeating the Biblical admonition, "Let him who is without sin cast the first stone."

During the time that the Liz-Eddie-Debbie scandal was front-page news there was a crescendo of fury, of personal hate, that filled the mailbags. To a slightly lesser degree, the mail poured in until Elizabeth and Eddie were married. When Debbie married Harry Karl, the letters slowed down to a trickle.

Then, in the winter of 1960-61, when Elizabeth was so desperately ill in London, the tide of letters swelled, reaching a crest when the newspapers reported her fight to stay alive.

The theme of those letters was pity and concern. They sent good wishes, expressed hope for her. I was amazed at the complete change of heart.

Then a false news report was circulated that Elizabeth had died. My phone started ringing, and there were tears in the voices of some who called to ask if it were true.

The same thing happened at newspapers, radio and TV stations whose phone lines were swamped with calls.

In London too the reserved English were reacting in a most unreserved way. Phone lines were jammed with enquiries. In addition, thousands stood outside the hospital, waiting through the long, dreary night for some word from the room where Elizabeth lay in an oxygen tent, barely alive. She had been given only a few hours to live and her own physician, Dr. Rexford Kennamer, had flown from Hollywood to her bedside.

Outside the hospital, the thousands waited and prayed for Elizabeth's recovery. Then, as the hours passed, the reports grew more hopeful and, finally, optimistic. There was a spontaneous reaction of relief and happiness.

Just who and just what was Elizabeth Taylor that she should cause this? How did it happen that she had created this intensity of emotion?

I have known her since she was a child. I don't know anyone essentially less anxious to be the center of public attention. She is not like some actresses who woo publicity by the way they dress, by hiring press agents, by purposely making news.

Elizabeth is inherently dramatic. Her beauty is soul, not skin, deep.

She is an actress by profession and not by nature. She doesn't—as actresses should and must—have a foremost feeling that she is always on stage, that she must always put her best foot forward because all the world is her audience. She doesn't believe that she owes that great audience anything more than her best professional performance. Outside of that, her life is her own.

But the world has refused to accept this. When she appears—raven-haired, beautifully cast features, violet eyes so alive beneath the long lashes—she is expected to stand center stage for public inspection and reaction. She simply has refused to accept this.

She will be herself.

She has insisted upon this all the years I have known her. I recall the time she came to a party at my house soon after she appeared in *National Velvet*. She walked in with a tiny chipmunk on her shoulder. This was "Nibbles," most beloved of her pets. He was her constant companion and she would permit separation from him only when she stepped before the camera.

She wasn't showing off. She wasn't trying to be different. Even then, she was insisting upon being herself. She loved Nibbles, she wanted him with her. So she brought him with her and felt that this made her no different from the other pretty young girls who had dogs or cats or new dresses.

Even then Elizabeth had the knack of saying things—so obviously true to her that she couldn't understand why people didn't accept them—which made good newspaper copy. She was asked, "Do you really like animals?" and she answered, quite candidly, "Of course. More than I like people."

I recall thinking, way back then, that she was always looking for objects to love. And in the book, *Nibbles And Me*, which she both

248

wrote and illustrated with pen-and-ink drawings when she was fourteen, she revealed this need for loving. It's all there, as I rediscovered recently when I read again the autographed copy she gave me and which I prize.

She has been in pictures so long, and seems so obviously to have been born for just that, it is hard to believe that she became an actress by accident.

Her mother, Sara Sothern, had been on the stage and was well known before she married Francis Taylor. They lived in England, where Taylor operated an art gallery, and Elizabeth was born in London.

Elizabeth's first ambition was to be a ballet dancer. When she was three she saw the Russian Ballet perform and pleaded to be allowed to study ballet. Her parents enrolled her in the same school which had as pupils the then Princess Elizabeth and Princess Margaret.

But, when war clouds loomed over Europe, Mr. Taylor decided it would be wise to return to their native United States.

While he was disposing of his business interests, he sent his wife, Elizabeth's older brother Howard and Elizabeth to stay with Mrs. Taylor's parents in Pasadena. Later he joined them and opened an art gallery in Los Angeles.

Mr. Taylor had no movie ambitions for his daughter yet it was he who was responsible for her going into pictures. Among his clients was Sam Marx, a producer at MGM. Talking with Taylor one day, Marx said, "Don't talk to me about your problems. Listen to mine. I have a picture all ready to go [the picture was *Lassie Come Home*] and I can't find a little girl for one of the parts. I've tested a dozen and they were all wrong."

That evening, teasing, Taylor said to ten-year-old Elizabeth, "Would you like to test for a part in the movies?"

"I don't think so," Elizabeth replied promptly.

"It was just a whim," Taylor said. "It's a movie about a dog."

"A dog!" Elizabeth's eyes widened. "I'd love to meet an acting dog."

That was the way it happened. Taylor called Marx. Marx signed Elizabeth without a test. "I knew she was the right girl the minute I saw her," he said.

The studio put her under contract and, because of her British accent, put her into *The White Cliffs Of Dover* and later loaned her to Fox where she played in *Jane Eyre*.

Then Elizabeth heard about a script, based on the famous Grand National steeplechase of England, which was being prepared at MGM by producer Pandro Berman. It called for a young girl, a girl who could ride, for the lead. Elizabeth was young and she could ride. She had owned her own horse when she was seven.

She went to Berman and asked for the part. "You're too small," he said.

"When are you going to make the picture?"

"Not for a while."

"I'll be back," she said.

Now here is a deep insight into Elizabeth's character. She wanted to play the part of Velvet Brown. Wanted it more than she had ever wanted anything before in her life. Moreover, she was convinced the part was for her and that she would get it.

If she had to grow to get it, she would grow.

She knew that nature was on her side. To aid and abet nature, she decided to eat well and get plenty of sleep. But, beyond any conscious efforts she made, there was that comforting conviction, secure in her mind. She would be ready to play the part of Velvet Brown before the part would be ready to be filled.

Call it fate, call it what you will—she *was* Velvet Brown.

In five months, she returned to Berman's office. She was three inches taller and fifteen pounds heavier. And the pounds, even then, were in all the right places.

Berman looked at her, shook his head and gave her the part.

It made a star of her but, at the same time, it presented a problem. She was potentially valuable property (how valuable was to be learned sometime later) but she was an adolescent. And the studio had learned, with other child stars, that there was always an "awkward age"; always a period when the pretty children became adolescents —gawky, unsure—neither children nor grownups. And, as had also been proven in other instances, the grownups could frequently have very little of the charm they had possessed as children.

But Elizabeth saved the studio worry. When she was fifteen, the

250

males on the MGM lot were turning their heads at her approach. One day she was a child. The next she appeared in the commissary in a costume with a plunging neckline. She was no longer a child.

Now came the game of "measurements." For whatever they were worth, Elizabeth got top marks. She was that rarity, a woman with a beautiful face who had a figure to match. Who could ask for anything more? Certainly not MGM.

She was put into picture after picture. The reaction? The consensus was expressed by one critic who wrote, "What did the story matter anyway? The audience lost itself in Miss Taylor's beauty."

We were friends and saw each other quite frequently. One day she unburdened herself to me. "Louella," she said. "I'm an actress. I wish they'd stop talking about my being beautiful. It makes people ignore any talent I may have."

We talked some more and I realized that her beauty frightened Elizabeth at the same time that she prized it. I suddenly thought of Barbara Hutton, so fearful that she could not be loved for herself, only for her money. And here was Elizabeth, fearful that she would only be loved for her beauty.

Males flocked about her. Glancing at the column I wrote at that time, I see how often I mentioned her dates, her first screen kiss. And there was the time when she was, as she put it, "engaged to be engaged" to handsome, all-American football star Glenn Davis. He was a lieutenant in the army at the time and gave her his gold football to remember him by when he was shipped out to Korea.

Was she serious about Davis?

"As serious as I've ever been."

Well, that was hardly an answer which told anything, but it was the only answer that I could get. Besides, Elizabeth was more preoccupied at the time with her parents' marriage. Mrs. Taylor had so involved herself in Elizabeth's career that she had almost lost her husband. For a time they separated but they reconciled and that reconciliation has lasted.

At about this time Elizabeth made a close friend. I wrote a story about her and the friend, remarking that MGM had under contract two of the most promising young stars in years; two girls who both had tremendous promise and yet, except for that, were completely unalike. One was Elizabeth, the epitome of glamour at all times, and the other was Debbie Reynolds, pigtailed, blue-jeaned; the kid next door.

I smiled wryly the last time I saw that story.

While Davis was in Korea, Elizabeth went to Florida. Soon she was being ardently wooed by William Pawley, Jr., son of a millionaire industrialist-diplomat. Elizabeth returned the gold football to Davis and accepted from young Pawley, in its stead, a massive diamond ring. This was a real engagement.

But it did not last. Young Pawley explained that if they married he expected her to leave Hollywood and her career. Elizabeth returned the diamond.

She was back on the dating merry-go-round, and after a time it seemed she had caught the solid-gold ring. This was Nicky Hilton, son of my friend Conrad Hilton, owner of my favorite New York hotel, the Waldorf-Astoria, and so many other hotels throughout the world. As his heir, Nicky was certainly a good catch.

Elizabeth brought Nicky to visit me when they became engaged. It seemed to me that they were both children. Sophisticated children, with an outward brittleness, but children still. There was a little too much "I" in their conversation and not enough "we." But, incurable optimist that I am, I assured myself this would change.

What a wonderful wedding theirs was in my own church, the Church of the Good Shepherd in Beverly Hills. Beauty radiated throughout that lovely building and seemed to touch all the people who were inside it. It's hard to explain but there it was—an aura of loveliness emanating from the starry-eyed bride, the handsome groom. It should have been an augury of happiness.

It was reported fully by the newspapers. And so were the doings on their European honeymoon. They had little privacy and the newspapers were able to give firsthand accounts of their quarrels, their disagreements. I have often thought that if they had had some privacy, some chance to get to know each other—the faults as well as the virtues each possessed—their marriage might have had a chance to succeed. As it was, pock-marked by spats, it was a very, very long shot.

Their biggest blowup came when they were in the south of France.

252

Nicky left his bride alone night after night in favor of the gambling tables. This was a new and unbearable situation for Elizabeth. No man had ever ignored her before; chosen to be elsewhere when he could be at her side. This was an insult she could not accept.

As soon as they were back in California, Elizabeth filed for divorce. Conrad Hilton attempted to bring the youngsters together, but failed. It would have required a great deal of compromise on the part of both Elizabeth and Nicky and neither was willing to make that compromise.

Each would have to mature before a marriage would work.

And now, for the first time, the radiant, healthy Elizabeth Taylor lapsed into sickness. Overnight she appeared to wilt. Her vitality was replaced by languor. It became an effort for her to work.

For a time there was hope that this would pass. But it continued and it soon became apparent to the press that she was a sick girl. It became necessary to issue the first of the "medical bulletins" that have since marked Elizabeth's life.

"Miss Taylor is suffering from incipient ulcers and colitis."

Hardly romantic, of course. But both of these ailments, many hold, are triggered by the emotions and I am not one to argue. I do know, for she told me, that her marital breakup was harder for her to take than most of us suspected.

How much of this had to do with her feelng for Nicky and how much with her feeling for herself, I don't know. I can't say that it was her heart rather than her ego, or vice versa, which had suffered the harder blow. But I do know that a hard blow had been suffered.

Her recovery was hastened, I believe, by the attentions paid her by Stanley Donen, the talented young director. She was cast in a picture he directed, *Love Is Better Than Ever,* and the pair were seen everywhere. He stood by staunchly during the time that she was waiting out her divorce, obtained on the ground of "mental cruelty." And they continued to be seen together until she went to England to make *Ivanhoe* with Robert Taylor.

At about this time Elizabeth made another of her controversial statements in an interview. She said, "I have a woman's body and a child's emotions."

Everyone had his own idea as to just what she meant. I'm not sure

253

that even Elizabeth had an understanding of how those words could be taken. Certainly I know she never anticipated the variety of meanings that would be given them through the years.

In another interview, given at about the same time, Elizabeth declared, "I'm happier being married than single." And, "Next time I marry, I'm really going to know the man I marry. I want an old-shoe courtship."

What this type of courtship meant was uncertain, but there was not very much "old-shoe" in her next romance.

In England she soon began to be seen with an old friend from MGM, Michael Wilding, then in the process of getting a divorce. They dated, went to parties together and generally came to be regarded as a pair to be invited together.

Wilding is, for lack of a better descriptive term, a gentleman. (I'm not sure that there is a better term than "gentleman" to describe anyone, now that I think of it.) He was never a top-ranking star, a magnetic box-office draw, but he was a most able and attractive film personality. At the time that Elizabeth and he started going together, Wilding was believed to be the semipermanent escort of another great film personality and beauty, Marlene Dietrich.

When, out of the blue, Elizabeth announced that she was engaged to Wilding and was going to marry him, a lot of eyebrows were lifted and there was much meowing about the child—Elizabeth—proving victor over the woman—Marlene—in this joust on Cupid's battlefield.

Now an engagement is one thing and getting married is another. I was among those who had doubts that this engagement would lead to the altar. After all, Elizabeth was not yet twenty and Wilding was about twice as old. And the engagement was followed by her return to the United States.

But when people talked with her, they learned that she was determined to marry Wilding. I got pretty good evidence of it myself.

I was well acquainted at the time with a handsome, shy millionaire who was very much in love with Elizabeth. He came to see me when I was staying in Palm Springs and said, "You've got to call her and tell her that she'll be making a mistake. That marriage can't work

254

out. Call her and tell her so." She was leaving for England the next day.

"How can I do that? She'll tell me it's none of my business and she'll be right."

"She likes you, Louella. She respects you. And she'll know the only reason you're calling her is because you're thinking of her."

I guess I was flattered by this and, against my saner judgment, I made the call.

"Do you think you'll be happy?" I started.

"Why should you call me?" she demanded. "I love Michael and I'm going to marry him."

"I just thought—" I said, but never got any further.

"I think I know who got you to make this call," she said. "Well, you can tell him for me that I love Michael and am going to marry him!"

I was angry with myself and took out the anger by repeating the message verbatim. He took it quite hard. "She'll never be happy with him," he said. "You'll see."

Then he left, still shaking his head dolefully.

Elizabeth returned to England and she and Wilding were married on February 21, 1952.

Now began a period of domesticity. She threw herself with a vim into being a wife. They set up housekeeping in a London flat and she was known as "Betty Wilding."

This was an interesting period in Elizabeth's life. The pampered, idolized young star, whose salary was astronomical, was for a short period just another young housewife. She was away from the glamour and excitement of Hollywood, married to a man she had assured me she loved very deeply. It was her first real domesticity.

Then MGM recalled her. She was too big at the box office to be allowed to rusticate. I wonder what would have happened had she refused to return. What course would her life have taken had she insisted upon remaining in England?

But there is little profit in trying to guess what didn't happen. My job has always been to tell what did.

When Elizabeth read the script which MGM had prepared, she

refused to do it. Then she followed this with another announcement. She was going to have a baby. MGM put her on suspension. (Not for becoming pregnant, but for refusing the role.)

Now Elizabeth put together a hillside home that was luxurious, beautifully decorated and had a panoramic view. It also was overrun with cats and dogs.

I recall visiting her at the time and being forced to duck, parry and shift as the pets insisted upon their squatters' rights to most of the house. Michael, wearing a slightly strained look, remained the perfect gentleman, debonair, smiling and apparently unruffled.

Michael Howard Wilding was born on January 6, 1953. After his birth, Elizabeth went into her second serious spell of sickness. She spent interminable weeks in hospitals in California, in England and in Denmark. They kept traveling in the luxury that was only normal living to her. In her world you never asked the cost of anything. You merely said, "Send me the bill."

When they returned to the United States, there was a definite change in their relationship. Elizabeth, a little healthier, was irritable most of the time and, when she was not, was bored. Wilding remained imperturbable; in other words, "veddy, veddy British."

Their second son, Christopher Edward Wilding, was born on her 23rd birthday. This time she did not get ill; instead she filed for divorce. Gentlemanly Michael Wilding took all the blame.

I have always felt that this marriage, like so many others I have known, was blasted by troubles over money. Elizabeth, when she was on salary, was very highly paid. Wilding, however, though he did very well by ordinary standards, was not in her class as a moneymaker. When they had to live on his earnings, she couldn't adjust. She continued to live—and spend—as if there was no tomorrow. She couldn't help it; she was used to it.

She is not mercenary. But she is luxury-oriented and, to a great extent, spoiled. This began when she was a child. She was the favorite niece of millionaire Howard Taylor and from childhood any desire she might express was always satisfied. Long before her own earning capacity made such luxuries possible, she was accustomed to diamonds and furs, to costly perfumes and more costly clothes.

Married to Nicky Hilton, she could still afford these, working or not. Married to Wilding, she still expected them. So, though Wilding could give her love, understanding and gentleness, he could not provide these other items which were just as necessary to her.

And now, while she was in the process of divorcing Wilding, she met another Mike—Mike Todd.

Blustering, explosive, the only man with built-in neon lights on Broadway, Mike Todd was a throwback to the days of Diamond Jim Brady, Bet-a-Million Gates and Phineas T. Barnum, consolidating in himself the more obvious characteristics of all three. He was a promoter in the field of show business and money was his hallmark.

Not that he was enormously wealthy, but that he lived as if he were. He had made and lost a half dozen million-dollar fortunes and was always in the process of doing one or the other. If Elizabeth lived as if there were no tomorrow, Mike Todd lived as if he were uncertain of today.

I recall the first time I ever saw her with Todd. It was at a party given by millionaire oilman Edward Pauley and Elizabeth was incredibly beautiful that night. No sign that she had been ill. No suggestion that she was the mother of two young children. Just the personification of beauty. And these two appeared completely unaware that there was anyone else in the world except Mike Todd and Elizabeth Taylor.

Sometime in the course of that evening, Mike took me aside to whisper in my ear "confidentially" that he was going to marry her the moment she was freed from Wilding. Well, Mike was given to such "confidences" about his most intimate affairs and, while I felt that he would like to marry Elizabeth the moment she was free, I wasn't sure about her. No, not even after that evening's display of affection.

After all, Mike was older than Wilding and had a son older than Elizabeth. His amorous track record was also fairly common knowledge, including both marriages and well-publicized romances.

Keeping in mind California law, which requires a year of waiting between granting of interlocutory decree of divorce and granting of final decree, I decided that this bright, gemlike flame might be giving a lovely light but the odds were against its lasting 365 nights.

But I underestimated Mike Todd.

He was in the process of putting on his two biggest shows, the filming of *Around The World In 80 Days* and the pursuit of happiness —with Elizabeth Taylor. And ultimately despite all the doubters, the nay-sayers, the handicaps and the worries, he put both over. First came the picture, destined to be one of the smash hits of all times.

Mike had hit a jackpot larger than any he had ever known before. So much the better, because now he could lavish even more gifts on Elizabeth. All of which were duly reported. I remember his calling me to tell me that he had just bought her an emerald-cut diamond that cost $92,000. "She said she liked it." And a fabulous necklace of rubies and diamonds. "The fellow who sold it to me said it was fit for a queen and I asked him what queen?"

They made the calendar too long for Mike Todd. He wanted to marry Elizabeth and he wanted to marry her right away. Who needed a final California decree when you could get an instant decree in Mexico? He gathered up Elizabeth, her jewels and her other possessions and flew to Acapulco.

Wilding, still fond of her, anxious to do what he could to make her happy, flew down to expedite the divorce when some technicalities arose. (However, he didn't stay for the wedding.)

Cantinflas, that wonderful, engaging comedian and one of Mexico's national heroes, had been one of the stars of *80 Days* and he helped to arrange for the wedding. Todd's best man was a curly-haired, slim, young singer—Eddie Fisher. And Elizabeth's attendant was Fisher's wife—Debbie Reynolds.

The four of them were photographed at the ceremony—D'Artagnan and the Three Musketeers. That news picture has since become a classic; probably reprinted more often than any other picture of modern days.

Mr. and Mrs. Mike Todd returned to the United States. Among those who wished them all happiness was young Mike Todd. "That really made me happy," Mike said to me.

Todd started looking for new ways to spend money, and if he couldn't find any he invented them. He hung fabulous jewels on Elizabeth until she looked like a department-store Christmas tree. He furnished a New York apartment at fabulous cost—"I'll take a dozen of those. No, those. They're more expensive." They leased

258

a big estate in Beverly Hills. They leased a resort home in Palm Springs.

All his life Mike had spent more time on his promotions than on his domestic life. Now it was reversed. He found it hard to stay away from her. He would "beef" to me that Elizabeth was interfering with his work, but he didn't show any signs that he resented this. In a sense, he was bragging that he, a middle-aged man, could captivate this young and lovely woman to a degree where she would not let him go away from her.

I saw them frequently and heard from them even more often. Mike called me one day—my birthday, August 6—and said, "Got a birthday present for you, Louella. Picked it out all by myself. Her name is Liza and she was born this morning."

He called me again later. "I want you to know she's as beautiful as her mother and that's all the beauty there is."

I was close to them the night he literally launched himself from his seat in the Pantages to accept the Academy Award for *80 Days* as the best picture of the year, and to cheer as so many other awards were given for the picture to those who had helped him make it.

Later, at Romanoff's, he told me, "Elizabeth was robbed." He was talking about the Oscar for best actress, given that year to Ingrid Bergman. Elizabeth had been nominated for her performance in *Giant* and I am one of those who believed then, and believe now, that it was a magnificent piece of acting.

I was in New York on the night Mike gave that lavish TV party —the first time in history and, I think, the only time a network picked up a tab for a publicity party. "You've got to come to my 'bash,'" he said, and bash it was. The TV critics called it a "flop" and a "dud." Mike didn't argue. All he said to me was, "They have to admit that it was the biggest so-and-so of a dud that was ever on TV. That's the way I do things. Bigger."

But all was not continually pacific with Elizabeth and Mike. You couldn't throw two such positive human beings together and not expect fireworks. There were explosions, rockets and sparklers galore.

The press photographers caught them in a real dilly at Orly Field, outside Paris. They had apparently begun an argument during the flight and weren't going to stop now that they had landed. Elizabeth

259

was shaking her fist at Mike, and he was shaking a finger at her and both of them had their mouths wide open, like a pair of screeching jay birds. That was Page 1 all over the world.

But it seemed that the more they fought, the more in love they became. Then Elizabeth's health started to fail. Mike changed from screeching jay to mother hen. Some newspaper writers said her problem was psychosomatic. Mike telephoned me in a rage.

"Louella, how can they write that?" he demanded. "That poor child is suffering so much—she's in such real pain!"

He watched over her so carefully it was pitiful. Let her temperature rise a part of a degree, and off she was sent to bed, and the doctors alerted.

She was suffering from a cold, and in bed, on the night of March 22, 1958. Mike received a call from New York asking him to go East on some important business. "Right away," he said. "The sooner I go, the sooner I'll get back." He had his own plane, "The Lucky Liz," in readiness at the airport. He notified the two pilots that they would be taking off. And then he called Art Cohn, the ex-reporter who was working on his biography, and suggested Cohn come along. "We can work that way," he said, "without interruptions."

He kissed his wife good-by and went to the airport.

A few hours later, over Grants, New Mexico, The Lucky Liz burst into flame and plummeted to earth.

Mike Todd died as he had lived, in a bright flame. A flame extinguished too soon.

The crash came at two in the morning. Elizabeth was asleep then and was still asleep when her doctor, Dr. Rexford Kennamer, and Mike's secretary came to the house to break the news to her. Servants had been fending off phone calls and reporters for hours. Debbie Reynolds had come to the house earlier and taken the two boys and little Liza to her home.

Elizabeth's grief was almost horrible in its intensity. First it shocked her so she was numb and then she refused to believe it. She pounded her fists against those who were with her and said, "You're lying. You're lying. He's not dead." After a long time, she accepted the fact. But now she wailed, "Why didn't I go with him? Why? Why?"

Hers was a half world for a time. A few moments when she accepted the reality of what had happened and then periods when she blotted it out. Finally, she emerged into reality. And another crisis.

She had been sick when Mike had flown off. Her grief and an inability to take any food had further weakened her. Some of her good friends told her she should not go to Mike's funeral, which was to be held in Chicago. She might not have gone had it not been for Rabbi Max Nussbaum of the synagogue at which Mike had worshipped.

"Go," he told her. "If you don't, you'll never forgive those who kept you away."

So she went and was part of the unhappy, irreverent proceedings. Then the widow returned to the empty house in Beverly Hills.

That spring, before Mike's death, Liz had been nominated for her performance in *Raintree County*. Mike had told me he was sure Liz would win the coveted Oscar this time. She had lost out on *Giant* the year before. But fate had other plans. Liz did not attend the Awards that night. She said she didn't care, since win or lose, Mike wouldn't be there. At the party at the Beverly Hilton afterward, I sat at a table with Joanne Woodward who won the award for her performance in *Three Faces of Eve*. Naturally, Joanne was ecstatic. Then came a little note and a beautiful orchid from Elizabeth, congratulating Joanne. There were tears in her eyes as she read it, and she reached over and held the hand of her husband, Paul Newman.

I'd like to digress and write briefly of Debbie Reynolds. I have known Debbie about as long as I have known Elizabeth. I've always been deeply fond of her, ever since I first met the pert, pretty, appealing schoolgirl from Burbank who started out to be a gym teacher and ended up a star.

She was entered in the "Miss Burbank of 1948" contest and won it. A Warner Brothers talent scout saw her (Warner's Studio is in Burbank) and signed her.

Almost a dozen years later she was fifth on the list of the top money-making stars in pictures; rated above Frank Sinatra, John Wayne, Glenn Ford, Jerry Lewis and Susan Hayward.

It took a deep personal tragedy to make so great a star of Debbie Reynolds.

I first got to know Debbie well when she was cast in *Susan Slept*

Here at RKO, on loan-out from MGM. My daughter Harriet produced the picture and kept telling me all during the making of it that Debbie would be a happy surprise. "She is not only charming and appealing," Harriet said, "she can act."

When I saw the picture, I agreed with Harriet and said so in print —quite often.

It was at my house that she and Eddie Fisher first felt the twinges of love. Eddie was a friend of mine who had been introduced to me by composer Jimmy McHugh. I had heard of him earlier from still another old friend, Eddie Cantor, who discovered Eddie Fisher if anyone did.

Eddie C. had heard Eddie F. sing at Grossinger's, the famous Catskill Mountain resort, and had immediately taken him under his wing. In a short time Eddie F. had become a bobby-sox idol and his records were automatic hits. He became one of the most wanted TV and night-club performers.

That evening at my home Eddie and Debbie were—all right, let me be more specific—Eddie and Debbie were the cutest couple we older people had ever seen.

And, a few days later, Debbie and I were on our way to Las Vegas where Eddie was to open at the Sands. Her strait-laced parents would allow her to go only if I went along as chaperone. They didn't think highly of Las Vegas.

That weekend love was really in bloom. I was a fifth wheel and wished I could find some place to hide. Each night Debbie filled me in on how wonderful Eddie was. Each day Eddie, when he could stop looking at Debbie, told me how wonderful *she* was. By the time Debbie and I left, she and Eddie were engaged.

"But," she said, "we're going to be really sensible. We're going to be engaged for a year just so that we'll both be sure."

Ordinary young people use engagements as means to get to know each other better. This is a time when they step away from the crowd, find moments for discussing the wonderful, serious and important things so universal to kids in love. But these two were not ordinary. And privacy was not for them.

This was great publicity and Debbie's studio and Eddie's manager and agents weren't going to let it go by default. So, instead of having

262

privacy, they became public exhibits. What use, then, being engaged?

Their wedding day was first planned for June but was delayed again and again. When they were married in September it was at Grossinger's where Eddie had been discovered by Eddie Cantor three years earlier.

When their engagement was announced, Cantor gave them a smashing party. It cost Eddie thousands and when I said this to him his answer was, "You know, Louella, that boy is the nearest thing to a son we ever had. And Debbie is a darling. What difference does the money make?"

Oh, she looked a darling! I wrote that she seemed "Pretty enough to eat with a spoon."

They certainly typified a happy couple. Both were successful. In time they had two wonderful children, a daughter Carrie and a boy Todd named after Mike Todd whom Eddie considered his best friend. He appeared to idolize Mike, even to aping some of his mannerisms. He was kidded about these but he just laughed it off.

And Debbie and Eddie and Elizabeth and Mike were an inseparable foursome whenever the wandering Todds turned up in Beverly Hills.

Then came Mike's tragic death.

When Elizabeth returned from Chicago and the funeral, she stayed out of public sight for a time. She was seeing only a few close friends —and none were closer than Eddie.

Before Mike's death she had started *Cat on a Hot Tin Roof*. I had been at the studio with her several times while she was working. After the tragedy she didn't feel she wanted to go on with the picture, but Liz was a trouper and the sad young widow with the violet eyes went back to work; probably the best thing for her. I hated the theme of the picture—felt it was degrading—but when I saw it I joined all those who said that Elizabeth had done a remarkable job.

She explained, "I acted my heart out for Mike. I wanted to win an Oscar for him; the one he thought I should have received for *Giant*."

She was nominated for the Oscar but she did not receive it. (And the reason for that, I think, had little to do with her acting.)

In April I remember that I felt she deserved some extra encouragement, some tribute, and I tried to give it to her in my column. I wrote

263

that Mike's tragic death had changed his pampered young widow from "a thoughtless girl into a woman—a woman whose deep suffering and heartbreak have given her a new understanding of other people and their problems." I closed by saying to her, "All Hollywood and all your fans all over the world salute you."

I guess my crystal ball wasn't working too well. For early in the summer of 1958, with the shock of a jet breaking the sound barrier, scandal detonated.

Elizabeth Taylor and Eddie Fisher, husband of Debbie Reynolds, were dating each other steadily in New York! And if there was any idea these dates might be innocent, the reports that came from a visit this pair paid to Grossinger's—of all places!—quickly splintered that idea.

The resultant publicity was worthy of a soap opera. Cast of Characters:

Debbie: the wide-eyed and unsophisticated little wife and mother, at home with two adorable babies.

Eddie: the misled, weak, husband.

Elizabeth: the wicked villainess, the home wrecker, the (as my letters were to declare time after time) brazen Jezebel.

I have been close to all three of these people. I have liked—still like—all three. I'm not happy about the tragedy that has marked their lives. But I can't judge. I know that I was shocked at what happened, found it hard to believe and even harder to understand.

Like millions of others, I had believed that Debbie and Eddie personified happiness in marriage. Hadn't I written it any number of times? Hadn't every other person writing about Hollywood written it time after time?

Certainly we had convinced the great American public that this was true, as well as convincing ourselves. But, as I look back now, I have to admit that I wanted this to be a happy marriage as I want all marriages to be happy. And I didn't know the real truth about Debbie and Eddie—and why should I have?

It may be that theirs was truly a happy marriage but it could hardly have been perfect if it was to break up as it did. On the other hand, it might never have shattered if there had been no Elizabeth Taylor.

To the public what was happening was a betrayal. And the mountain of letters that I received were just about unanimous in saying so. I can't recall receiving even one that expressed anything less virulent than extreme distaste. And many of those letters came from the same people who had written soon after Elizabeth's bereavement. They wanted to go on record very quickly.

If the public and the reporters were taken unawares, so too was Debbie. She telephoned me; asked if she could come to see me. "I need help."

My heart ached for her. I saw her often in those days and she poured out her heart to me. One day I was at my doctor's office (the same Dr. Rex Kennamer who took care of Marilyn Monroe, Gary Cooper and Elizabeth Taylor shares offices with my doctor, Myron Prinzmetal). "An urgent call for you, Miss Parsons," said Pam, his nurse.

I took the telephone. It was Debbie. She had written a statement for the press. "I want to read it to you," she said.

That statement, which later was so widely quoted, began, "How can you know a man doesn't love you when you have been living happily together?"

I had seen Debbie and Eddie and the children at their home just before he went to New York on that ill-fated trip. He had played with the children and the four of them seemed happy.

Over the telephone I tried hard to tell Debbie that difficult as this moment was, it was not—must not be—the end of the world for her. But it was she who was going through this and not I. What good were my words when she was knowing the heartache?

All this—thank goodness—is ancient history now.

But there is still, stacked in my files, a record of venom, calumny and hatred that is shocking and frightening. Even now, just glancing at it, I shudder. I recall the days when I didn't want to look at my mail. And I was certain that the tenor of that mail, so long as it referred to Elizabeth Taylor, would never change.

How did I know how short a time "never" could be?

Time passed.

It seemed as if the fates were moralists. Debbie's career took a sudden swing upward. She had been a bright young star for some time but now she became "hot as a pistol." It was as if hurt had given

265

her a new dimension and, further, as if all the world was anxious, by seeing her pictures, to show her that it was on her side.

Eddie's career came almost to a dead stop. And I could hear the "Serves him—serves her—right" whispers and shouts.

Elizabeth, fighting occasional illness, was also fighting her studio. She had been cast in *Butterfield 8,* but didn't want to play in it. And when the 1959 Oscars were awarded, she was passed by despite her fine performance in *Cat on a Hot Tin Roof.*

The Academy members, apparently, were passing as much a moral judgment as a professional one.

Fate continued to play favorites. Debbie appeared to have fallen in love with millionaire Harry Karl. She kept getting bigger and better roles. Her salary kept on increasing.

Elizabeth, on the other hand, was signed to play *Cleopatra,* but nothing but hard luck continued to dog her. She became ill again.

Debbie married Karl, moved into a new domestic phase. (And the violent anti-Elizabeth, pro-Debbie letters became a mere trickle.)

The news about Elizabeth became worse. She was really sick this time. How sick became general knowledge shortly afterward when the doctors made their glum statements about her chances of recovery.

And now came the switch, the reversal, the complete upside-down public reaction. I started getting mail about Elizabeth again. But what mail! The whole world appeared to be, with some nasty exceptions, on her side.

When she finally won her battle for life, it seemed as if millions all said at the same time, "Thank God."

Meanwhile, she had received still another Oscar nomination, this for her role in *Butterfield 8,* a part she had fought against playing. And on the night of the Awards, she was in her seat, a muted beauty, showing many of the ravages of her illness. Eddie sat beside her— protective, his jaw set—as if he dared anyone to say a word against her.

Finally came the moment for awarding the Oscar for "The best performance by a female star." And millions watched, their hearts, I know, agitated, as the slip of paper was removed from the envelope. And then, "Winner"—a breath's pause—"Elizabeth Taylor."

That brought the roof down.

And then the long walk as, leaning on Eddie's arm, she went down the aisle and up onto the stage. I wondered if she was thinking of the night that Mike Todd had catapulted toward the stage, then turned and run back to kiss her, as she had just kissed Eddie. I wondered what she was seeing in her thoughts.

This last Oscar night will always be known as "The night Elizabeth Taylor won." But she won a great deal more than a statuette. She won a place, again, in the world of acceptability. This night she was pardoned.

I wondered that night, and I wonder now, what lies ahead. I see one hopeful sign. For in addition to Elizabeth having been granted her pardon, it appears that Eddie too has been accepted.

I like that boy.

It seems fitting he should also have his chance to regain his proper place. And it is cheering news, as I write this, that he is once more preparing to move forward. His fine singing voice has been missed and it will be good to hear it again.

I hope, with all my heart, that he attains success. And I wish him and Elizabeth, Debbie and Harry Karl all happiness.

➔➔➔ *Chapter 17*

MUSIC TO MY EARS

The Amusement World is like a piece of tapestry these days, with movies, television, the stage, records and night clubs all part of the strands woven together.

Music has always been an integral part of my life. When I was a young reporter in Chicago and New York, I became an opera enthusiast. One season in New York I saw thirty-two operas. I not only heard Geraldine Farrar and Mary Garden sing many, many times, but they were my friends as well.

The first time I met Geraldine Farrar was when she came to Chicago, the happy bride of Lou Tellegen. All of us reporters went to the station to meet her and I was the only woman among the group which included Ben Hecht, Charles MacArthur and others of my contemporaries. Miss Farrar spotted me, an eager beaver with my notebook in hand, and whispered to me, "Come up to my hotel and I'll give you a story." Of course, I went. Later I was to know the golden-voiced Geraldine when she was starring at the Metropolitan in New York and I went every time she appeared. Now Miss Farrar is retired, living near Boston. Very often she sends me messages. She was my favorite and I had a mad crush on her.

Years ago Enrico Caruso was making a motion picture for Jesse Lasky in New York. I took myself out to the Lasky studio to interview him. We discussed in detail the operatic roles I had heard him sing at the Metropolitan—in *Pagliacci, Samson and Delilah* and others.

"Young lady, you really know a lot about music," he praised. I glowed at this compliment from the Great Caruso. All the time we were talking, he was busily sketching me. He was famous for his caricatures and I was flattered that he thought me worth sketching. If I do say so myself, in those days I was pretty fair to look at— young, animated and full of enthusiasm and excitement over my job.

I expected he would draw me as a beauty, but when I saw the sketch my heart fell. What he had put on paper did, I suppose, resemble me but it ignored—no, not ignored—punctured my girlish vanity. When I got home I tore the caricature to bits. Now, how I wish I had kept it.

In Hollywood I became so wrapped up in reporting the news of the movie world that I neglected my love of music. Perhaps it was more than coincidence that when Dr. Martin and I were courting, we had "Our" song, and it was Jimmy McHugh's "I Can't Give You Anything But Love, Baby." If anyone wants to call this trite, let him. What was "Your" song?

Jimmy McHugh in time came to be a part of the circle of which Dr. Martin and I were members, and he has remained a dear friend of mine through the years. After my husband's death, Jimmy's kindness and understanding helped me when I felt completely alone. Jimmy's humor, his ability to make others laugh and his enjoyment of life itself eased my loneliness. Furthermore, he is always interested in some philanthropic cause and this became of interest to me.

Jimmy has written more than a thousand songs, among them "Louella, Louella," which many people think was written for me as a sentimental gesture. But let me tell the real story of "Louella, Louella" which has such a lilting melody that Pat Boone recorded it, and whenever I walk into a night club the orchestra starts playing it.

In 1944 when William Randolph Hearst celebrated my twenty-seventh anniversary with the paper by giving a dinner, attended by all of the Hearst executives, stars and then California Governor Earl

Warren—you name them, they were there—Jimmy McHugh, who was at MGM at the time, was asked to write a song for me.

(Mr. McHugh, do I have your permission to reprint it?)

> Louella, Louella, Louella
> Everyone loves you
> Louella, Louella, Louella
> What can a fella do?
> Press agents go for your column
> Oh, how they really love you
> Louella, Louella, Louella
> And your 1200 newspapers, too.

Some years later, he revised the last four lines, i.e.

> Someday you'll pick out a sweetheart
> Maybe my dreams will come true
> Louella, Louella, Louella
> Can I be the fella for you?

Through Jimmy, who is a walking IBM machine when it comes to vital statistics about the music industry and movies, I have met many persons important in the field of popular music; composers, musicians, performers. He kept pounding away for me to get "on the beam" and to accept the new type of rock 'n roll, rhythm and blues, ballads and folk music. Suddenly, I found myself surrounded by young people, the very mention of whose names makes teen-age hearts flutter—Elvis Presley, Fabian, Frankie Avalon, Paul Anka, Bobby Darin, Jimmy Rogers, Brenda Lee, Connie Stevens, Joni James, Steve Lawrence and Edye Gormé, Tommy Sands, Connie Francis, Johnny Mathis.

Some of these—such as Elvis Presley—I first met when they came to Hollywood to make pictures. All I knew about him was what I read in the papers, and I must admit I wasn't one of his admirers—until I got to know the real Elvis.

He arrived at my house all alone and ill at ease. He seemed frightened at meeting me. That was fair enough. I was a little intimidated myself. I noticed his sideburns weren't as long as I thought they would be and he had a nice, attractive face. After all, he's only a

270

youngster, I thought, even if he is earning a million dollars a year.

Then I noticed his shoes—and my eyes became riveted to them. On each shoe was a full color picture—of Elvis!

After so many years in Hollywood, nothing shocks me, but never —never had any star I knew worn his or her picture on his shoes.

Elvis mistook my hypnotic glance as one of admiration.

"They're really something, aren't they?" he said.

I nodded dazedly.

"I'm glad you like them. I'll get you some pink ones just like these." (Fortunately he never sent them to me. All I would need is to go for a stroll on Maple Drive wearing Elvis' pink shoes and the over-sized sweater Fabian gave me.)

I removed my gaze from Elvis' feet to his fingers. He was wearing four rings. Happily, he extended his hands so I could examine his jewelry.

"I bought one of them for myself," he explained, "girls gave me the others."

Times certainly have changed. In my day boys gave girls rings.

As we talked, Elvis ate. My cook had prepared hors d'oeuvres, mainly small hamburgers, and she refilled the plate four times.

"I'm hungry," Elvis said unnecessarily. "I've been working all day and didn't have time to eat."

Both of us relaxed now, we talked leisurely. "I was a twin," Elvis told me, "but my twin died at birth. I guess my parents felt they had to love me twice as much on account of it."

He loved them much in return and lavished everything he could upon them; this I know to be true.

Ninety minutes later, Elvis suddenly looked startled.

"What's the matter?" I asked him.

"My friends," he said, "my friends. I forgot about them. They're waiting outside for me in the car."

"Well, for heaven's sakes, have them come in."

In they came—lovely Natalie Wood, not yet married to Bob Wagner; Nick Adams, who was only famous then for attaching himself to stars, first the late Jimmy Dean and then Elvis. But Nick's drive, ambition and talent later resulted in his own TV show and his own hangers-on. The third member of the trio was Elvis' cousin, Gene, probably his closest friend. Gene never says a word, just sits and listens.

Later it was a different Elvis who came to see me after he returned from two years in Germany where he served with distinction with the United States Army. He wore a dark suit, his hair was trimly cut. There were no rings on his fingers, no pictures on his shoes, and his only companion was his ever-silent cousin Gene.

"I had to come to see you to thank you," Elvis told me. "When my mother died, you wrote such a beautiful story about it. I always carry it with me."

Not only did Elvis change after the army experience, his career has taken on another aspect. He is solidly entrenched in pictures as a star who acts as well as sings. Like Bing Crosby and Frank Sinatra, Dean Martin and Doris Day, his career in movies was launched because he was a singer; but talent, ability and the intangible qualities of the plain old sex appeal—call it what you want—that all our big stars possess, have taken Elvis out of the ranks of being a freak swivel-hipped singer and made him a number 1 box-office draw. His records still sell in the millions.

While talking about Elvis, let me digress a moment to speak of Colonel Tom Parker, Elvis' mentor, manager and friend. I first met Colonel Parker long before he met Elvis, when the Southern Colonel came to Hollywood to promote a patent medicine called "Hadacol."

At the cocktail party in honor of Hadacol, none of the liquid was served and not many weeks after, we were surprised to learn that Hadacol "had a call" from the government.

No question about it, Elvis Presley is the purest and best product the Colonel ever launched. Where others believe that the way to make money is to spend it, the Colonel believes that the way to make money is just to make it. When fans want autographed pictures of Elvis, they pay for them. I once asked the Colonel for a picture of his protégé and, by return mail, got one so small I could put it in a wallet. Under the Colonel's auspices, there have been Presley ties and shirts and musical instruments, and Elvis dolls and toys and games. The Colonel found avenues of revenue that showman-wise Hollywood had never dreamed of, but Hollywood had never known a Colonel Parker before. Bob Hope said it best, as only Bob can say things: "Colonel Parker is the greatest con man since Barnum and the best of it is, he knows it."

In my playroom, where Elvis and so many young singers come to visit, their recordings are stacked to the ceiling. The record business does over $500,000,000 a year, and the motion-picture producers have come to learn how important a hit song is to a picture. Most of the studios own their own recording companies now, to cash in on the musical bank notes that hit songs bring in. The melodies will linger on long after the pictures are forgotten: "Love is a Many-Splendored Thing," "Three Coins in the Fountain," *The Third Man* theme, which popularized the zither and has become a classic and "Never on Sunday."

As good as the picture *Bridge on the River Kwai* was, the marching song, with lyrics much laundered from the original war parody, made it an even greater success.

Pictures have been named after popular song titles and producers have paid great sums for the privilege. Popular singers who have nothing to do with the pictures—which, incidentally, have nothing to do with music—have been paid astronomical fees to record title songs. Johnny Mathis received $25,000 just for singing "A Certain Smile" under the main title. But he is well worth it.

When Gary Cooper made *High Noon,* Harry Cohn of Columbia Pictures told me they were ready to throw the picture down the drain, he thought it was so bad. Then came Tex Ritter's recording of that haunting tune, "High Noon," written by Dmitri Tiomkin, which retrieved this now historic western and gave Gary an Academy Award. For a time the song also revived the career of ex-cowboy star Tex Ritter, who was much in demand for television appearances.

When *Tammy* was released it was a real dud at the box office. Then Debbie Reynolds recorded the song which sold a million copies and won her a gold record. There were those who said that Eddie Fisher who was supposed to be—and was—the singer in the family, wasn't too pleased at this unexpected competition from his talented wife. I don't believe this is true because Eddie had Debbie sing "Tammy" on his own television show.

Sometimes songs are born, not made. I have often heard Jimmy McHugh tell how they needed a song for a newcomer, Frank Sinatra,

273

when he went to RKO in 1942 to make the musical, *Higher and Higher*. Jimmy couldn't sleep worrying about the deadline for his song so he got up and wrote "I Couldn't Sleep a Wink Last Night." Harold Adamson wrote the lyrics. Another song written for that musical, which Sinatra sang, was "A Lovely Way To Spend An Evening," now—almost twenty years later—the theme song for the great and talented Nat "King" Cole and the night-club act of the Crosby Brothers, Philip, Dennis and Lindsay.

Gosh, how I remember Bing, whose musicals for Paramount were always sure fire at the box office. For ten years Bing sang on my radio show every Christmas. If I didn't call him, he'd call me and say, "Louella, when are we going to do the Christmas show?" He was so relaxed he'd put me at my ease on radio, which wasn't always easy. We could go through a show without a rehearsal.

Bing was the first of the millionaire crooners and set the pattern for the others to follow—Perry Como, Sinatra, Dick Haymes, Vic Damone, Bobby Darin, and even Sinatra's son-in-law, Tommy Sands.

Many of the current crop are criticized, and rightly—I'm sorry to say—because they've ridden to fame on the crazy, mixed words of some hit song rather than the musical magic of their voices.

One of those who's the first to admit he can't sing very well is Fabian, a favorite of mine. He was very unhappy when he came into the limelight, because he was criticized so for his bad voice. He came to see me to ask what I thought he should do.

"Study voice and pay no attention to your critics," I told him. "My mother once said, 'When they're attacking you, they're leaving other people alone.' "

No matter where he goes on his personal-appearance tours, Fabian telephones to tell me any news about himself. Like many of the youngsters, he has capitalized on the craze of lending his name to endorsements of products; sweaters, among them. He even gave me one, a really king-sized garment that was big enough for two. Through Fabian—born Fabian Forte—I met his closest friend, another teen-age idol, Frankie Avalon. The boys grew up together and it was just coincidence that they became famous at the same time.

Fabian and Frankie took me to church one Sunday, then to lunch at the Beverly Hills Hotel. The young fans surrounded us, and one

274

has to have youth and vitality to cope with their enthusiasm. Well, I'm no teen-ager, but I love to be surrounded by young people. They keep you young—and you know me—I'd like to tap that Fountain of Youth.

Doris Day looked like a teen-aged tomboy the first time she came to my house for an interview. She wore a cap pulled down over her eyes, blue jeans and sneakers. I could hardly believe it when she told me she had a son Terry, who at the time was back in Cleveland with her mother.

Today, Doris is not only a top money-maker in films, she is also one of the top recording artists of our era. That clear, sunny voice of hers has been heard on records and albums that have sold in the millions and her "Que Sera, Sera" is a classic rivaled only by her "My Secret Love."

She is so established now as a star of the first magnitude that she has essayed purely dramatic roles, such as that in *Midnight Lace* in which she sang nary a note. This graceful, slender girl has earned a reputation now as one of the screen's best-dressed women, a far cry from the tomboy in blue jeans who first called on me.

Another female vocalist who has had several picture roles, is Patti Page, a very good friend of mine. Patti turns out one gold record after another and has a golden voice to match. I remember when she and Charlie O'Curran were married. Charlie originally was married to Betty Hutton and he had a pretty bad time of it. Never were two girls so dissimilar. Patti isn't temperamental. Charlie is her man and he can do no wrong as far as she's concerned.

The day of their wedding in Palm Springs, Jimmy McHugh and I went first to a cocktail party at the desert-resort home of the Gregson Bautzers. He's my attorney. My dress caught on fire from some candles and literally burned off my back. Never did I have so many men rush to put out my fires. The dress was ruined, of course, but fortunately I had a spare to wear to Patti's wedding.

Patti and Charlie have bought a house just a few blocks from me. Long before President John F. Kennedy popularized the rocking chair, Patti not only sang about one, she rocked in one, making all her telephone calls sitting in a rocker.

You can't write about music in Hollywood without mentioning The Queen, Dinah Shore. I remember Dinah when she first came to Hollywood and had no luck with motion pictures. Today Dinah is one of Hollywood's most popular hostesses, best tennis players, hardest workers and foremost fashion plates. Her television program is a must, and many stars known strictly as dramatic actors have sung with Dinah for the first time; Craig (Peter Gunn) Stevens, Laurence Harvey, Robert (Wagon Train) Horton.

Dinah's made a lot of money from records, television and infrequent appearances in the high-paying Las Vegas night clubs. Both Dinah and her husband George Montgomery, who builds beautiful custom furniture when he isn't making westerns, are excellent parents. Missy, their daughter, is a beautiful teen-ager and Jody, their adopted son, is full of mischief. When it became known that Dinah's Sunday TV show, which had stayed on the air longer than that of any other female star's, was finally going off, she was swamped with offers.

Television and Music. Television and Music. They're as much a part of the industry today as the movies themselves.

It's all music to my ears—a far cry from the twenties when I first came to Hollywood and the only music was the piano in the pit of the darkened movie houses playing tinny, spine-tingling accompaniments to the silent flickers.

⤜ *Chapter 18*

THE NEW RAINBOW

ONE of the most exciting experiences in my entire career was
Judy Garland's second concert at Carnegie Hall in May, 1961.

From the moment Judy stepped on the stage, cheers and bravos
went up before she even opened her mouth, and then after hearing
that God-given voice the audience was so hysterically excited, they
kept urging more and more songs. The thing that interested me the
most was that after the concert teen-agers en masse rushed to the
stage to try and touch her.

Judy, who has gained poise, shook hands over the footlights with
this group of half-hysterical kids and when she had sung every song
in her repertoire, she brought out her daughter Liza Minnelli, now a
pretty, dark-eyed teen-ager, who sang and danced with her mother.
To cap the climax, Liza brought out her little brother, Joe Luft.
The happy mother hugged the little boy and laughingly said: "*Time*
magazine called me corny for introducing my children at my first
concert. They will have a field day with this."

Nothing could have done my heart so much good as to have wit-
nessed this triumph.

Judy has been a part of my Hollywood for more than a quarter of
a century and I've been writing about her all that time. Writing about

her when she was happy and writing about her when she was dulled with heartache. Writing about her when she was on top of the world and when the whole world appeared to have descended on her.

I wrote about her when she was a doll-faced, chubby girl and when she was a nerve-ridden, ailing woman.

If ever there has been a Hollywood story that has encompassed the entire gamut of emotions, it has been the story of the girl born Frances Gumm, who became Judy Garland.

I have heard it said that much that happened to Judy was the fault of Hollywood. I can't agree. I can only say, however, that it could only have happened in Hollywood.

The last time we visited she was easy, relaxed and happy after the upturn her career had taken.

She was in Hollywood to play a small part—what is called a "cameo"—in *Judgment in Nuremberg*. Judy Garland playing a small part! Why, once a studio—MGM—was happy to spend a million dollars for a story in which she could star.

I had the feeling when I talked to her that Judy was far more in command of herself than she had been in those other days. And I was happy for her. Happy as I have been all during the years whenever it seemed that she was going to fight her way back from the miasma which all too often enveloped her. If ever anyone has had a faithful rooter, a one-woman cheering squad, Judy has had it in me.

In my playroom are all the records that she ever made, beginning with the first ones. (Remember "Somewhere, Over the Rainbow" from *The Wizard of Oz*?) And at times, when I have felt a need to cheer myself—to realize that things are not as bad as they seemed— I have played some of those records. When that golden voice has come out of the speaker, I have been able to pull myself together. Judy's singing has always had that quality for me. I hope that it has had the same quality for others.

"How did *Judgment in Nuremberg* go, Judy?" I asked her one afternoon as we sat in my garden.

"Good, I think. I hope so." Then she broke into a big smile. "I know it did, Louella." She stopped smiling. "The crew all told me so. You know, there were people on the set who knew me when I was a kid. It was like being home."

After she left me I sat and let my memory go back to the time when she was a child, because that was when I first knew her. She had been one of three sisters in a vaudeville act, "The Gumm Sisters." They had been on the same bill with George Jessel and, looking at them, he had said, "You kids look like a garland of roses. That's what you ought to call yourselves. Garland."

And thus was created Judy Garland.

A whole generation has been born since she first sang in pictures. She was one of a group of talented youngsters who all grew up about the same time and were big box-office names before their heads were high enough to reach a box-office window. Judy. Deanna Durbin. Mickey Rooney, with whom Judy appeared in so many hits.

Judy and Mickey were under contract to MGM. (Leo the Lion thought he had a hold on Deanna too but found out, too late, he didn't and so that lovely, talented young woman became Universal's biggest box-office draw.) They went to the studio school, played on the back lot, practiced dancing and singing routines together.

These were the glory days of MGM and of Judy. The sound stages were always in use. Pictures were being prepared, not by ones and twos, but by the dozens. And there was Judy, right in the center of it all. A girl of twelve.

At this time I find myself wondering if Judy never grew up or if she grew up all at once. If the first, it explains so much of her life since. If the second, it implies that growing up hardly solves the problems of childhood. I suppose both could be true.

Certainly when Judy was sixteen, she was no longer a child. She was a star who, in 1940 and 1941, was listed among the ten biggest box-office draws. She lived in a huge home in exclusive Bel Air, bought with money she had earned. And she lived like a star, in the grand manner.

Even at that time I knew her quite well and was aware that she had conflicts which were already causing her to fight herself. She was always "on." Always performing. The excitement, the nervous tension which so many others could leave at the studio when the day's work was done, were always around her shoulders like a cloak.

Judy needed frenzy to exist. And she sought it out. Ahead of her years, her friends were older, more sophisticated, more worldly.

They lived on excitement, sensation, jam sessions and late hours.

When she was fifteen, she fell desperately, completely in love with a married man. And there was nothing her friends could do for her. She had thrown herself without reservation into this love affair and carried a torch a mile high for a man who couldn't marry her.

When she met him, she was a chubby child. To impress him, to make herself more desirable, she fought against weight; a fight that has been never-ending with her. Because it meant so much to her, she managed to slim down and her figure was envied by a lot of women. However, when her romance proved unhappy, when it seemed—and rightly—as if it could never get anywhere, her first reaction was to eat. That was her way of finding solace.

Now her friends were caught in a dilemma. Eating was her way of recompense for unhappiness. Yet, at the same time, putting on weight only made her more unhappy. And would interfere with the one solid thing that she did possess—her career.

And now Judy became involved in more self-destruction. Dieting and unhappiness had sapped both her strength and her energy. A so-called friend, an older woman, suggested a solution. Why not try "pep up" pills? She did try them and they effected a cure for her lethargy but had an even worse effect. They pepped her up to such an extent that it was necessary to give her sedatives each night so that she could sleep.

This was the beginning of a vicious circle—so vicious that, as I think of it, I wonder that she was able to save herself at all.

Love came to the rescue—or appeared to have come to the rescue. This was when she was nineteen and the man with whom she fell in love was David Rose, the talented composer—then just beginning to make his mark. He was some years older than Judy, just enough, we felt, to be a steadying influence.

They married in July, 1948, and all Judy's friends told themselves that this would prove an answer to her problems. She was in love. Her husband loved her. They both had talent and the world was their Oyster, Rockefeller.

Only it didn't work out that way.

In a short time it was obvious that they shared the same lovely big house but not a real marriage. Here were two people whose careers,

280

while not competitive, were still dominant in their lives. One or the other would have to make compromises; would have to accept the minor role. Well, neither apparently could. They were divorced.

Now came one of Judy's really sad times. It must be remembered that she was at the top of the heap, with the money rolling in. And in Hollywood, as everywhere, there are stooges, leeches, parasites; all seeking someone on whom to implant themselves, off whom to live. And the poor girl was made to order for them.

After a bad session with nerves and illness, she was cast in *Meet Me in St. Louis,* still one of my favorite musicals.

Vincente Minnelli, a famed Broadway director, was making the film. He was in his mid-thirties and had never been married. Vincente is a man who shows great strength in his work; who commands and gets respect. He believes that when a picture is being made the director is the boss and he lets his actors know it.

I have always felt that this was what first attracted Judy. Here was a man with certainty, a man who took command. And she, I felt, realized that she needed such an influence in her life. Judy fell in love with him and they were married in 1945, when she was twenty-three.

I suppose I should have known that marriage might be a step toward discovering the answers to problems, but that it didn't provide the answers. That was the way it was with Judy during the period when she and Vincente were married.

She began to have long periods of deep depression and finally she had a severe breakdown and was hospitalized in New York.

I called her and talked with her and her voice—that lovely, deep voice—was thin and fading. "I'll get over this," she said. "It's just one of those things. Please call me again, Louella. It helps to talk to you."

I did call her and was delighted when she told me that not only was she feeling better, but that—and now her voice was suddenly alive and vibrant again—that she was going to have a baby.

All her friends went through another period of rationalization about her. Marriage hadn't effected the change we had all hoped for, but motherhood would. This was the special magic that could undo the conflicts, the hurts, the miseries. It was so simple.

Except, of course, that it wasn't.

True, Judy found delight and pleasure in little Liza; a miniature of her mother with the same enormous dark eyes and the same fawn-like smile. And, for a while, it appeared that she had thrown off her depressive state. When she returned to work, she seemed in better form than ever. This was the period when she made hits like *The Ziegfeld Follies, Till the Clouds Roll By,* and *Words and Music.*

Up until this time, Judy had lived by the trouper's credo, "The show must go on." No matter what her problems, her state of health or her insecurities, she could be depended upon to be on stage on time, to work as long as she was needed and to give the best perform-ance of which she was capable. Suddenly this changed. She ap-peared to fall apart.

She was cast opposite Fred Astaire in *The Barclays of Broad-way,* and didn't show on stage when shooting was to start. A new starting date was set and, again, Judy failed to show. The same thing happened a third time.

She was suspended. Ginger Rogers went into the picture with Astaire.

I talked with Judy soon afterward, not as a reporter but as an old friend. "What is the matter?" I asked. "Can I help?"

"I don't know what's wrong," she said. "I just feel terrible. I don't know what to do."

"This is so unlike you. The studio must understand that."

"I begged them to give me another chance. I told them it wouldn't happen again. They said they'd see."

Now I did what little I could. I reminded old friends of mine of how many millions Judy had made for MGM and of debts that were owed her. Others joined in the battle. Finally the studio took her off suspension and cast her opposite Van Johnson, then at the peak of his popularity, in *In the Good Old Summertime.*

Judy was the old Judy in this picture. On the set when needed. At the top of her form. And the picture was a success.

MGM then bought the biggest musical hit of the season for her, *Annie Get Your Gun.* They paid a tremendous sum for it and spent at least a million dollars getting it ready for production. She was there when the picture started.

But this was a strange star. She complained about the director. She didn't like the script. There were a score of other things that displeased her. Work was disrupted daily. And then Judy just didn't show up at all.

This might have been a gambit on her part, but if it was it failed. The studio simply found a new star—Betty Hutton—and put her into the picture. The MGM executives weren't hardhearted; they had a large investment to protect and could take no chances.

To prove that MGM felt both affection and gratitude toward Judy, the studio arranged for her to be rushed to a hospital in Boston for care and treatment. One day she simply left the hospital without a word to anyone. When next heard of, she was in New York and the old crowd of sycophants were surrounding her. Their meal ticket was back.

Some months later Judy returned to Hollywood. She was at least twenty pounds overweight.

While she was off the screen, the public was demanding that she be cast in a picture. MGM was deluged with letters to that effect. I was getting stacks of mail asking when Judy would be seen again. So were most other Hollywood reporters and writers.

MGM decided to take another chance. The studio cast her in *Summer Stock* and she went into it while she was still on a stringent reducing diet. If you watched carefully when the picture was shown, you could see her growing slimmer and slimmer as it progressed.

One big help to her while the picture was being made was Gene Kelly. I have heard it said—and have seen instances to prove it—that most actors rarely recall what someone has done for them; only what someone has done to them. But Gene Kelly is a different kind of man. He told me once that Judy had helped him tremendously in his first picture, *For Me and My Gal*.

"Without Judy," he said, "I don't know how I would have made the picture. I'll never forget."

Now he had a chance to prove that he hadn't forgotten and prove it he did.

Gene's confidence, his help, were tremendously important to Judy. She needed someone to show faith in her, someone who could make her believe in herself. And that was what Gene did. He also helped her greatly in the dance numbers which were so integral a part of the picture.

I recall the night that the film was previewed. The audience reacted as if it was attending the first night of a Broadway hit. And cheered Judy loud and strong.

Once again it appeared that she was back in form; but not for long. Her marriage broke up. Not even little Liza could cement Judy and Vincente.

She decided to take a badly needed vacation, but MGM had a casting crisis. June Allyson was about to have a baby and had to be replaced in *Royal Wedding*. Judy was assigned to replace her.

The responsibility for what happened next should be placed on both Judy and the studio. Had she told MGM that she was ill and upset and couldn't take the part, I feel the studio would have accepted this and given her a vacation. On the other hand, her physical and mental state were not unknown to the studio. They should have taken them into consideration when they assigned her to *Royal Wedding*.

What happened was that Judy just wasn't available when the time came for shooting to start. MGM suspended her, and almost at once the studio dropped her contract.

What happened next was shocking and inevitable. Ever since she had been a child, she had "belonged" to MGM. It was her home. It gave her what little security she had because, no matter what happened, she could always go "home."

And now there was no longer any "home."

The headline on the story told the simple facts of Judy Garland's complete collapse.

Vincente immediately rallied to her side. He devoted himself to her during her long recovery. There was talk that this would bring them together again, but that did not happen. Vincente was very fond of Judy but their marriage could not be salvaged.

Now she crawled into a cave from which she would not emerge. She cut herself off from all her old friends. And, after a time—as always happens—yesterday's sensation was forgotten.

Suddenly there was news of her. She was making a comeback. She

284

had a new manager who had booked her into London's famous Palladium.

When it became evident that this wasn't rumor, but fact, all of her friends started beating the drums for her. I took every opportunity to plug her and her comeback. I held my breath for fear that something would interfere with it. How pleased I was when it did happen.

Judy opened to raves at the Palladium. The audiences loved her. The critics praised her.

And from London I got word that the success was easing her mental and physical anguish. Her ego, so battered, was reacting favorably to kind words and cheering people.

Much of the credit for the success was being given to Sid Luft, the new manager. He had once been a test pilot; later became a business manager and promoter. He was married to Lynn Bari, a talented young actress, but was in the process of getting a divorce. As soon as both Judy and he were free, the reports went, they would marry. (Which, of course, did happen. What's more, they phoned me the news, so I was the first to know.)

From the Palladium, she went to the Palace in New York. For years it had been the height of every performer's ambition to play the Palace. To headline the show there was an accolade. To *be* the show, which was what she was going to try, was unheard of.

But Judy did the impossible. She bowled over the critics and the SRO sign went up, to stay up all during the long weeks when she appeared at the theatre. This was Judy of the golden voice, belting out songs in a way that was peculiarly her own.

For nineteen weeks, eleven shows each week, she had them hanging from the rafters. It was, as it turned out, too much to ask of her with her still depleted strength. She suffered from hepatitis and had to be taken to a hospital.

I talked with her and knew from her voice that it wasn't true that her past had caught up with her. It was hard to convince people that this was hepatitis plus a case of physical exhaustion, and that Judy had so completely thrown herself into her work that she had used up all her strength.

Hollywood didn't believe it either, as Luft found out when he came to Hollywood seeking a movie contract for her. The studios

285

weren't interested. Hard times had hit the movie capital and studios couldn't gamble millions on even a Judy Garland when they couldn't be certain that she would ever make the picture for which she was signed.

Luft came to a decision. He would find the right property for her and produce it himself. The property on which he decided was *A Star Is Born*, which had been a great picture years earlier when David O. Selznick produced it with Janet Gaynor and Fredric March playing the leads.

Judy was afraid of the role. "I'm a singer," she said. "And this is a dramatic role."

Luft assured her that she could play the part and that, in rewriting the story, music would be added to take full advantage of her talents.

When Luft had convinced her, he completed negotiations for the property. And, proving that he was a great salesman, he sold Warner Brothers on the idea of producing it.

There were trials and tribulations during the course of the shooting. This wasn't one of those pictures that went from "Fade-In" to "Fade-Out" smoothly. But finally it was done at a cost of about $4,000,000; considerably more than had originally been budgeted.

And, once again, Judy came through. The picture was good, but the star, everyone agreed, was superb. She received an Academy Award nomination for her performance and many felt that she, like Janet Gaynor, would win an Oscar.

I had a long talk with her soon after the picture was released. She had just returned from a personal-appearance tour in conjunction with the film, concluded abruptly when she was told that she was pregnant. (She and Luft already had one child, a daughter.)

"I hope it will be a boy," she said. "Liza and Lorna need a brother."

"Are you happy?" I asked.

"Terribly happy. And I feel so good when I'm pregnant. Absolutely nothing bothers me. I'm calm and easygoing. I sleep like a lamb. My mind is free from worries."

As we talked, the two little girls came into the room. Both of

286

them are copies of their mother and have the naturalness that I recall Judy's having as a child.

Soon Sid's son, John Luft, joined the group and I thought how handsome and carefree all of them were; how much a part of a family.

On Oscar night, Judy was in the hospital having her baby. All her special, hopeful, cheering squad—with me as cheer leader—was heartbroken when she didn't win.

I called her the next morning to tell her this, but she needed no comfort. "I got a special Oscar of my own," she said. "The boy we wanted. Only we're calling him 'Joe.' "

So I wrote a story about the happy Judy and said that it seemed she had at long last found happiness. I had put that word "seemed" in the story because I knew better than to make any absolute statements about her. And I was, unhappily, right.

She and Sid had a raucous argument and she announced she was going to get a divorce. Then, shortly afterward, she telephoned me they had reconciled.

Her career was slumping again, and for some time it seemed as if not even all her natural talent could ever bring her back to the top again. But that wasn't so.

In 1960 she again played the Palladium. Again she was a triumph. This was a different Judy; an older one than the girl who had appeared there some years earlier. Reporting on the two hours she had held her audience captive as she sang thirty-three songs, *Newsweek* magazine declared that she was "pudgy and plump" but her voice, her stage-presence, her ability to sell a song were greater than ever.

I remember so well one time when she came to a party in my home. It was a warm, summer evening and we sat out in the garden. Famous song composer Jimmy McHugh sat at a small piano on the patio and played while Judy sang song after song. She sang many of Jimmy's tunes. I remember especially "I Can't Give You Anything But Love, Baby," for which she had a special arrangement and which she recorded; "The Man Who Got Away," by Harold Arlen from *A Star Is Born*; "Meet Me In St. Louis" and of course, "Over The Rainbow." It was 3 A.M. before she left for home. I never stay up that

287

late but we were so fascinated and spellbound with the charm of Judy's singing that the time went by without any of us realizing it. That is the hold she has on the public and that is why she has had such a success on her concert tours and a demand for more and more.

The ovation Judy received when she gave a concert at Carnegie Hall—when she was called back again and again for curtain calls—was proof positive that she had her greatest moment of triumph. By popular demand she gave a second concert at Carnegie and again received an ovation that I was lucky enough to witness.

Very wisely, Judy engaged Freddie Fields, Polly Bergen's husband, to manage her. Freddie said he would do so on one condition—Judy must do as he said, there must be no outside interference.

In the beginning, Sid Luft was content to go along with this. He was interested and engrossed in his airplane invention—a device that pipes music into planes—but all this takes a lot of money.

Throughout their marriage money had been a problem between Judy and Sid chiefly because of his love of gambling, not only on the dice tables, but in business enterprises. Despite the large sums Judy had made periodically, the Lufts seemed always to feel the pinch of lack of finances.

Judy, with Freddie Fields in control, was now hanging on to her money for the sake of their children, and this wasn't easy for Sid who had always spent whatever he wanted.

At first, they denied any trouble although it was obvious they were no longer happy. As this is being written, Judy says there will be no divorce—but I believe eventually there will be.

Sid was bitterly opposed to selling their huge and very costly home in Holmby Hills. Now it has been sold and Judy has no home in Hollywood.

I am convinced that the Judy of today is stronger and more emotionally poised and is better able to handle this new emotional crisis in her life than she has ever been in the past.

I sincerely believe Judy knows where she stands—and where she is going.

My last glimpse of her before she left Hollywood was when she was presented with an award at the Foreign Correspondents' Golden Globe Awards dinner. I've never seen anything like it in all the years

288

I've been in Hollywood. The entire audience rose to its feet and cheered The Rainbow Girl.

She glanced over at the table where I was sitting close to her and her eyes were wet as she struggled to overcome her emotion.

I believe now that Judy has a firm hold on herself. Not in the years I have known her have I seen her as self-possessed and as in control of her nerves as she is as I write this chapter of her life.

Yes, Judy, who has gone over the Rainbow so many times, now has it draped around her shoulders.

⇝ Chapter 19

MARRIAGES ARE NOT (NECESSARILY) MADE IN HEAVEN

IN THIS book I have told many stories about unhappy marriages and the divorces that have resulted. It seems to me that there is a place for some happy marriages in these pages, for the uncluttered reason that a happy marriage takes a lot more doing—particularly in Hollywood—than throwing in the towel in a divorce action.

People often ask me, "Why can't movie stars stay married?" My answer to this is, "For the same reason the butcher, the baker, the candlestickmaker can't stay married—plus *dozens* of added complications."

In any town—a happy marriage is an achievement. When the principals are actors—worse, *stars*—it is a conquest!

I've never held with the theory that married life in Hollywood is just like that in any other place. It isn't. The hazards are far more dangerous.

In addition to the "natural" battle between the sexes planted by good old Mother Nature, a great majority of the married people with career lives have to face the unnatural rivalry of which partner is the more successful, the more catered to, the biggest money-maker—in short, who's running the roost?

The great god Fame is a jealous god. Even when people are in love. I should correct that to read—particularly if people are in love.

When eye meets eye and lip meets lip—love is a tender emotion. When *ego* meets *ego*—POW!

Because it is their business, the way they make their livelihood, love or a reasonable facsimile, comes easily to actors and actresses— even married ones. They spend their working days moving in an illusion of "perfect romance." When it begins to go sour at home, the natural inclination seems to be to look around for a more flattering partner. And believe you me, there are plenty of contestants lurking around, of both male and female variety, waiting to be the first to say—"You're wonderful—and soooooo *misunderstood.*"

It's an old situation—but kept eternally fresh and new in the clover fields of movie marriages.

This is why I think a big salute should go to those people who make a go of marriage in the movies.

I shall not bore you with a long list—and there *is* a long list—of couples who have achieved the state of happy, or at least contented, marriage over a period of many years in our town. You know who they are; to mention just a few, the Robert Youngs, the Robert Cummings, the Bob Hopes, the Jack Bennys, Gracie Allen and George Burns, the Charles Boyers, Rosemary Clooney and José Ferrer, Irene Dunne and Dr. Frank Griffin, Maureen O'Sullivan and John Farrow—I could go on and on.

Instead, I think we will take as Example "A" the marriage of Tony Curtis and Janet Leigh. To me, Janet and Tony are an outstanding case history because there are so many ways their marriage could have hit the rocks—and almost did, time after time.

That it has survived, and steadied and grown stronger each year of the ten they just celebrated, is a tribute to two people who came from radically divergent walks of life, met, fell in love and married in Hollywood with tremendous odds against them.

Actually, theirs is really the marriage story of Jeanette Helen Morrison, of Stockton, California, and Bernie Schwartz, the kid from the Bronx, New York, U.S.A. Those are the "real" names of Tony and Janet; the ones that appeared on the marriage license this popular young movie couple took out ten years ago just before they eloped and everyone started saying, "Well, start writing the breakup stories. This one can't possibly last."

Why?

The most important thing was—almost everyone liked Janet. Almost no one liked Tony. Janet was an uncomplicated, well-mannered, eager-to-learn young novice who had been "discovered" by Norma Shearer at a Ski Lodge in Soda Springs, California, and catapulted into a surprisingly successful movie career at Norma's studio, MGM—surprising, most of all, Janet.

Tony was cut off an entirely different piece of material. He was all brass—and a couple of yards wide. While he didn't wear zoot suits, he looked and acted as though he had been born to fit one. Most of the time he carried a chip on his shoulder that was more of a wood stack.

I remember the first time I met Janet. She was fresh and pretty and so wide-eyed about Hollywood in her youthful enthusiasm that it was hard to believe she had survived *two* short-lived, impulsive marriages in her early teens—the first taking place when she was fifteen. Frankly, the disillusioning tender marriages did not show on her.

In her first picture *The Romance of Rosy Ridge*, Janet registered as a happy, typical American girl (incidentally, who is this character?). The fan mail started pouring in, her happy studio gave her the full treatment in build-up, and by 1950 she was getting star billing and attention.

She had a lot of suitors ranging from a shy millionaire to any number of smitten young actors and businessmen.

Then, one night, she met Tony Curtis at a party. With him it was love at first sight—and when Tony fell in love it was done like everything else he did—with a vengeance.

Later, he told me, "I was jealous from the moment I set eyes on Janet. I wanted her so much it hurt. I knew she was more successful than I, that there were a lot of reasons why she might never love me, but I was damned if I was going to let anyone else get her."

What manner of man or boy was he then—who was already known for fighting for what he wanted?

292

Tony was born in 1925 in one of the poorest sections of the Bronx. His father was a World War I refugee from Hungary who started out as an actor but ended as a tailor, primarily because he never completely mastered the English language. Tony was the elder of two sons.

As far back as he can remember he felt he *had* to fight. Because of the length of his eyelashes, his deep blue eyes, his unruly black curly hair which brought on the irritating tag of "Pretty Boy."

The second, and most important, was because he was a Jew. "Jew boy . . . Pretty boy . . . Jew boy . . . Pretty boy" was the insulting background music throughout most of his youth.

The safest place of all, he learned, was the cool darkness of the neighborhood movie theatre.

A lot of things happened to Bernie Schwartz as he sat alone, almost daily, and watched the films on the screen. He escaped from the bare-knuckled reality of the outside world and lost himself in fantasy. The movies became almost the only *good* thing in his life. He was a devout acolyte from his earliest impressions.

To hide the hurt he deeply felt, he assumed a smart-aleck attitude toward the world. He was cocky, he knew everything, he bragged and boasted and strutted. "I was," he has told me, "impossible."

The "impossible" Mr. Schwartz was seventeen when he enlisted in the Navy and was sent to Guam as part of a submarine crew. Once again the movies were to play an important part in his development. The only movie on the sub was *Gunga Din*, starring Cary Grant.

"Night after night," Tony recalls, "the crew sat around and watched the picture. Finally we got to know it so well that the projectionist turned off the sound and we provided all of the sound effects and most of the dialogue ourselves. Only our dialogue wouldn't have gotten past the censors. It was during this time that I learned to imitate Cary Grant." (Some fifteen years later, Tony used that mimicry to good effect in *Some Like It Hot*.)

It was the most natural course in the world that his path should lead him straight to Hollywood when he got out of the Navy, except for a brief stopover at an acting school in New York.

It was also natural that he should still be on the defensive. Hollywood can be as tough as the Bronx for a newcomer. They don't call

293

names like "Pretty boy . . . Jew boy"—but your heart can be bruised just as badly by the coldness and the rebuffs.

Tony's good looks and his natural ability rated him interviews and some good opportunities. But his smart-aleck attitude almost threw him. Early in his career he was invited to sit in on a studio powwow about changing his name to something that sounded more like a movie star than Bernie Schwartz.

"Anthony Adverse," flipped Tony—and flapped himself out of the deal. He was more careful the next time—but the cynicism remained. He felt people didn't like him. All right, he didn't like people. He could turn on a big smile and not mean it—just like the others. If that was the way the game was played—deal him a hand.

The only thing he wasn't flip about was his career. Without talking about it he was studying, being coached and preparing himself —and this he kept up even after he rated a very good contract at Universal-International and was getting leading roles.

In the beginning, he was no prize with the critics. One wrote of him, "The only way to make Tony Curtis believable is to explain he's an exchange student from the Grand Concourse" (that being the main street of the Bronx). They hurt, those digs.

But he made a vow that no one would know how much they hurt —or anything else about his "inside" life.

And that's the kind of boy he was when he met the kind of girl Janet was—and he went out to get her "whether we would be happy forever—or not," were Tony's exact words.

Everyone told Janet she was making a big mistake. "He's some kind of a nut" was one of the kindest descriptions she heard of Tony.

But she was falling more and more in love, his brash persistence was wearing her down—it wasn't too hard to do, she admits—and so they were married, via the elopement method, in Greenwich, Connecticut, "to live unhappily ever after," most people said.

One forecast which did not come true—in fact just the opposite happened—was that marriage between two such teen-age idols would wreck both their careers. It was prophesied that young girls would stop squealing over Tony and ardent young male fans forget about Janet after they became Mr. and Mrs.

Instead, the union seemed to intensify their popularity with the younger set. The fan magazines were so flooded with stories about them that it was wisecracked that an issue couldn't be salable unless their photographs adorned the cover.

"It was the 'ickiest' type of publicity—the stories so sweet and—untrue—they made me gulp," Janet said later.

What actually *was* true was that Tony and Janet were having their troubles. The very ones that throw so many young movie couples.

She was zooming in her career. He was rocking in his—just going along as another juvenile leading man. She was making more money —which he resented, as any male animal usually does. He also had family financial obligations which he wanted to, and did, shoulder. They could afford only a small apartment.

Janet had acquired social graces. Tony didn't want to.

Instead of the billing and cooing they were pictured and printed as doing, there were many arguments and harsh words between them. Tony had to take out his seething frustrations on someone. Janet was closest at hand.

At this juncture of what was fast becoming a shaky marriage, Blake Edwards, a writer-director at U-I and one of Tony's few close friends, stepped in. Edwards was fond of both of them. And, in Tony, he saw many of the same emotional disturbances which had once threatened to destroy both his own career and personal life.

He had been greatly helped by psychoanalysis. He suggested that this might help Tony. Result—Tony went into analysis and stayed in for three years. During this time he learned a great deal about the reasons for his fears and insecurity. And, once learned, he acted upon this knowledge—much to his advantage and ultimate happiness.

I am not suggesting that psychoanalysis is the key to happy marriage in Hollywood—or anyplace else. Never having undergone analysis, psycho or otherwise (and I don't want to hear any cracks) I've nothing to say about it pro or con.

But the fact remains that many motion-picture people go in for it on a big scale—some successfully, some without too noticeable results.

At a very emotionally disturbed stage of his personal life, Danny Kaye underwent analysis and is quick to admit that it was very beneficial to him. "I can't say that I am fundamentally a changed person thanks to analysis," Danny says with his usual honesty. "But it pointed out to me where I was making mistakes, helped me correct them, and eventually taught me to live comfortably with *myself;* one of the most important lessons we have to learn. It has brought me contentment out of chaos—and that is much to be grateful for."

Cary Grant, in a burst of psychoanalysis-plus-hypnotism "confessions," admitted he had been under treatment for several years and credited analytical hypnosis with breaking his habit of chain smoking even if it didn't save his marriage to Betsy Drake.

With complete cheerfulness, if somewhat backhanded philosophy, Cary said, "The results of the treatments have been wonderful, simply wonderful. Sort of prepared me for falling in love for the first time in my life. I seem to have had some kind of a block against love in the past. Now I am prepared to know real love no matter what it brings me—happiness or pain." Well. So much for love. Smoking was more clarified. It was completely out of Cary's life.

Marlon Brando has also undergone analysis from time to time with no noticeable change in his personality: that is—no change in his relationship with the press (consistently bad); his marriage, or marriages (equally unfruitful); his ability to get along chummily with his fellow man.

All of which has brought on some wisecracks—the most notable being, "Think what Marlon might be if he *hadn't* had analysis!"

With this joke over, let us return for a brief summary to Tony Curtis and Janet Leigh and the obvious benefits to their marriage which Tony is quick to mark down on the credit side of his emotional ledger.

He has given out many detailed accounts of the great help he received in "being introduced to myself," and in learning that "the Bronx and its battles which marred the life of Bernie Schwartz had no place in the potentially happy life of Tony Curtis." With these realizations came many changes in his life and career.

He soared to such sensational success as a personality, and as an actor, that he was this year voted (a tie) with Rock Hudson as "the most popular Hollywood actors in the world"—by the Foreign Press. As he has grown in stature and understanding, he has grown as an actor—and as a man, a husband and a devoted father.

In 1956 a daughter named Kelly was born to the Curtises and in 1958 another little girl, Jamie, arrived.

Today this handsome young couple's marriage is recognized as one of the most stable in our town; they are popular members of one of our best social sets, and ardent workers in all fields of charity and many civic and national public events (strong for John F. Kennedy in the last election—if you're asking).

My point is this—I believe Janet and Tony deserve a world of credit for putting the time and effort and heart they have into making a *good* marriage from a *bad* start. And I say they should be a shining example to other young couples in and out of pictures, many of whom do not have to face half the hurdles the Curtises courageously met —and conquered—together.

The world—and even Hollywood—is most assuredly peopled with many happy couples who may be thinking, "Well, we've made it—and didn't have to do it the hard way." But to them and to almost every marriage couple, I must add this thought: no matter which way *you* have solved your problems—through religious understanding, through kindness and sympathy, through philosophy, through marriage counselors, through your own good common sense—I doubt if you will boast of a "perfect marriage." Each brings its particular problems—and to the lucky ones, the successful solutions.

And this, by a rather odd set of reasoning, brings us to the case of Kim Novak—one of the rare cases in film history of a beautiful screen star who has *never* married! Happily—or otherwise.

You can't even say of this beautiful blonde "always a bridesmaid —never a bride," because she doesn't even get as close as that to matrimony. In love? Yes. Many times. Wedded? No.

Kim's rumored engagements have been many, but they never seem to get beyond that "rumor" stage.

When she first arrived on the Hollywood scene and was still an unknown quality around her home studio, Columbia (pre-*Picnic,* her first, and still one of her best acting opportunities), her constant and devoted companion was man-about-town Mac Krim.

So glued to Kim's side was Mac that many people thought them secretly married—or on the verge of being wed any minute. They attended church together (Kim's Catholic church); all the social affairs they accepted, which were few, together; lunched, dined and went to the movies each night, their shadows merged.

Kim seemed to desperately need Mac for self-assurance, for advice (although he is a nonprofessional); even to help her make up her mind what she should wear—usually something in pale lavender.

Suddenly, for no particular reason that anyone could make out—least of all Mac—Kim changed. This cannot be laid to the fact that she was beginning to soar as a personality of Columbia motion pictures, because she had become quite a hit before she got around to saying *adios* to Mac.

Nor did a quarrel or a set of temperamental differences break up this close companionship. The parting was so gradual—Kim going to New York for personal appearances, Kim going on location with one of her pictures, Kim accepting first one "date" unescorted by Mac, and then several—that Krim himself hardly knew he was "out" until it was an accomplished fact. Kim never became Kim Krim.

Mac was succeeded by a whole bevy of "rumors"—the present dictator of the Dominican Republic (a role inherited via the assassination of his father), Rafael Trujillo, fell like a ton of bricks for Kim and presented her with an imported car; a little habit he had of showing his esteem. She later returned it to him along with some other "trinkets" of jewelry, etc.

This was followed by much talk of a sensational love in her life which provided a lot of fodder for the "exposé" type of periodical —and which I never believed was as close to marriage on Kim's part as the "exposers" tried to make out.

After this glaring flash in the headlines, a period of relative quiet descended on Kim's emotions when, two years ago at the age of twenty-six, she met and fell in love with attractive and talented young director Richard Quine.

At this time, Kim told me, "Dick is the only man I have really loved. We are good for each other. We understand each other. We haven't discussed marriage [at the time Quine was in the process of being divorced by his wife Barbara, granddaughter of old-time matinee idol Francis X. Bushman] but Dick and I may be married when I go to London for a picture."

298

Kim went to London. Dick followed her. But they were not married—nor are they yet.

I think that Dick's divorce, plus his being the father of two little girls whom he adores, had a lot to do with Kim's decision not to marry him. She has more than once told me, "I was brought up a Catholic and my religion means everything to me. I won't marry unless I can be married in my church." As this was out of the question under present circumstance, this big love went the way all the others had—out of her life; although Quine is directing her in *Notorious Lady* as this is written and there's some talk the flame is being relit.

Already they are beginning to write stories asking "Will Kim Novak be a Spinster?" Which seems to be writing her off pretty fast —if you ask me. She's only twenty-eight.

I like Kim very much—and I think she likes me. I sincerely believe that she would make a very good wife and wonderful mother.

Several years ago, not knowing her then as well as I do now, I asked her if she would go with me and some other stars and entertainers to an annual church "festival" put on by my good friend Monsignor (then, Father) Tom English, on the school grounds adjoining his church in Pomona.

I explained to Kim that it was a venture to raise funds for the playground Father had started and continued to operate for the children of all faiths in Pomona; a place to play, with supervised instruction from the young priests in all the sports children love—baseball, football, basketball, swimming.

Kim's enthusiasm surprised me. Most stars can hardly wait to beg off such affairs. "Why how perfectly wonderful," she said with real feeling. "What a fine thing to do—and how great for the children."

Kim rode down in the car with me and her interest in the afternoon was contagious. She seemed so glad to be part of helping to keep youngsters off the streets. She was horrified by the waves of juvenile-delinquency crimes we were experiencing in practically every large American city.

"I can't do much to entertain," she apologized, "but I can talk and sign autographs—and do anything else they might call on me for like *selling* things."

We arrived to a big burst of applause for the smiling and so very pretty Kim. After waving to the crowd and promising to be right back, she left me for a moment and I saw her slip into the little chapel on the grounds, to pray.

When she came out, she was gay and very happy and caught some of the younger children up in her arms; linked arms with two of the older girls—and soon there was a swarm of eager, excited children surrounding her. They just seemed to take her to their hearts—and she took them to hers. Usually, in past years, I had thought the children "thrilled" but shy about the movie stars.

Another indication of Kim's deep maternal instinct is the way she returns to her "home base" in Chicago over all the sentimental holidays such as Christmas, Mother's Day and the like.

She loves going home for Christmas—getting her sister's young children and all the little cousins and relatives tucked in early on Christmas Eve—and then helping to decorate the tree for all the fun of present-opening the next day. Kim is good to her family, constantly thinking of surprises to delight them; particularly her mother.

A very talented artist, her portrait of her father, and more recently her mother—both in oils—have attracted much favorable comment.

"I'm really a home girl," she told me once, quite unnecessarily, I can assure you.

There's something a little wistful in the amount of affection Kim, "the spinster," lavishes on her cat Pywack—and a little pet monkey she's more recently taken into her life.

Feeling as she does, and reaching out eagerly for affection (a marked trait in her personality) one can only deduce that she has such deep feeling she must be afraid of marriage—or the possible failure of marriage.

But I personally don't hold with the idea that the longer she waits, the harder it will be for her to take the step. Some day an attractive man will come along—one who fills all this unusual girl's strictest requirements—and she will take the plunge. Even if she is afraid that marriages are not (necessarily) made in heaven.

300

➤➤➤ *Chapter 20*

WHERE DO WE GO FROM HERE?

THE pulse of Hollywood and the motion-picture business has been taken so many times and the patient pronounced "dying," that I often feel like saying, with Mark Twain, "The report is greatly [and continually] exaggerated."

Ever since I've been covering the town and reporting its people, Hollywood has been on the "critical" list for one condition or another. Bring up the question "What's going to happen to Hollywood?" and the prognosis is certain to be gloomy to—black.

In the days of the roarin' 20's, the diagnosis was that the movies were too prosperous for their own good—the market was being flooded with machinetype boilermakers.

This was immediately followed by the threat of the "TALKIES," an oral ailment of such magnitude it threatened to kill off some of the biggest stars who, alarmingly, couldn't sound like they looked.

The early 30's brought the GREAT DEPRESSION which sent the blood pressure of the entire industry down so low, the heart (box office) was barely beating.

Then came the killer TELEVISION, a knockout disease creating such blocking off of all arteries that poor old Hollywood, for the mo-

301

ment, went down on its back, and was heard gasping, "Help—if it isn't *too* late"—and just about everyone thought it was.

But, as always seems to happen, the sinking movies continued to breathe, to gain a bit of strength, to regain wobbly legs and finally to check up the biggest financial year of its history in 1960.

But was the pestered patient out of the sickbed? Not on your life!

Came the plague of "the inmates taking over the asylum"; another way of saying that the actors, by some nightmarish series of events not yet understood, were demanding all the *profits* (genuflex and face East when you say that word) and the poor producing executives—the only ones who really *knew* how to make movies—were being "cut up" by sharing percentages and paying out $1,000,000 contracts to the likes of John Wayne, Jimmy Stewart, Cary Grant, Ingrid Bergman, Frank Sinatra and Doris Day.

More recently, specialists have been called in to report that Hollywood is "killing itself" with pro-Communist scripts turned out by pro-Communist script writers. Pickets bore placards condemning Dalton Trumbo (Unfriendly Witness of years ago), openly credited with the scenario of *Spartacus*.

And coming up fast as a brand-new ailment is the "fear" that Hollywood is being contaminated by the busty box-office success of foreign imports and that some of the "filth" is rubbing off on the native product.

I refused to be an obnoxiously cheerful nurse, with that irritating bedside manner of saying all this was harmless nonsense. Many of the dangers were very real and threatening—at the time.

But the result has always been the same. With each onslaught Hollywood has rallied and come up strong.

You may think I'm one of the "inmates" myself when I tell you I think that—at this very moment—Hollywood is on the verge of the most bloomin' health kick of its life! A blooming BOOM—no less. I mean:

PAY TV.

So insatiable is this monster due to become, so demanding will be the cry for more more MORE films, stars, stories; *fodder* to be pumped, like blood, into the medium of the smaller screen—that good old ailing Hollywood is due to get a shot that will lift it permanently off its invalid's couch.

And this happy state of events is just around the corner. Very quietly, tests are being made in "specified zones"—and the results are fabulous.

You may be saying—"But this is TV. Not movies." That is where you are wrong, my friends. It will be the biggest bedside marriage ever culminated—the merging of the two greatest sources of entertainment in the world. And the resulting *zoom* will be heard around the world.

What difference does it make what size screen entertainment will be projected on? Or whether the customer goes to his neighborhood theatre or a luxury movie palace to pay an admission; or merely sits in front of a TV set and drops his dollar in a receptacle?

It has been conservatively estimated that *one* feature length film, either fiction or fact—if of sufficient general interest—can bring in $50,000,000 to $80,000,000 in a single beaming! Those figures are the *Wall Street Journal*'s—not mine. I can't count that high myself.

But the thing that really interests me most is that studios will be a dozen times busier than they were back in the bad, old days when the industry was flushed with too much prosperity; actors will be in enormous demand—ditto for all technicians, writers, directors, producers.

My friends, the golden days of health of this great business—or art, if you prefer—are ahead of us. Not behind.

Of course, there will be changes. But I predict—they will be *Up* —*Rosier*—*More Affluent*—not less of the same.

If it makes your temperature soar to read that Elizabeth Taylor is being paid $1,000,000 to star in *Cleopatra* (which, even if it is as big a hit as *Gone With The Wind*, which in twenty-two years has taken in $72,000,000), what do you think Liz might be offered to star in an offering earning $30,000,000 in *one* night? Not to count the "take" on reruns? Once again I must admit my brain, never too able to cope with figures of this magnitude, refuses to reckon with what could be a "fair wage" from Pay TV.

So much for the happy financial future of where we are going. Hollywood not only is going to *Live*—It's going to *Jump!*

But if you think I am turning my back on some of the ills that afflict my town—if you think I am being an ostrich with my head in the ground, refusing to face some unpleasant factors—then you do not really know your reporter.

My chief charge against Hollywood, and it is a serious one: The American motion picture, one of the most potent propaganda forces in the world, has been feeding ammunition to the Soviets in far *too* many pictures made here. Pictures which distort our American way of life into evil, careless morals, violence and—worst of all—perversions.

I repeat that I believe Hollywood is standing on the horizon of its most brilliant world-wide success.

But what does all the money and triumph in the world mean if we use the great medium of film to sell out to our enemies?

Recently, in my "home" newspaper, the Los Angeles *Examiner*, I wrote an article, "How Hollywood Can Meet The Challenge Of Communism." I have seldom had such public response by letter, telegram and telephone to a serious-type article. I am not the only one who is direly concerned about the distorted view American motion pictures are giving about our American way of life.

The paying customer is beginning to be thoroughly aroused—and to the industry I have loved and championed for so many years, I say—*Beware!* Take care!

In my newspaper article I quoted from a searching indictment of American movies by writer-traveler Norman Cousins, who took the gloves off his typewriter to pound out some cold, unflattering facts under the title of "Little Good Will In U.S. Films."

After stating that he had just returned from Europe where he paid his way into movie theatres for the express purpose of observing our motion-picture output as Europe sees us, Mr. Cousins let Hollywood have it. I quote:

> In all countries, the reaction to American motion pictures is frightening—to an American. They laugh, they jeer, they poke fun where no comedy is intended. They scoff at the simple, wholesome pictures yet thoroughly believe all the distortions painting Americans as cocktail swilling, lawbreaking, drunken, brawling, speed crazy and neurotic.

304

Whether Hollywood cares to recognize the fact or not, it happens that a full-fledged propaganda war is being waged at the moment and the stakes are large and real. Ironically, the Russians are winning it with the material we hand them under the name of entertainment.

There are times when I felt like standing up in film theatres and yelling over the sound track, 'This is a *lie*. Life in America is *not* like this.' But it would have been a futile effort.

The millions of dollars we are pouring into the Voice of America, our official propaganda agency, I warn you is going down the drain as compared to the damage done by Hollywood holding up our women as high-class tarts and our men as wastrels—or worse.

Which brings me to another point sorely troubling me about many pictures being turned out today in Hollywood—the *filth*.

That is not a pretty word. But these are not pretty movies. I am not going to make a list of the offenders; not because it would take up too much space, but because I do not care to further publicize them.

Suffice it to say that some of our finest talent, creative and technical, has in the past few years been bent toward producing films about CANNIBALISM, HOMOSEXUALITY, INCEST, INFIDELITY, SHOCKING JUVENILE DELINQUENCY, RACIAL INTOLERANCE, CONTEMPT FOR LAW AND LAWMAKERS.

I have to laugh when such themes are termed "Art" and are said to be made for "adult audiences." They are made for *Money*.

We all know that motion-picture producers are not in the business for wholly altruistic reasons. They have a right to expect profits on their offerings—or they jolly well won't be in business long.

I offer you Mr. Walt Disney as example "A" of a producer who has made millions from his motion pictures and his lovable cartoons without once stooping to the gutter. There are many other fine producers of a quality product; Sam Goldwyn, William Wyler, Billy Wilder, George Stevens, Frank Capra, Jack Warner, Sol Siegel, David Selznick, the late Harry Cohn, Louis B. Mayer, Y. Frank Freeman and many, many more. They deserve the accolades they have won for their consistently high product.

But there are far too many sensationalists who are getting their story inspirations from the dirty words written on back fences.

Quoting again from my *Examiner* article, I said: "Obviously, we must do something to correct this dangerous and false impression of the American national character and way of life as fast as we can.

"*How?*

"That's a difficult question—but it must be faced. A whole *new* way of thinking must pervade Hollywood. Let us use our magnificent *know-how* to flood the movie markets of the world with fine, dramatic motion pictures which will be to our credit.

"Before it is too late, let us turn our best writers loose and pour some of our profits back into entertainment that will reflect credit, not shame, on America and Americans.

"There is great drama and stirring story material in our glorious history; our inspired statesmen, our inventors, scientists, branches of the service. Let us show the world how the majority of our teenagers *really* live as members of 4-H Clubs, cadets, young servicemen, students—not as rioting hoodlums.

"Above all—how about stories of just every-day *decent* Americans? Let's have some good, clean fresh air blowing through movie plots.

"There can be no alternative choice. We Americans are *not* going to Hell in a sports car. If Hollywood continues to foster such a false impression, it will write its own epitaph:

"HERE LIES THE INDUSTRY THAT SHOT ITSELF IN THE HEAD—BOTH HEADS.

"I, who have known and covered and loved Hollywood for so many years I hate to think of how many, refuse to believe this will happen.

"Despite the sensationalists, Hollywood is not in its 'decline and fall.'

"It is young, vital, virile—and has the potentiality of being one of the greatest thought-molding forces of propaganda in the world. As I see it, this is the larger over-all picture of the future of Hollywood."

Emotionally, during this past year particularly, and even previous to that, Hollywood has suffered irreparable losses in the deaths of great personalities who for twenty-odd years and longer colored the history of Hollywood.

I mean, Humphrey Bogart. Tyrone Power. Clark Gable. The loved Gary Cooper. These stars were "kings" of an industry; their passing was mourned around the world, and the meaning of their loss to Hollywood cannot be measured—in a far wider sense than financial returns. Every place their pictures played they made friends for themselves and for their country. To me, their loss was personal and shattering. Each was my friend. Each has left his particular void.

I think often of the "snarling" Bogey who loved the world to look on him as a tough guy—the same type he played on the screen. To me, and others close to him, he was an incurable sentimentalist. I recall so vividly his last days when, wasted and shrunken from the ravages of cancer, Bogey kept up his gallant pretense as long as he was able to.

The last time I saw him is indelibly printed on my memory. Desperately ill, but still able to come downstairs by crowding his thin body into the dumb-waiter lift of his Holmby Hills house, Bogey had asked his beloved Lauren "Baby" Bacall to ask Louella over for a cocktail.

When I arrived he was sitting in the library, wearing one of his innumerable beautifully tailored silk dressing gowns, and smoking a cigarette in a long holder. On the table beside him was a glass of white wine on-the-rocks. It was the effect he preferred and I couldn't help thinking that Bogey had "dressed the set" to make me feel that all was well with him. In his strange way, I believe he was as fond of me as I was of him.

And his "dialogue" was just the same—he was cheerfully griping about, of all things, a lawsuit he was planning against a columnist who had printed that he was so ill he would never make another picture.

"I oughta shove the column down her throat," he said in true Bogart fashion. "I've been on the telephone all day talking to Harry Cohn about my new picture. It starts as soon as the doc lets me out of this wheel chair. I'm getting stronger by the day." (We both knew just the opposite was true.)

Getting back to his pet peeve, the columnist, he barked—"This dame had me never getting out of the hospital. Well, I'm here ain't I?" A college graduate, Bogey preferred to mess up grammar and talk like a "character."

It was only when he spoke of his wife that he permitted his true self to show through. His voice choked up when he said, "She's the greatest, Louella. The greatest."

It was the last time I ever saw him—but that final meeting typified all the hundreds of talks we had enjoyed together over so many years. A week later, Bogey was dead.

Of my close friendship with Clark Gable I have dealt at length elsewhere in this book.

Tyrone Power was forty-one when he died of a heart attack on the set of *Solomon and Sheba* in Madrid. Yet I always thought of him, and continue to, as a wonderfully handsome youth, the dashing romantic fearless young hero of his finest films.

Ty was like a member of my family. I had known his father well, the great Tyrone Power of Broadway stage fame, and his regal Patia. Ty had the power of the gift of acting in his blood; it was his birthright.

But as a man, he never lost his deep sincerity and simplicity. His marriages—first to Annabella, the vivacious French actress, and later to Linda Christian, the overly vivacious Mexican beauty— were not happy and ended in divorce. He remained friendly with Annabella and paid her $40,000 a year to his death. His break with Linda was more bitter—but I never once heard Ty utter an unkind word about either Annabella nor Linda, nor any woman.

He was a gentleman in the truest sense of the word—a gentle man—and the impression his stardom left on the world was of gallantry and derring-do and shining, triumphant youth.

The other giant to go—Gary Cooper's final days were such emotional heartbreak to relatives, friends and strangers—the great and the unknown—that the beloved "Big Coop" triumphed as a *man* over even the enormous shadow of his screen fame.

During those last bittersweet, tragic weeks as the world looked into the lives and hearts of Gary and his loved "Rocky" and Maria, more words were written about an intimate tragedy than have ever gone out about a Hollywood star.

A Queen in England, for the first time in history, sent a personal message via her consul to the home of a screen star. A President of the United States put through a personal call. A Princess in Monaco sent her love and devotion and prayers to a beloved friend and co-star. Perfect strangers knelt in prayer for the one and only Gary.

The "coverage" was unsurpassed as leading news services kept their wires open night and day for the latest flash on Gary's condition or any change in it. On the same day we sent a man, Commander Alan Shepherd, into space; the stories ran side by side. Gary Cooper's doctor had issued the statement that the end was close at hand.

I wrote my remembrance of the many, many years I had known him as a dear friend and as a star, for the Hearst newspaper syndicate —and my bosses tell me that there was enormous reaction to it. Certainly no added words of mine can convey more deeply what Gary Cooper stood for to Hollywood, to the world, to me—one of his million friends.

And now they are gone—these four great ones. The question is asked, "Who can take their place? Who can fill their shoes? With the loss of the great box-office champions—will Hollywood produce other actors who can so successfully catch the imagination and affection of the whole world?"

To this, my answer is—no one will take the place of Bogey, Ty, Clark or Big Coop. No one has taken the place of that idol of another era, Rudolph Valentino. Or of William S. Hart. Or of the loved Will Rogers.

No one, including myself, has ever successfully defined a Star— and what makes one. But take my word for it, there's magic in it— the magic of a single personality who is able to reach out by way of gesture, lifted eyebrow, drawn-down lip; a certain shining appeal to all peoples in all walks of life in all countries—as though they were saying, "I am *your* friend. You are mine."

Each age and stage of film history produces its particular brand of Star. And the influence of their appeal does not happen overnight. Many years go into the creation of a great personality.

We are not bereft today. Perhaps the new candidates are not yet as "tall" as Cooper, Gable, Bogart, Power—but already we are beginning to feel the influence of such actors as: the very handsome Rock

Hudson, who along with Tony Curtis, was voted in a tie for World's Most Popular Actor; the moody, temperamental Marlon Brando, a fine actor who hasn't yet found himself as a human being; Frank Sinatra of whom the same may be said; Cary Grant (not a newcomer by a long shot) but charming and far-reaching in his sophisticated-romantic appeal; the perennial John Wayne, close to being a screen legend in his own time; lovable Jimmy Stewart; the Continentally charming Yul Brynner; the fast upcoming Efrem Zimbalist, Jr. There are many more on the horizon with enormous potentialities.

I can tell you that seldom before has Hollywood been on such an earnest quest for new faces and new talents.

That is the way it has always been—at least while I have been covering Hollywood. And that is the way it will always be.

Hollywood is not in its "decline and fall."

➤➤ Chapter 21

THIS ONE'S ON ME

In 1925, after working as a newspaperwoman in Chicago and New York, I came to Hollywood. I was a widow with a young daughter, a typewriter and a medical statement declaring that I was a victim of tuberculosis.

My boss, William Randolph Hearst, felt Southern California would be a healthy place for me, and he was willing to take less than his pay check's worth for that reason.

Hollywood was a lazy country town. Meadows and sweet-smelling orange groves; grape arbors and pepper trees shaded the dirt roads that later were to become so famous. Even the palm trees were pristine and any man with a megaphone, a pair of puttees and a little nerve could call himself a director. Movies weren't made, they were born—out of notes scribbled on the backs of envelopes and pieces of wrapping paper. Cameramen filmed scenes and then tried to work them into the scripts; providing they had a script.

A man walked into a scene accidentally and became an actor. No one took Hollywood seriously then, even the money men who kept their investments low and their hopes not much higher. It was strictly a gamble to these financial backers who stayed close to the sources of their regular incomes in New York and Chicago.

The pioneers actually involved in creating the pictures loved California with its balmy weather and constant sunshine, so practical for outdoor shooting the year round. Indoors, too, films could be ground out cheaper than in the East. There was land, lots of land, more than enough for the studios which later were to become the trade-mark of Hollywood.

In the golden bathtub giddiness of the 20's, the great stars of the flickering silver screen were Mary Pickford and Douglas Fairbanks, Charlie Chaplin, Fatty Arbuckle, Charles Ray, Marion Davies, Gloria Swanson, Bebe Daniels, William S. Hart, Francis X. Bushman, Harold Lloyd, Mabel Norman.

I knew them all; their tragedies and loves, their successes, their disappointments. Taxes were low, and even for those times, salaries were fabulous. Many of them tried to live the roles they portrayed on the screen, and their heartbreaks made headlines.

Nowadays nearly 500 ladies and gentlemen of the press in one form or another cover Hollywood, but in those rip-roaring twenties, I really had a monopoly on the news. There was but a handful of reporters and I was the only syndicated columnist. I've been first on the scene more often and longer than I care to remember. They say a lady who will tell her age will tell anything, and at this late date in my life, I'm not going to tell whether I'm thirty-five (even younger than Jack Benny) or ninety-five (even older than Grandma Moses). One thing you can say about all three of us. We're not lazy.

Many of the Hollywood scribes are my good friends and this includes Mike Connolly of the *Hollywood Reporter,* Army Archerd of *Daily Variety,* Jim Bacon of A.P., Cobina Wright, Sheilah Graham, Jimmy Starr and Harrison Carroll.

Two disasters hit Hollywood when we all were young: the Wall Street crash and the talkies. What a searing, heart-rending moment it was when we first heard John Gilbert's squeaky voice. And who will ever forget the thrill of Garbo's husky, sensuous, throaty tones?

Sound, a private disaster to so many, was the savior of the motion-picture business. The parade of stars of those glorious years can never be equaled: Valentino, Norma Shearer, Jean Harlow, Ramon Navarro, the Barrymores, Clark Gable, Katharine Hepburn, Spencer Tracy, Jimmy Stewart, Gary Cooper, Ingrid Bergman, Joan

312

Crawford, Humphrey Bogart, Jean Arthur, Robert Montgomery, Luise Rainer, Irene Dunne, Rosalind Russell; the musicals of Fred Astaire and Ginger Rogers, Jeanette MacDonald and Nelson Eddy, Dick Powell and Joan Blondell. Bing Crosby and Bob Hope found the Road pictures they made paved with gold. Who can list all the stars? I could but neither space nor necessity allows for it.

When we think of these Hollywood greats, we don't remember as much of the films that made them famous as we do of the personal dramas of their lives and times.

The movies have had their ups and downs, but the world's interest in the stars themselves has never flagged, even when box-office returns were at their lowest. Elizabeth Taylor's near fatal illness and Gary Cooper's death knocked world news off the front pages.

The public wants to know. My job is and always has been to keep them posted. Make light of it if you will; reporting on Hollywood is my life. I've made a fortune and spent a fortune, and I've never been bored a moment. Someone once said of me, "The secret of Louella's success is she has never stopped being a movie fan herself. She really believes that what she is doing is important." When I stop believing that, I'll stop reporting.

Not so long ago I was watching a TV panel show and heard my name mentioned by a fellow Hollywood reporter who said scornfully that my speciality was "births, marriages and divorces," and he added, "These hardly make news."

The moderator (no admirer of mine) leapt on this and asked, "What do you consider news?"

The reporter was stumped.

I have been asked many times if I really believed that everything I wrote warranted being written. The answer is no. I have to fill eight columns a week, every week of the year, for the Los Angeles *Examiner*. These columns are syndicated around the world. In addition, I must write one Sunday feature story each week—usually an interview with a star—and I have contracts calling for a certain number of magazine articles monthly.

I can't write "no news today" and let it go at that, so I fill it with whatever I can find. The bigger the better. I want news. I beg for it and I go out of my way to get it. I have a staff which has been with me a long time and they're all first-rate newsgatherers. They're tops in the field. I'm grateful for their loyalty and the longevity of their services.

Heading the staff is my chief assistant, Dorothy Manners, a fine reporter and writer and a dear friend. She has seen me through many crises, several severe illnesses, disappointments and triumphs. When I have been on vacation, ill or enroute to distant places, Dorothy has pitched in and written the column with her own by-line. She has been with me for twenty-eight years.

Usually when people associate themselves with me—hard as I make them work—they seem to like it and make no threats of having better offers. They stay for years. I don't like changes myself, so this is a break in my favor.

Lewis Collins, my butler-chauffeur, has been with me for twenty-seven years, and he knows more stars—and they him—than anyone outside the professional movie area. He gives me a devotion above and beyond the call of duty.

One of the amusing stories about him was during the war, when he was called before the draft board. He said he couldn't possibly go to war because he had two dependents—his mother and Louella O. Parsons!

I have had my cook, Lucille Collins (no relation to Lewis), for six years, and since the Dorothys and I have luncheon in my office every day, and the girls are always dieting in some form or another, Lucille's favorite literature is the cookbook.

Of course the most important person in the world to me is my daughter, Harriet. All through my life she has been a guiding force and an inspiration for me. It is not mere maternal pride which causes me to say that she is a brilliant girl.

A graduate of Wellesley College, she began her own career as a magazine writer and went on to become a successful motion-picture producer. She has produced such fine pictures as *The Enchanted Cottage, Night Song, I Remember Mama, Clash By Night, Susan Slept Here.*

Harriet and I have always been a very close mother-and-daughter team, considering we have lived such full and consuming existences.

She has written my column (although not in recent years) when I have been on vacation, and she frequently took my place on my radio shows. And she was good. Sometimes too good for comfort. Although I have never felt anything but pride in her achievements.

I seem to have an affinity for girls named Dorothy. Dorothy May Cochard, "Dottie May," has been my secretary for seventeen years. She has a built-in filing system in her pretty head. Dorothy Treloar, "D.T.," is a comparative newcomer. For four years she has helped with the newsgathering, busy telephones and answered my fan mail.

There is one man in our midst, Neil Rau, who covers the studios, does the legwork, checks tips which are checkable through standard sources. Neil has been on my staff for more than twenty years.

I have unlimited volunteer help. My phones are always ringing (thank Heaven—when they stop ringing, I'll be worried) with news tips and stories from actors, directors, writers, producers, office boys, parking-lot attendants, headwaiters and the ubiquitous press agents. I check every story that comes from these sources and some of my biggest exclusives have derived from them.

Publicity is the vertebrae of Hollywood, and press agents the puppeteers who pull the strings that move the stars out of the shadow into the limelight. Hollywood could not exist without press agents. They want to get their clients' names in print. Where better than in Louella's column?

Some are glib. Some aren't. Some are ethical. Some aren't.

Every day a dozen or so of these fast-talking fellows will call and announce blithely, "Hello, Louella. Here's the lead for your column."

That's like waving a red flag before a bull. To me, the lead which heads my column and usually headlines it, is the most important story of that day. I don't want anybody telling me what my lead should be, especially some young man with no newspaper experience and less news judgment.

The veteran press agents in Hollywood came off city desks and news beats; men like Harry Brand and his assistant, Perry Lieber, at 20th Century-Fox; Howard Strickling at MGM; John Flinn at Columbia; and Bill Hendricks at Warner Brothers. They knew the difference between fact and fiction and never try to pass one off as the other. When they say a story is exclusive, they mean just that. When they verify or disclaim a story, they are telling the truth.

This mutual trust is necessary to any sustained relationship, whether it's business or pleasure. None of them has ever said, as so many do, "I'll lose my job if I don't get this item printed."

I would have lost mine long ago if I printed every item that was given me. I've kept secrets and watched others profit from my keeping them. I've covered up infidelities and scandals and then seen them publicly proclaimed, frequently by the protagonist himself. In order to merit trust, you have to be trustworthy. I think I can truthfully say I've never broken a confidence, never used an "off the record" item. And through the years there have been many hundreds of these. Nor do I print "blind items," a popular sport of many columnists who want to print some provocative, juicy news that may or may not be true, but sounds good, anyway, sheer fantasy though it may be.

The world of Hollywood is like any other community; the good, the bad, the local gossip about members of the town. The only difference is that in my town, the citizens live under a microscope. Everything they do is magnified, multiplied. Some of them are richer, more beautiful, more famous, more infamous. If they weren't they would have stayed behind in Podunk. And no one outside of the other Podunkians would care what happened to them.

Hollywood is my Podunk. I love it.